15⁺

Bucks on Dewel — 152⁰

**PUBLIC OPINION
IN OCCUPIED GERMANY**

PUBLIC OPINION
IN OCCUPIED GERMANY

The OMGUS Surveys, 1945-1949

Edited by
ANNA J. MERRITT and **RICHARD L. MERRITT**

With a Foreword by
FREDERICK W. WILLIAMS

UNIVERSITY OF ILLINOIS PRESS

Urbana   Chicago   London

For Christopher, Geoffrey, and Theo
—*our wanderers between two worlds*

CONTENTS

CHARTS

ACKNOWLEDGMENTS

Many people and institutions assisted us in the preparation of this volume. For providing us with the OMGUS survey reports, we are indebted to Professor Robert E. Lane of the Political Science Department and Mrs. Gretchen Swibold of the Political Science Research Library of Yale University; Dr. Donald V. McGranahan, Research and Development Branch, United Nations; Dr. Frederick W. Williams; and the Archives Branch, Washington National Records Center. Drs. McGranahan, Williams, and Leo P. Crespi of the United States Information Agency gave us words of encouragement. Pamela C. Tilling assisted in preparing some of the summaries included in Part II. Harriet Stockanes typed the bulk of the manuscript. And the University Research Board of the University of Illinois gave us a grant to facilitate the task of summarizing the reports. We would like to express our appreciation to all these individuals and institutions.

An earlier and shorter version of Part I appeared as "Political Perspectives in Germany: The Occupation Period, 1945-1949," *Social Science Information,* 8:2 (April 1969), 129-140.

A.J.M. & R.L.M.

Urbana, Illinois
4 March 1969

FOREWORD

I first set foot in Germany late in the summer of 1945. But acquaintance with the German people, their history and culture, had deep roots in my personal experience. That experience had been topped by nearly six months of intensive interviewing and sampling of opinion among captured German soldiers in the prisoner-of-war camps in England.

When I left England for Germany, I was assigned briefly to the Psychological Warfare Division of Supreme Headquarters, Allied Expeditionary Force. On arrival in Bad Nauheim, the assignment was transferred to Information Control Division (Office of Military Government, U.S. — OMGUS). The interests and personnel of the Psychological Warfare Division and the Information Control Division overlapped closely. Both were focused upon understanding the motivations, drives and interests of the German people so that operations could be planned and carried out which would help to guide the German people to reacquire responsibility for and management of their nation in freedom.

Brigadier General Robert A. McClure, the head of Information Control Division, had recommended to General Lucius D. Clay, the deputy military governor, that McClure's Intelligence Branch be authorized to establish an organization which would sample German public opinion and report regularly the analysis of such samplings. General Clay wrote in *Decision in Germany*: "In October 1945 a public opinion survey unit was created. We had much faith in these polls, although it was shattered somewhat by the election at home in November 1948."

The planning for the work of the survey unit was accomplished in Bad Nauheim prior to establishing its headquarters in Bad Homburg. Essential to making the plan a reality was acquisition of personnel, transportation and a sample design. Personnel were acquired from the staff of the U.S.

Strategic Bombing Survey when their assignment was completed in early fall, 1945. Jeeps for each man were acquired. The sample design was more troublesome.

Germany in 1945 was a nightmare of dislocated persons. Typically, 90 per cent of the buildings in major population centers were destroyed. Bridges were out. Roads were torn up. People lived under the rubble. Refugees streamed west from Soviet-held territories. Soldiers, released from captured armies, walked home. Wives and children who had been evacuated from the cities returned to start rebuilding. Occupying armies settled into those hotels and homes which were still in sound condition.

The scarcity of food and the highly professional administration of a food ration card system made possible the design of a practically ideal sample under nearly worst possible conditions. In essence, there was a current and continuously up-dated listing of all persons living within the German economy. This meant that every person was attached to an administrative center and that any community selected for interviewing could be systematically and randomly sampled by drawing cards from a card file. Selection of communities for sampling, below the largest cities, within each *Land* (State), was randomized by random number selection of cells within a grid applied to an enormous map which displayed all communities throughout the American-controlled area. The authority and prestige of the occupying force was such that requests made to individuals to grant an interview were almost universally honored.

The Strategic Bombing Survey staff members, heavily trained and experienced, personally drew the samples and conducted the interviews for the early studies. At the same time, they were responsible to recruit and train German interviewers to whom that particular task was assigned before the end of 1945.

Supervision of the organization, training and scheduling of the field operations was commendably handled by William Diefenbach. Within the several *Laender* regions, Robert Speagle, George Florsheim, Dr. Richard H. Williams, Norman Sharp,

Fred Brauckmann and Dr. Henry Hart directed the coordinated efforts. Dr. Max Ralis worked with these units on special assignment.

During the planning period in Bad Nauheim, skepticism was frequently heard about the possibility of constructing an organization which could, in practice, meet strict time schedules. That skepticism was almost immediately overcome once operations were started. But skepticism was also voiced about the worth of the findings. Would the German people tell military government representatives what was *really* in their hearts and minds?

The determining factor, of course, was the attitude of the interviewers themselves. Given honest, thoughtful, sensitive, decent interviewers, it was reasonable to expect that individual Germans would respond in kind. Tests were made comparing responses given to the original set of American interviewers with responses given to newly trained German interviewers. But the ultimate test was to be made in elections of public officials. The first elections for city-wide positions were held in January 1946. The problem posed was to determine in advance the turnout of voters. Estimates were simultaneously drawn from all official and responsible sources channeled to the military governor's office. General Clay reports in *Decision in Germany* how important the size of turnout was to him: "I have listened to election returns in the United States many times and with eager interest, but never have I waited so anxiously to know how many voted. . . ." Among all the estimates reported to the military governor's office, the projection from our small sample was closest to the actual proportion voting, being well within the margin of error.

The success of that one report placed the operation on a well-accepted foundation. It did not presage a flow of requests from the highest level for additional subjects to be explored.

The fact is that the Intelligence Branch had had a proud history throughout the European campaigns and had earned the highest respect for the quality of its work. It had continually brought information to the attention of commanders which was believed to be critical from the point of view of behavioral scientists. That practice was continued within the military government organization. Guidance on topics to be explored through samples of German public opinion was derived from internal staff meetings in the Information Control Division's Intelligence Branch. Mr. Alfred Toombs and Dr. Alexander George provided continuous and thoughtful counsel.

Supporting the Intelligence Branch's position of professional anticipation of requirements for essential information was the emphasis given to repeating identical questions on successive surveys. Such repetition permitted subsequent reports of trends of public opinion.

Military government was centrally concerned with change – change interpreted as the political maturing of the German people, an increase in their readiness to accept responsibility as individuals and as a great nation, a deepening in awareness of the nature of a free society, with its strengths and weaknesses, an improvement in the peoples' knowledge of the history of their own nation and the character of the tyrants they had supported. Reports of trends of public opinion, in these respects, went far to satisfy a deep interest among military government and German officials for any information which might limit speculation and guide interpretation as to changes occurring.

Reports of the surveys of public opinion were disseminated to all major divisions of military government. Wider distribution was assured through incorporation of highlights of surveys into publications of the Intelligence Branch which regularly reached all top commanders and, through the intelligence community, all operational arms of military government.

The daily contacts of the survey staff – especially its field representatives – with German officials (mayoral, administrative, police, for example) built, in time, good relations with the German government which was being erected parallel to military government. Particular studies of public reception of the mass media opened doors to conversations with executives in radio, newspaper and magazine offices. A continuous effort was made to tell such officials informally about aspects of public opinion which were related to their areas of responsibility. As regards the topic of anti-Semitism in Germany, a major effort was made to bring the findings of our studies to the attention of the broadest range of German leadership so that they could, in mutual consultation, consider the implications to their own fields of interest and activity.

Analysis and interpretation of the survey findings were more easily coped with in the early days of the work than later, toward 1948. Public issues, at first, appeared sharp and well-defined, the meaning of the data seemed to be clear. The addition of analytical staff, as time passed, brought fresh views from the United States, generous and warmly humanitarian in outlook toward the German people, tolerant and indulgent toward Soviet power. Important contributions toward richer interpretations and presentation of the findings were made by Dr. Hedvig Ylvisaker, Ann Schuetz, and Henry Halpern.

But all those interpretations are now historical curiosities. They tell us, perhaps, as much about the situations of the day and about the interpreter as the facts being analyzed. But the facts reported remain as given.

The reports issued by the survey unit were made enduring by the elegance of the sample design, the dedication to wholesome interview procedures and the impeccability of the card counts (thanks to Louise Hopwood's insistence). The studies merit careful consideration by historians, political scientists, sociologists, psychologists, communications specialists and other persons who seek to understand the hopes and fears, the judgments, the expectations and the response to events which characterized German outlooks after the collapse of Hitler's Reich.

Frederick W. Williams
New York, New York
August, 1968

LIST OF ABBREVIATIONS

AMG	American Military Government
AMZON	American Zone of Occupation
CDU	Christian Democratic Union
CSU	Christian Socialist Union
DM	Deutsche Mark
DP	Displaced Persons
DVP	Democratic People's Party
ECA	European Cooperation Administration
ERP	European Recovery Program
IMT	International Military Tribunal (Nuremberg Trials)
JEIA	Joint Export-Import Agency
KPD	Communist Party of Germany
LDP	Liberal Democratic Party
MG	Military Government
NSDAP	National Socialist German Workers Party (Nazi Party)
OeVP	Austrian People's Party
OMGUS	Office of Military Government of the United States for Germany
PG	Party Member (of NSDAP)
RIAS	Radio in the American Sector (Berlin)
RM	Reichsmark
SED	Socialist Unity Party of Germany
SPD	Social Democratic Party of Germany
SPOe	Socialist Party of Austria
VOA	Voice of America
WAV	Economic Reconstruction Party

PART I

POLITICAL PERSPECTIVES IN OCCUPIED GERMANY

Throughout the years since the end of World War II, as Germany was rising from a shattering defeat to resume its position as a leading member of the international community, American policy makers and scholars have closely watched developments in German public opinion. Just after the first American troops penetrated the crumbling Third Reich in 1945 came batteries of social psychologists. These men, responsible to the United States Army, were charged with the formidable task of ascertaining the potential for resistance among the population, singling out those citizens − preferably democratically oriented − most likely to be most useful in restoring municipal and other services, and in keeping the Army administrators informed about the mood and concerns of the defeated Germans.

The Army quickly saw the need for formalized procedures to gather information on public perspectives. In October 1945, less than six months after the capitulation of Hitler's Germany, the Intelligence Branch of the Office of the Director of Information Control, Office of Military Government for Germany (U.S.), set up its Opinion Survey Section, under the direction of Dr. Frederick W. Williams. This agency conducted 72 major surveys during the course of the next four years, an average of one every third week. The reports based on these surveys went to the highest levels of the American occupation authorities.[1]

Even after West Germany regained a measure of sovereignty in September 1949, with the promulgation of the Federal Republic, American officials retained their interest in the political perspectives of its citizens. The Opinion Survey Section within the Office of Military Government, United States (OMGUS) became the Reactions Analysis Staff, Office of Public Affairs, Office of the U.S. High Commissioner for

Germany (HICOG). From 1949 until 1955 this agency, too, conducted a multitude of public opinion surveys. Meanwhile the United States government had become aware of the utility of such surveys, not for occupied West Germany alone, but for other Western European countries as well. A small survey research section within the Department of State ultimately developed into a major arm of the United States Information Agency. More than twenty times since September 1952 the USIA has commissioned extensive surveys in at least four major Western European countries.[2]

THE OMGUS SURVEYS

This volume deals specifically with the surveys of West German attitudes conducted under the auspices of OMGUS. Its body comprises summaries of the reports prepared by the Opinion Survey Section. These introductory remarks, after discussing some technical aspects of the surveys, will outline some of the main findings of interest to present-day students of public policy issues.

Questionnaires. A review of its procedures by the Information Control Division's Opinion Survey Section reported:

> The questionnaire is prepared in consultation with Division or Branch heads who are most closely concerned with the problem under investigation. The studies are usually designed to produce evidence which is zone-wide in its implication. But special segments of the population or special areas are also studied on occasion.
>
> The questionnaire is pre-tested. That is, the questions are tried out on small groups of Germans to determine whether they are meaningful and understandable to the wide variety of types of Germans to be studied.

A set of the questionnaires is now available through the United States National Achives and Records Service.[3]

Sampling. The Opinion Survey Section's initial intent was to concentrate solely upon the American Zone of Occupation in the south of Germany, that is, Bavaria, Hesse, and what was then called Wuerttemberg-Baden. By March 1946, however, it had begun surveying the opinions of West Berliners, and somewhat later expanded operations to Bremen (together with its harbor city of Bremerhaven), a city-state under American control in the north of Germany. The first eight surveys, conducted between 26 October 1945 and 13 December 1945, rested upon area samples of 39 to 45 communities, with a sample size that ranged between 331 and 466 respondents. Beginning on 27 December 1945 the Opinion Survey Section interviewed approximately 1,000 persons in 80 communities; in April 1946 it increased this number to about 1,500 respondents in 141 communities; and by April 1947 it was surveying roughly 3,000 persons in 241 communities (Table 1).

The earliest surveys made little attempt to stratify the sample even by *Land*. By April 1947, when the Section formalized its sampling procedure, it could note that ". . . communities under 10,000 in size are systematically selected at random from lists which order all communities in [the American Zone of] Germany according to size within the eight administrative areas. Towns over 10,000 in size are weighted out in the sample as separate items." The determination of individual respondents rested upon the selection of every *n*th name from the list of rationcard holders – which, in the earlier years at least, doubtless constituted a complete enumeration of residents of American-occupied Germany. A visiting expert, Elmo C. Wilson, commented in August 1948 that the use of such lists offered a "samplers' paradise" unparalled in the United States. He went on to characterize the Opinion Survey Section's entire sampling procedure as being "of the highest order."[4]

Field Work. The field staff carried out the interviews in the respondents' homes or offices. For surveys in October and November 1945, American service personnel who could speak German "like natives" conducted the interviews; thereafter,

TABLE 1. **THE OMGUS SURVEYS**

The dates listed below are those printed on the questionnaires, and represent the days on which the field workers began interviewing. For approximate sample sizes, see the text: an asterisk (*) denotes that the entire sample was split into two halves, with each half getting a separate questionnaire.

1.	1945	26 Oct	37.	1947	7 Jan
2.		5 Nov	38.		3 Feb
3.		12 Nov	39.		17 Feb
4.		19 Nov	40.		7 Apr*
5.		26 Nov	41.		5 May
6.		1 Dec	42.		5 Jun
7.		6 Dec	43.		Jun*
8.		13 Dec	44.		8 Jul*
9.		27 Dec	45.		4 Aug
10.	1946	14 Jan	46.		25 Aug*
11.		21 Jan	47.		15 Sep*
12.		31 Jan	48.		6 Oct
13.		7 Feb	49.		10 Nov*
14.		14 Feb	50.		2 Dec*
15.		21 Feb	51.	1948	5 Jan*
16.		1 Mar	52.		1 Feb
17.		8 Mar	53.		23 Feb
18.		15 Mar	54.		29 Mar
19.		22 Mar	55.		19 Apr*
20.		29 Mar	56.		17 May*
21.		5 Apr	57.		8 Jun*
22.		15 Apr	58.		30 Jun
23.		26 Apr	59.		19 Jul
24.		8 May	60.		2 Aug*
25.		7 Jun	61.		23 Aug*
26.		21 Jun	62.		17 Sep*
27.		1 Jul	63.		12 Oct
28.		25 Jul	64.		11 Nov*
29.		9 Aug*	65.		2 Dec*
30.		Sep	66.	1949	8 Jan*
31.		4 Oct*	67.		3 Feb*
32.		3 Sep*	68.		1 Mar
33.		14 Oct	69.		15 Apr
34.		28 Oct*	70.		8 Jul*
35.		25 Nov*	71.		1 Aug
36.		10 Dec	72.		12 Sep*

Germans trained by the Opinion Survey Section carried out the field work. In all cases the interviewers informed respondents of OMGUS sponsorship of the surveys and assured them that their anonymity would be preserved.

Given the fact that Germany was an occupied country, and that the agent of the armed occupier was conducting these surveys, one might legitimately ask what influence this fact had upon the type of responses given by those polled. In November 1948 the Opinion Survey Section designed a survey specifically to determine how much bias OMGUS sponsorship introduced into the findings. Two sets of interviewers, one representing the "Military Government" and the other a "German public opinion institute," asked separate samples in West Berlin a variety of questions focusing upon political attitudes, particularly issues of occupation policy. In summarizing the results of this survey, Leo P. Crespi, at that time chief of the Opinion Survey Section, wrote:

> Without in any way denying the importance of the sponsorship problems that were uncovered in some areas of questioning, it would not be unreasonable to hold that the major import of the present experiment is not so much the presence of sponsorship differences on MG [Military Government] questions but their relative absence. With only a third of the questions exhibiting differences at the 95 per cent level [of significance] and only 14 per cent at the 99 per cent level; with a maximum difference of 17.1 per cent and a non-significant average difference of 6.6 per cent on questions in large part selected to show up sponsorship differences if they exist, the conclusion seems fair that on the score of sponsorship MG polling is an entirely workable method of inquiry in occupied Germany. . . .[5]

The areas of greatest difference seemed to be questions bearing upon American prestige and, to a lesser extent, questions about militarism and National Socialism. In these areas, Crespi continued:

> It is on the side of caution not to take the obtained percentages entirely at face value. Perhaps a feasible suggestion

is to apply in such instances a 10 per cent safety factor—
the nearest round figure to the 11.1 per cent average
sponsorship difference found on questions passing the 95
per cent level. . . .[6]

But to this must be added the fact that sponsorship differences
do not necessarily mean that the OMGUS-sponsored surveys
were less valid than those conducted by the "independent"
German agency. Respondents may simply have given different
versions of the "truth" to interviewers from different agencies,
with neither version necessarily being a more accurate reflection
of the respondents' "true" perspectives than the other.[7] Those
who would use the OMGUS surveys, however, must bear in
mind the possibility of bias.

Analysis. The staff of the Opinion Survey Section
transferred the information from the questionnaires to punchcards, produced sometimes elaborate cross-tabulations of the
data as well as longitudinal comparisons, and wrote reports for
distribution to other OMGUS agencies. Unfortunately, the
punchcards for these surveys have disappeared. All that remains
is the set of 194 reports based upon these data. The reports,
ranging in length from two to 71 pages, analyze specific aspects
of the data. They frequently contain tables of data broken
down by demographic characteristics, or cross-tabulated according to expressed opinions on related subjects. Taken together,
these reports (despite the absence of punchcard data) comprise
a veritable wealth of information which social scientists have
not yet begun to mine thoroughly.

The purpose of this volume is to make this material more
widely available to the scholarly and policy-making community.
Its bulk is comprised of short summaries of each of the 194
separate reports, together with an index. Where possible we have
taken these summaries directly from the reports themselves.
Similarly, information on sample sizes and interviewing dates
stems from the individual reports. The complete set of reports,
in microfilmed or xeroxed form, can be obtained from the
United States National Archives and Records Service.[8] The

remainder of this introductory survey will suggest some uses to which social scientists could put the information contained in the OMGUS reports of public opinion in occupied Germany, as well as some findings that emerge from the reports.

IMMEDIATE OCCUPATION POLICIES

The OMGUS surveys were oriented toward policy problems facing the American occupation authorities. Particularly at the outset of the occupation years this meant short-range policy — that seeking to deal with the day-to-day issues arising in this massive effort to control an alien population. Cardinal among these issues were the attitudes of Germans toward the occupation itself, the effectiveness of the American information policies, and a host of specific problems such as food rationing, refugees and expellees, currency control and reform, the division of Germany, and the city of Berlin.

Attitudes toward the American Occupation

Doubtless few nations relish the prospect of falling under the control of a foreign country. The remarkable thing is that Germans in the American Zone of Occupation (AMZON) and West Berlin did not regard the occupation of the late 1940s as a national humiliation for Germany: For every person who considered it as such (an average of 30 per cent of the population), more than two (62%) did not view it as a national humiliation (#22).[9] Moreover, there was a general feeling among AMZON Germans that they received better treatment, particularly with respect to food rations, than did their compatriots in other zones of occupation (#64); and they had more confidence that the Americans would treat Germans fairly than would the other occupying powers (#76).[10]

Attitudes toward the American occupation forces were ambivalent. On the one hand, few Germans came into direct contact with soldiers. A survey in September 1946 revealed that only 28 per cent of Mannheim's citizens had struck up some relationship with white soldiers, 16 per cent with black soldiers (#24). For the American Zone as a whole, only one in seven had come to know an American soldier well or rather well, although as many as one in five had had an opportunity since the beginning of the occupation to talk with an American (#27). A year later almost twice as many AMZON Germans (27%) could claim that they had become acquainted with an American since the end of the war (#94) — a figure that rose to 32 per cent by December 1949 (#II/6).

On the other hand, the lack of direct contact did not prevent Germans from forming images of these American troops. These images were by and large positive. There seems to have been little basic hostility toward the soldiers: Almost three-quarters (74%), for instance, would not have expressed opposition to German girls from their circle of acquaintances or family who dated Americans (#94). And surveys taken at various times revealed the overwhelming German belief that both the behavior and the popularity of the American troops were improving rather than worsening as the occupation months progressed (#94, 110, and II/6). Minorities felt in November 1947 (#94) that the Americans enriched themselves through barter (30%), had heard that the troops wasted or destroyed food (36%), knew of cases where American negligence had destroyed German property (21%), or had had unpleasant or irritating experiences with Americans (13%). But to this must be added the fact that, among respondents who claimed to know Americans, the share reporting such negative images averaged 13 percentage points greater than among those who knew no Americans. Negro troops, although seen as friendlier than white soldiers, seemed to arouse somewhat greater anxieties among Mannheim residents (#24): Most of these respondents described the behavior of black soldiers either as decent (37%) or as decent with some exceptions (33%), as opposed to a small minority (17%) characterizing their behavior as not decent; but as many as 29 per cent reported their fear of black soldiers (a self-description that the interviewers' estimates, based upon the tenor of the respondents' comments, more than confirmed).

Germans in the American Zone were not sanguine about the prospects for an early end to the occupation. In April 1946, of those willing to estimate how long the occupation would last (62 per cent of the entire sample), two-thirds suggested at least a decade or "many years." Only one in nine of those willing to make an estimate thought that the occupation would end within the next three years (#22). The same question was asked a half year later of 188 community leaders in areas under American control. Three-quarters of this sample felt that the occupation would last for at least another ten years, and a quarter even thought it might last until 1966 or longer. A large majority (76%) backed up their best guesses about the duration of the American occupation with the assertion that the Americans "should" stay that long (#44). Incidentally, of those willing to estimate how long Germany would have to continue paying reparations (67 per cent of the entire sample), less than one in seven thought it would be under 20 years (#59).

More problematic was the German view on reconstruction. In early 1946 residents of the American Zone were optimistic despite their recognition that the road to full recovery was long. Only a seventh (14%) expected reconstruction within a decade; four times as many (57%) thought that it would take two or more decades; and a fifth (20%) anticipated that it might require at least 50 years (#22). About as many (41%) were satisfied that recovery was proceeding more quickly than expected as the number seeing it proceeding more slowly than expected (40%). Over half (56%) were nonetheless optimistic that reconstruction could be accomplished with some degree of speed and energy (with 35 per cent expressing pessimism).

American Zone Germans expected and felt that they were getting more assistance in reconstruction from the United States than from joint Allied efforts (#22, 76, 100). Satisfaction with the American contribution declined, however, from November 1945, when as many as 70 per cent of AMZON respondents expressed the view that the United States had furthered rather than hindered the reconstruction, to September 1946, when this percentage stood at 44 per cent; after remaining at this level until the following August, it rose again to 55 per cent in January 1948 and 63 per cent in August of that year (#60, 85, 175).

The Marshall Plan evidently played a large role in increasing German confidence in the United States. In August 1949 as many as 69 per cent of the AMZON Germans were aware of this aid program, and all but a handful of these knew that Germany was to benefit through it (#190). Asked what underlay the Marshall Plan, the bulk of the respondents saw America's self-interest: Almost two-thirds (63%) felt that America wished to prevent Western Europe from becoming communist, and almost half (48%) thought that America wanted to win friends in Western Europe so that it would have allies in the event of a war with the Soviet Union. Purely altruistic motives found third place in this ranking, with 45 per cent stating that America was earnestly anxious to help homeless and starving people. A few saw sinister motives – a desire to use the Marshall Plan to dump surplus goods (18%), to achieve dominance over Western Europe (7%), or to penetrate the European market (6%).

On all these points – attitudes toward American soldiers, the American contribution to German reconstruction, views of the Marshall Plan – West Berliners were consistently more ready to express an opinion and more likely to take a pro-American position. This trend was in evidence even before the crises that led up to the Berlin blockade of 1948-1949. During and after the blockade, however, West Berliners were even more predisposed to look upon the Americans as their friends in an otherwise hostile environment.

American Information Policies

The occupation authorities were quite naturally interested in the effectiveness of their information program. This program included the licensing and publication of newspapers and magazines, radio programs, pamphlets, special programs, and the facilities of the so-called *Amerika-Haeuser,* or United States information centers.

Although newspaper readership was high in all segments of the German population under American control, with roughly 70 per cent consistently reporting themselves as regular readers (#175), it was nonetheless higher among the more educated, men rather than women, and city dwellers, particularly West Berliners. The American-sponsored newspaper, *Neue Zeitung,* found its greatest readership in West Berlin, where 20 per cent of the sample reported reading it regularly, in contrast to ten per cent in the American Zone. Of present and past readers, 63 per cent said that they liked the paper; 22 per cent felt that it was one-sided (#154). More generally, AMZON Germans felt that the licensed press contained fair and trustworthy news, particularly when compared with newspapers published during the war (e.g. #58).

Other written media reached smaller audiences. Less than a quarter of the respondents in the American Zone, and 42 per cent of those in West Berlin, reported that they regularly read magazines (#53, 108). Together, the American-sponsored *Heute, Neue Auslese,* and *Amerikanische Rundschau* accounted for about half of the magazine readership (#43). In February 1946 as many as 55 per cent of the respondents in the American Zone reported that they did not read books at all, but by October 1948, 50 per cent (64 per cent in West Berlin) said that they did (#13, 153). Generally, Germans claimed to prefer novels, fiction, and short stories to other types of books; specifically, they listed the *Bible* (71%), the *Prayer Book* (27%), and the works of Goethe as their favorites. Occasionally the American Military Government published information pamphlets on political issues for sale to the general public. Studies among those who had received these pamphlets as gifts revealed that the readership ranged between 35 and 75 per cent, although it was higher among men, upper socioeconomic groups, and the better educated (#89, 97, 103, 112, 129). In most cases only minorities claimed to have learned something new from these pamphlets. Majorities nonetheless felt that they presented a fair rather than one-sided picture of the facts.

Slightly more than half of the American Zone Germans described themselves as regular radio listeners (#175). Most preferred the radio station located in their own *Land* (or state), particularly in West Berlin where RIAS (Radio in the American Sector) had to compete with programs beamed from the Soviet Zone of Occupation (#45). The most popular type of program in both AMZON (72%) and West Berlin (85%) was musical. Regarding political controls, substantial majorities in both the American Zone (64%) and West Berlin (72%) felt that the Allies had censored the programs; but in contrast to West Berlin, where 58 per cent thought that the programs contained too much propaganda, in the American Zone 66 per cent did not think that this was the case (#45). The share of the AMZON public listening to the "Voice of America" varied, from 63 per cent in January 1946 to 75 per cent in October of that year and 41 per cent in May 1949 (#1, 45, 176).[11] Again, those most likely to listen to VOA programs were men, upper socioeconomic groups, the better educated, and Protestants. Although the bulk of VOA listeners (56%) considered the programming good, criticism focused on its propagandistic tendencies and its dullness (#176). More generally, however, Germans tended to rely upon the radio rather than the newspapers as their chief source of news: In January 1946, almost two-thirds (65%) thought the radio more truthful than newspapers (#1); but by the spring of 1947 only 24 per cent were more inclined to rely upon the radio, with eight per cent preferring the press and another 37 per cent finding them equal in their trustworthiness (#68).

The movie audience was not large, fluctuating around a quarter of the population (#20, 116, 171). Love themes were most popular. Allied policies sharply restricting the number of pre-1945 films that theaters could show, and the absence of extensive German production companies in the immediate postwar period, meant that foreign films, and particularly those made in the United States, dominated the market. Germans nonetheless indicated that they would have preferred German films, in large part simply because they corresponded more closely to traditional German culture.

An important aspect of the United States information policy was the establishment of information centers. Almost every major city had its own *Amerika-Haus,* where its citizens could read books and see films about the United States, hear lectures relevant to American foreign policy interests, and participate in other activities. It is remarkable that, although a majority of the people knew of these information centers and about four in ten knew what they offered, only four per cent had ever been in one. And most of these were the better educated, especially community and opinion leaders (#145).

A study conducted in early 1948 on the cumulative impact of all mass media revealed that 12 per cent of the AMZON population seemed to have no source of information whatever, and another 17 per cent had no regular source of information (#192). The more sources of information a person had, it turned out, the more likely that he had a favorable attitude toward the United States and its government and economics. Similarly, the more information the respondent had about the Soviet Union, the more likely it was that his attitude toward American capitalism was favorable.

Specific Issues of the Occupation

The number of specific issues on which the occupation authorities wanted to know German attitudes was too great for each of them to be discussed here. A few, however, deserve special attention: rationing, expellees, currency problems, the division of Germany, the question of Berlin, and more specifically, the Berlin blockade.

Food Rationing. Questions about food rationing produced mixed reactions among AMZON Germans. On the one hand, they definitely felt that they were suffering from the

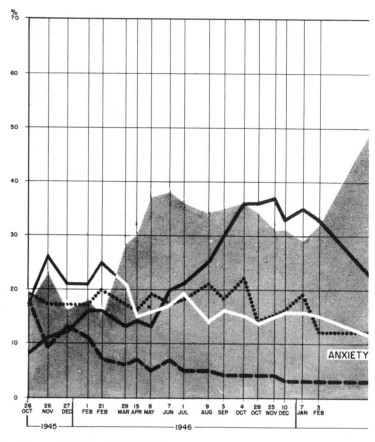

Fig. 1. *Major Cares and Worries of AMZON Germans*

Question: "What are your greatest cares and worries at the present time?"
Source: OMGUS Report 175, June 1949, p. 3.

shortages, particularly in the earlier part of the occupation (see Figure 1). Even before a cut in rations, which took place in April 1946, three in five respondents (61%) stated that they were not getting enough food to be able to work efficiently; by late April this proportion had reached 72 per cent, and it remained at 71 per cent in the following month (#15, 18). Only one in eight (12%) was satisfied with his food allotment, and another two in eight (24%) considered it adequate. Even as late as January 1949, four in ten continued to feel that they were getting insufficient food to permit efficient work (#175).[12]

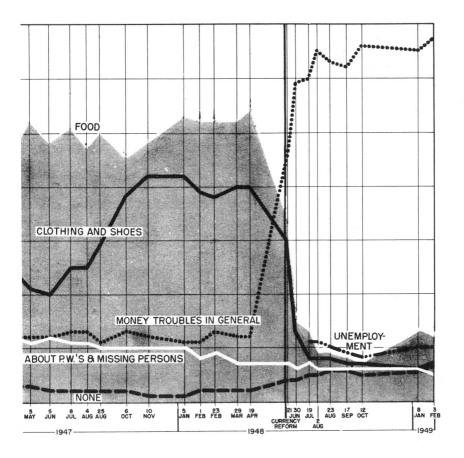

On the other hand, rationing evidently did not pose an overwhelming hardship for most Germans in the American Zone. For one thing, the rationcard system seemed to be equitable (although the number seeing it carried out unjustly rose from three per cent in November 1945 to slightly under a third in January 1948 before dropping off to about a fifth in February 1949). For another, eight out of ten AMZON Germans were able to supplement their rations by canning foods from their gardens, obtaining food from friends or relatives who lived on farms, or securing special supplements because of the nature of their work (#18). Third, and what may have been most important, they saw themselves in a good position compared to that of the residents of other zones. In May 1946, two-fifths (41%) believed that food rations were largest in the American Zone, with 29 per cent citing British Zone residents as the best fed. Less than a half of one per cent felt that rations were smallest in the American Zone, with 22 per cent naming the Soviet Zone and 18 per cent the French Zone (#18).

An interesting shift occurred in the perceived causes of food shortages. Asked in May 1946 why rations had been reduced, the responses given most frequently stressed either food shortages in Germany and/or the world (41%) or else insufficient stocks and poor crops (27%). In third place (15%) stood perceptions that available supplies had to feed others in Germany, that the country was overcrowded, or that too many occupation forces were in the country (#18). General causes, however, soon became specific. In November 1946 and July 1947, the reason given most frequently for food shortages (46 and 44 per cent, respectively) was overpopulation due to displaced persons, evacuees, and so forth (#70). Other causes listed included the loss of the war or wartime destruction (22 and 10 per cent, respectively), the loss of the eastern territories (20 and 22 per cent), an imbalance between imports and exports (19 and 17 per cent), and the black market (8 and 26 per cent).

Refugees and Expellees. The data on underlying causes of food shortages are indicative of growing hostility in postwar Germany toward refugees and expellees. The October 1946 census revealed that no less than 16.2 per cent of the entire AMZON population comprised refugees from the Soviet Zone of Occupation, expellees from Czechoslovakia, Hungary, and elsewhere in Eastern Europe, and other displaced persons. By the end of the occupation period their numbers amounted to one-fifth of the total population in the American Zone. In most of their characteristics and political attitudes the evacuees did not differ greatly from the natives. Exceptions were that the evacuees were more likely to be Catholic, adherents of the Social Democratic Party, and from unskilled occupational groups (#84, 162). Integrating these masses of refugees and expellees proved to be one of the most serious problems that the Western Allies, and later the Federal Republic, had to face.

The native inhabitants of the American Zone resented the circumstances that had led to the influx of the refugees and expellees. In March 1946, before food shortages seriously hit the AMZON Germans, as many as 14 per cent of them saw some justification in the expulsions; thereafter, only about three per cent did so, as well over 90 per cent felt them to be unjust (#14A, 175). Asked who was responsible for the expulsions, over half (51%) attributed them to the Allies, to a desire for revenge against the Germans, to antipathy in Eastern Europe toward Germans. About three in ten (29%) blamed the defunct Nazi government or Hitler himself, one per cent said that the Germans themselves were responsible, and a quarter would not or could not assign responsibility (#14A). But the question of responsibility raised the further question of who should care for the expellees. In March 1946, about two-thirds of the AMZON respondents (63%) felt that Germans should perform this task, almost half (48%) that it should be up to the Allies or the countries which expelled them (#14A). By November of that year respondents were inclined to place the main burden on the state expelling them (46%), rather than either the Germans (28%), or the Allies (14%), although it must be added that West Berliners were considerably more willing to place the burden on Germans (#47). Somewhat less than a year later, in September 1947, almost half of those asked (48%) thought that Germany should provide for the expellees; a quarter continued to feel that the native countries of the expellees should bear the costs, and 13 per cent continued to name the Allies (#81).

These native inhabitants were not much less resentful toward the expellees themselves. Throughout the occupation period, whereas about half expected the expellees to be able to get along with the native population, a solid third expected trouble (#14A, 28, 47, 175). In November 1946, at the height of the food crisis, as many as 46 per cent foresaw trouble, in contrast to a more optimistic 47 per cent. In March 1946, substantial majorities despaired of finding solutions to food (71%) and housing (64%) problems. More than a third (35%) thought the matter of jobs insoluble. In November of that year, 78 per cent of a sample in Wuerttemberg-Baden expressed their conviction that the expellees constituted an economic burden for the American Zone.[13]

It was a burden that the native residents were nonetheless willing to accept, if sometimes begrudgingly. Large majorities agreed in March 1946 that the expellees should have both economic equality (81%) and full political rights (74%). In November of the same year five in six Wuerttemberg-Badeners (83%) wanted to permit the expellees to participate fully in politics. The share of native residents seeing the expellees as German citizens rose from 49 per cent in early 1946 to 67 per cent in late 1947, during which period those viewing them as foreigners dropped from 28 to 18 per cent. Even so, throughout the entire occupation years roughly 90 per cent expected that the expellees would return to their homelands if they were permitted to do so.

The perceptions of the expellees themselves differed sharply in important respects. To be sure, most expressed a desire to return to their homelands, but the percentage expressing this desire declined steadily, and it was persistently lower than the percentage of native inhabitants expecting the expellees to return to their homelands if given a chance.[14] Moreover, almost three in four (73%) viewed themselves in September 1947 as German citizens. By June 1947 almost two-thirds (64%) were expressing the expectation that they would not get along with the native Germans. The share of those expressing actual dissatisfaction with their treatment by local populations rose from seven per cent in March 1946 to 50 per cent in June 1948. And majorities persistently felt that the *Land* governments were not doing all within their power to assist the expellees. To all this, however, must be added the fact that, after the severe food and economic crises were over, the level of latent hostility among the expellees declined.

The Currency Reform. The key to ending the economic crises that contributed so much to such problems as mounting tensions between the expellees and the native residents was the currency reform, carried through in June 1948. In their earliest surveys the American occupation authorities focused on popular perceptions of inflationary trends, the standing of the *Reichsmark*, rent and price controls, rationing, the black market, and still other problems emanating in part from the Allied inability to cooperate fully on currency reform.

The first two years of the occupation saw increasing desperation among AMZON Germans. In January 1946, 67 per cent of the respondents reported that their incomes were adequate; two years later only 57 per cent felt this way (#100). Between January and June 1946 half the population believed that anti-inflationary measures would not succeed (#60). Confidence in the *Reichsmark* fell to the point where, in June 1947, about as many persons felt that it would maintain its then-current value as thought it would not (#100). We noted earlier a declining belief in the fairness of the rationcard system, accompanying increasing worries about the adequacy of food rations. Meanwhile, there was a growing recognition of the importance of the black market in German economic life. Although in February 1946 over half (51%) denied the existence of a black market in their community, two years later 71 per cent knew of one (see Figure 2). A more general mood of pessimism underscored all these trends: Whereas in December 1945 nearly eight in ten thought that economic conditions would improve, by April 1947 only 45 per cent thought so (#100).

There was a measure of confusion about the sources and solutions of their economic woes. Asked why ten times as much currency was in circulation in July 1946 as before the war, most attributed it either to black market dealers (66%) or Nazis and war profiteers (33%), and 17 per cent were unable to suggest a reason. And yet pluralities of 40 per cent in the

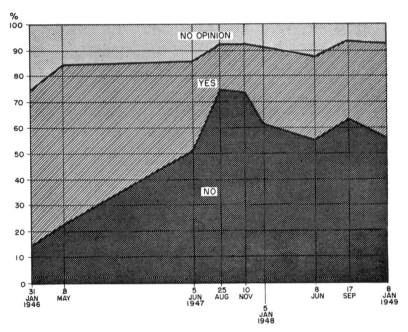

Fig. 2. *Government Efforts to Overcome the Black Market*

Question: "In your opinion, are the government officials doing everything to overcome the black market?"
Source: OMGUS Report 175, June 1949, p. 37.

American Zone and 52 per cent in West Berlin opposed a currency reform at that time (with 36 and 40 per cent respectively, favoring it). Presented with alternative schedules for carrying out such a reform, however, a plurality in the American Zone (44%) favored an immediate adjustment rather than delaying it until economic conditions should improve (12%) or until a new government should be formed (16%). In the meantime, most of those with opinions preferred to keep their reserves in goods rather than cash or bank accounts (#32).

Once instituted, the currency reform received hearty approval (#133). Nine in ten termed it necessary, and over half (53%) thought that it should have taken place earlier. It tended to create an optimistic mood: Over half (54%) expected the new currency to retain its value, 58 per cent believed that they would get along better during the coming year because of the currency reform, seven in ten intended to make additional purchases, and most expected the reform either to limit (71%) or overcome (14%) the black market. There was nonetheless some dissatisfaction. It focused particularly upon the ten to one conversion ratio which, according to more than a third (35%) of the AMZON Germans, treated the small savers more harshly than the rich. And 77 per cent expected – correctly, as it turned out – that the currency reform would lead to greater unemployment (see Figure 1).

The actual effect of the currency reform was a bag of blessings mixed with curses. On the one hand, after some temporary dislocations, it permitted the three western zones of Germany and the three western sectors of Berlin to get their economies moving again. That these West Germans could, before another decade was over, establish themselves as the economically strongest state in Europe is in no small measure an indication of the success of the currency reform and similar decisions made during the occupation. But, on the other hand, for Germans throughout the occupied territories it was a symbolic step that sealed the division of Germany into East and West.

The Division of Germany. The occupation years witnessed growing uneasiness about the prospect for ending the "temporary" division of Germany. Germans in territories under American control saw clearly a split emerging along east-west lines, due in large part to the inability of the victorious wartime Allies to agree upon the course of Germany's future. The percentage seeing the Allies as having furthered the reconstruction of Germany increased from a quarter in September 1946 to a half in January 1948, with the share of more optimistic responses declining from four to three in nine (#100). By January 1948 some 85 per cent of the respondents thought that the Four Powers were not cooperating successfully in the reconstruction (see Figure 3). Four in five did not think that a unified Germany would survive the end of the occupation (#175).

The failure of successive conferences of foreign ministers in 1947 enhanced this pessimistic mood. AMZON Germans thought that the Soviet Union had torpedoed the Moscow

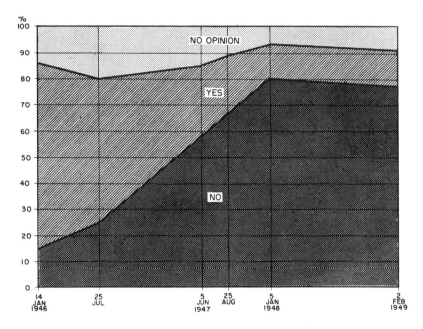

Fig. 3. *The Prospects for a United Germany*

Question: "Do you believe the Allies will cooperate successfully to leave behind a united Germany at the end of the occupation?"
Source: OMGUS Report 175, June 1949, p. 58.

Conference (10 March-24 April). A substantial plurality (49%) did not expect the Allies to conclude a peace treaty by the summer of 1948 (#62, 63). To be sure, Berliners in the American-controlled borough of Neukoelln hoped that the London Conference (25 November-16 December) would produce such a peace treaty, but only 14 per cent dared to believe that it would (#75). A spot survey after the breakdown of this conference revealed an overwhelming sentiment among West Berliners that the Soviets were to blame (#86). One in three (32%) felt that it meant the final division of Germany, another 26 per cent expected a continuation of the status quo, and as many as one in seven (15%) said simply that conditions would deteriorate or that war would ensue.

By the spring of 1948 Germans were prepared to accept a government for the three western zones of occupation. American, British, and French representatives, together with their colleagues from Belgium, the Netherlands, and Luxembourg, met in London during the first half of 1948 to lay the groundwork for such a government. Of the relatively few respondents who later claimed to know anything about the London proposals, the bulk favored them (#131). And, when apprised of these proposals, 78 per cent of all respondents in the American Zone (89 per cent in West Berlin, 93 per cent in Bremen) reacted positively. Support dropped to 72 per cent, however, when the interviewers pointed out the possibility that only representatives from the western zones would be able to help set up the government. A subsequent survey in August 1948 found 70 per cent favoring the creation of a provisional government for western Germany, with only one in eight (12%) opposed to the idea (#136).

In agreeing to a West German government, the respondents were evidently well aware that it meant a continued, and perhaps permanent, division of their country. The comment made most frequently by informed respondents (26%), when asked about the disadvantages of the London proposals, was "the division of Germany" but, it must be added, more either expressed no opinion (35%) or saw no disadvantages (8%). Told that, according to the London proposals, the French Zone would be added to the bizonal (American-British) economic arrangements, 72 per cent of the entire sample saw it as a step toward unification, six per cent as a step backward (#131). A more explicit question in August 1948 seemed to clarify this apparent ambiguity: Almost half (47%) of the respondents in the American Zone thought that the establishment of a provisional government for western Germany would widen the East-West split, with only two-thirds as many (33%) feeling that it would make no difference (#136).

The reasons for favoring a West German government were diverse. Asked what advantages the London proposals meant for western Germany, 36 per cent of the respondents who knew what these proposals were pointed to better living conditions and another 14 per cent mentioned that they were a step toward independence. Five times more respondents either saw no advantages (18%) or had no opinion (24%) than the number (8%) mentioning that the proposals would constitute a bar to communism (#131). And yet, as subsequent questions and surveys revealed, a fear of communism was very prevalent.[15] In July 1948, 95 per cent of all AMZON respondents expressed a preference for a democratic government in western Germany alone and only one per cent for a communist central government for all of Germany. More generally, Germans were becoming increasingly outspoken in asserting their dislike of the Soviet Union and distrust of its intentions (e.g. #185). Throughout the period from January 1947 to February 1949 approximately half agreed with the proposition that "The Americans should reconstruct Germany as soon as possible in order to avoid her becoming a prey to Communism" (#175).

We shall return later to the question of German attitudes toward communism and the Soviet Union. The point to be stressed here is that these negative views helped induce Germans in the western zones of occupation to accept a specific policy. This policy sought to strengthen the ability of these areas to resist pressure from the East, at the cost of steps aimed at restoring German unity. And perhaps in no place in that portion of Germany under Western controls and at no time was this hostility to the East more prevalent than in West Berlin during the blockade months from June 1948 to May 1949.

Berlin and the Blockade. The breakdown of interallied cooperation, the currency crisis, and the competition to create a Germany that would be an ally in the raging Cold War all met in June 1948 on the banks of the Spree River in Berlin. Using the Western currency reform as its justification, on the 24th of that month the Soviet Union closed the roads and canals leading to the western sectors of the city. The West's response was quick to come. American officials agreed that it would be technically feasible, however difficult, to airlift sufficient supplies to the two and a quarter million West Berliners. But the effectiveness of this tactic in countering the blockade would rest upon the morale of the city's leadership and its people. Ernst Reuter and other leaders gave their assurances immediately. But what about the mass of West Berliners?

Spot surveys, bolstered by more substantial investigations later, revealed that Berliners in the western sectors stood solidly behind the West and the Allied air lift. Four weeks after the imposition of the blockade 98 per cent of a Berlin sample expressed the view that the West was pursuing the correct policy (#130). From the very outset and throughout the blockade about nine in ten were confident that the Americans would stay in Berlin as long as they remained in Germany. This is not to say that they were without worries. Although three in four (77%) felt that the Western Powers were doing their utmost to relieve distressed conditions in Berlin (see Figure 4) and five in six (84%) thought that the air lift could provide them with sufficient food, more than half (52%) doubted that the air lift could carry them through the winter months.

Confidence grew as the air lift proved increasingly successful. By September 85 per cent – and by October 89 per cent – expected the air lift to provision them adequately during the winter months (#141, 150). Meanwhile, however bad their circumstances were, 88 per cent of the West Berliners preferred them to uniting their city under the communists (4%). And the percentage of those reporting that, if given an opportunity, they would leave Berlin dropped from 43 per cent in July to 30 per cent in October. Respondents in the American Zone were somewhat less sanguine about the Berlin situation. Only seven in ten were convinced that the Americans would remain in Berlin, nine in ten thought the Western position to be the correct one, and only somewhat over half (56%) thought that the air lift was providing sufficient food to maintain rations at their preblockade levels (#144, 175).

Ultimately, of course, the air lift exceeded all earlier hopes. The Soviet lifting of the blockade in May 1949 was widely seen as a triumph both for the American policy of hardness and the West Berliners' firmness. It is this perception that West Berliners celebrate down to the present day in their loyalty to the West in general and the United States in

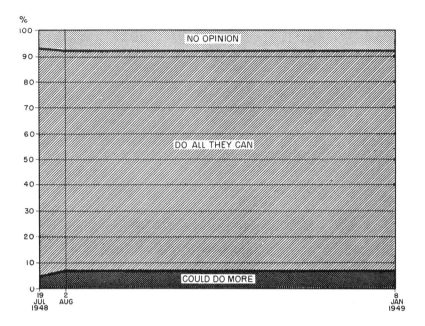

Fig. 4a. *The Allies' Efforts to Aid Blockaded Berlin: AMZON Views*

particular.[16] But the blockade also left a divided Berlin in its wake – a divided Berlin that symbolized the division of Germany as a whole. What is more, the Federal Republic that emerged in West Germany no longer had Berlin as the focal point of its attention. If 58 per cent of the residents of the American Zone agreed in August 1947 that Berlin should be Germany's capital, it remains a fact that the founding fathers of the Federal Republic located their capital in Bonn, a choice in which two out of three AMZON Germans with opinions concurred (#71, 180). Berlin itself became a symbol – a symbol of the united Germany that used to be, a symbol of the united Germany that many hope for in the future.

In their concern with these and a plethora of other issues stemming both from the need to make immediate policy decisions and from changes in the environment of interallied cooperation, the researchers of the Opinion Survey Section did not lose sight of the long-range issues that had brought them,

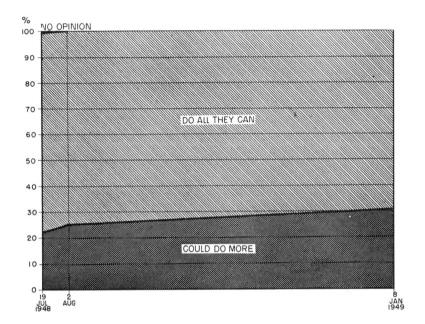

Fig. 4b. *The Allies' Efforts to Aid Blockaded Berlin: Berlin Views*

Question: "In your opinion are the Western Powers doing all they possibly can to relieve the needs of Berlin or could they do more?"
Source: OMGUS Report 175, June 1949, p. 52.

and indeed the entire structure of the military occupation, to Germany in the first place.

DEMOCRATIZING POSTWAR GERMANY

Among the purposes announced by Churchill, Roosevelt, and Stalin when they were formulating plans for the postwar occupation of Germany, the democratization of the country was particularly important. This policy implied several things. Most immediately, of course, it meant the punishment of those guilty of the Nazi excesses, the removal of Nazi sympathizers from important posts in governmental or private life, the effective disarmament of the country, and, more generally, the elimination of symbols of the Nazi past. More problematic was a second task – democratizing Germany's political culture.

Removing the leaders and reminders of the past was one thing, but revising the predispositions, perceptions, and values of an entire population was quite another. For the Opinion Survey Section it meant, on the one hand, an assessment of the state of German political culture and, on the other, a continual evaluation of the effectiveness of Allied programs aimed at changing this culture.

Nazism and Denazification

Many Americans, no less than Europeans, harbored deep resentments toward their wartime enemy, Germany. What explained the fact, many asked themselves, that Germany had initiated major wars of expansion three times within the past century? Was it something inherent in German national character? A common assumption was that in the breast of every German beat the heart of a Nazi. It was this assumption on which rested some of the early wartime policies for the postwar occupation – the Morgenthau-White plan, which called for a demilitarized, dismembered, and pastoralized Germany, and even Joint Chiefs of Staff Paper 1067 (JCS 1067), which set down guidelines for the American Military Government to follow. And one even sees it in the initial questions and reports emanating from the offices of the OMGUS Opinion Survey Section. But how true was it? To what extent were Germans blind adherents of National Socialism?

Attitudes toward National Socialism. It is not entirely clear how thoroughly mobilized in their support of Adolf Hitler the German population was. Few (7%) claimed to have read his *Mein Kampf* in its entirety, although another 16 per cent remembered reading part of it (#2; cf. #92). Only one in eight (12%) recalled trusting Hitler as a leader up to the end of the war; over half claimed either never to have trusted him (35%) or to have lost their faith in him by the time war had broken out in 1939 (16%). Asked whether they would like to have seen

Hitler before the International Military Tribunal at Nuremberg, interestingly enough, 72 per cent of AMZON Germans responded positively in October 1946, and only 12 per cent felt it better that he had spared himself this ignominy.[17]

Attitude toward Hitler notwithstanding, large numbers of postwar Germans in the areas under American control continued to express perceptions characteristic of National Socialist ideology (#19). To cite some examples, nine per cent agreed that "a civilian is an unworthy (lower) person compared to a member of the army"; ten per cent that "in all probability foreign nations and races are enemies; therefore, one should be prepared at all times to attack them first," and that "if a pure German marries a non-Aryan wife he should be condemned"; 12 per cent that "the horrors committed by the Germans are an invention of the propaganda of our enemies"; 15 per cent that "the Communists and the Social Democrats should be suppressed"; 18 per cent that "only a government with a dictator is able to create a strong nation," and that "this war was caused by a conspiracy between the International Bankers and the Communists"; 19 per cent that "the German people were the victims of a conspiracy by other nations"; 20 per cent that "it would have been much better for the Allies to have had a war with Russia instead of with Germany"; 29 per cent that "the publication of no book that criticizes a government or recommends any changes in government should be permitted"; 30 per cent that "Negroes are members of an unworthy (lower) race"; 33 per cent that "Jews should not have the same rights as those belonging to the Aryan race"; 37 per cent denied that "extermination of the Jews and Poles and other non-Aryans was not necessary for the security of Germans"; and 52 per cent agreed that "territories such as Danzig, Sudetenland, and Austria should be part of Germany proper." Two caveats are important in interpreting these findings. First, we must wonder whether these response patterns are typically German or whether, to the contrary, Americans, Frenchmen, and citizens of other industrialized countries might not agree to similar propositions. Second, these data say nothing about the extent to which such perceptions antedated the emergence of Nazism in Germany.

The Opinion Survey Section made an interesting attempt to test the latter point. Using the split-sample technique, it sought to find out what differences would emerge on perspectives according to whether assertions were explicitly identified as stemming from Hitler. Thus half of a sample responded to the question, "Before the war it was often said that parts of Europe with considerable German minorities (e.g. Sudetenland) should be legally reincorporated in Germany; did you agree to that or not?" and the other half got the question, "Before the war Hitler often said that parts of Europe with considerable German minorities (e.g. Sudetenland) should be legally reincorporated in Germany; did you agree to that or not?" In response to the questions, 36 per cent of the first sample reported having agreed, as did 39 per cent of the second sample. A similar pair of questions dealt with the prewar sentiment that "international Jewry alone would profit from the war." In this case 14 per cent agreed with the generalized proposition and 11 per cent were willing to identify themselves with Hitler in accepting it. A third pair of questions asked about the putative superiority of the "Nordic race," with results similar to the second. In short, there were no statistically significant differences in the responses to differently-worded questions. This in turn suggests that Hitler may merely have tapped a set of underlying perspectives while, to be sure, reinforcing them at the same time through his propaganda.

Further indications of this are to be found in the postwar population's unwillingness to reject Nazism completely. In eleven surveys between November 1945 and December 1946, an average of 47 per cent expressed their feeling that National Socialism was a good idea badly carried out; by August 1947 this figure had risen to 55 per cent remaining fairly constant throughout the remainder of the occupation (#60, 68, 175). Meanwhile, the share of respondents thinking it a bad idea dropped from 41 to about 30 per cent (see Figure 5).[18] A breakdown of the August 1947 survey revealed that the respondents most likely to describe National Socialism as a

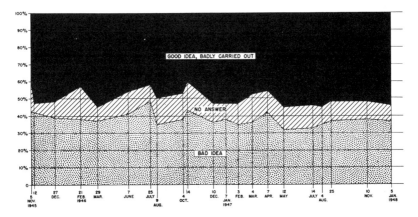

Fig. 5. *Views on National Socialism*

Question: "Was National Socialism a bad idea, or a good idea badly carried out?"
Source: OMGUS Report 175, June 1949, p. 9.

good idea badly carried out were those with nine to twelve years of schooling (64%), people under the age of 30 (68%), Protestants (64%), former NSDAP members (67%), West Berliners (62%), and Hessians (61%). They also tended to be more critical than others of the postwar news media, to be more likely to find fault with democracy, and to prefer a government offering security rather than one stressing liberty. Moreover, asked to choose between National Socialism and Communism, the number opting for the former increased from 19 per cent in November 1945 to well over twice that figure in February 1949, with the number preferring the latter alternative declining from 35 to 3 per cent (#60, 175).

The Nuremberg War Crimes Trials. The relatively cool attitude that postwar Germans displayed toward Hitler carried over to other leaders of the Nazi state. This view came out clearly in their reactions to the trial of the major war criminals before the International Military Tribunal in Nuremberg. Originally, the IMT brought an indictment against 24 top Nazi leaders, three of whom ultimately did not stand trial. After sessions lasting from November 1945 to October 1946, the Tribunal handed down 11 death sentences (plus another death sentence for Martin Bormann, tried *in absentia*), seven prison sentences ranging from ten years to life, and three acquittals. The Tribunal also declared the leadership corps of the Nazi Party, the Gestapo and the State Security Service, and the SS to be "criminal organizations."

Generally speaking, popular interest in the trial was high. In January 1946, 78 per cent of German respondents in the American Zone of Occupation indicated that they had read newspaper articles about the trial. Subsequent surveys, however, revealed both a declining interest in following the press treatment (67 per cent in March and 72 per cent in August) and that less than half of these read the reports in their entirety (34 per cent in March and 31 per cent in August). In October 1946, 93 per cent of the respondents claimed to have heard about the judgments (#16, 33). Confidence in the completeness and reliability of the press also dropped, from 79 per cent in October 1945 to 67 per cent in August 1946. In October, after the trial's completion, 48 per cent indicated that the newspaper reports had been complete, 65 per cent reliable (45 per cent complete *and* reliable), and six per cent thought that they had been neither.

The trial increased AMZON Germans' knowledge of the Nazi era. In December 1945, 84 per cent of these respondents indicated that they had learned something new from the trial: 64 per cent specified the concentration camps, 23 per cent the extermination of Jews and other groups, and seven per cent the character of the Nazi leaders; one out of eight (13%) said that he had known nothing about the evils of National Socialism prior to the trial.[19] In October 1946, the share of Germans saying that they had learned something new had dropped off to 71 per cent, and the number claiming that they had not learned anything new doubled to 27 per cent from 13 per cent in December 1945.

Asked about the guilt of the accused, AMZON Germans gave increasingly differentiated answers. The share of respondents holding all the accused to be guilty rose from 70 per cent in December 1945 to 75 per cent in the following March, only to drop to 52 per cent by August 1946. (In March, 71 per cent indicated that all the accused shared guilt for the preparation of the war, with another ten per cent wanting to except some of them; 59 per cent did not feel that the accused could defend themselves in the face of the charges levied against them.) Conversely, the share holding none to be guilty dropped from five per cent in December 1945 to one per cent in March 1946 and to less than a half of one per cent by August. After hearing the verdicts, the respondents were generally satisfied: 55 per cent felt that the sentences had been just, but 21 per cent felt them to be too mild and nine per cent too harsh.[20] Well over half felt it proper that organizations should be indicted for their criminal activity; the percentages varied from 56 per cent in October 1945 to 60 per cent in December 1945 to 59 per cent in October 1946.

Most AMZON Germans with opinions felt that the trial was being conducted fairly (an average of 79 per cent in seven surveys conducted from October 1945 to August 1946, as opposed to four per cent who saw them as unfair). To this, however, must be added the fact that the perception of unfairness crept up slowly over this period. In October 1946, after the conclusion of the trial, 78 per cent of the respondents thought that it had been fair, and six per cent thought it unfair.

These data lend themselves, of course, to varying interpretations. One possible interpretation is that the postwar Germans were truly desirous of seeing those responsible for the Nazi excesses punished by the International Military Tribunal. Others may see in these findings a large body of politically apathetic and irresponsible Germans looking for scapegoats to exonerate themselves of any blame for the crimes of the Nazi era (see Figure 6). Either interpretation clearly needs additional information (such as that provided by close readings of the German press, the works of postwar publicists, and memoirs) before it can be accepted. Another line of collateral data stems from public attitudes in postwar Germany toward the extensive denazification proceedings.

Denazification. Set up under JCS 1067, the denazification proceedings aimed at removing from "public office and from positions of importance in quasi-public and private

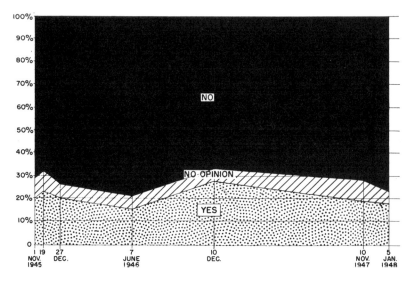

Fig. 6. *Collective German Responsibility for World War II*

Question: "Do you think that the entire German people are responsible for the war because they let a government come to power which plunged the whole world into war?"
Source: OMGUS Report 100, March 1948, p. 8.

enterprises" those Germans who had been "active supporters of Nazism or militarism and all other persons hostile to Allied purposes." This meant searching the records of some 13 million residents of the American Zone of Occupation, and ultimately processing some 3.5 million cases. By the beginning of 1947 the American authorities had removed 292,089 such persons from public or important private positions and excluded an additional 81,673.[21]

Unlike the war crimes trials, which focused upon a handful of very prominent Nazis, the denazification proceedings affected the AMZON population more directly. In principle, at least, every fourth citizen was subject to punishment. The immensity of the task of trying all such persons, together with the implications for the efficient operation of German industry and government should this many people be removed from positions of responsibility, soon led the occupation authorities to lower their sights.[22] Even so, the potential disruption of German life was great.

What at first glance is most surprising is the fact that Germans in the American Zone seemed to endorse the idea of denazification. Indeed, in January 1949, when the hearings were coming to a close, two-thirds (66%) thought it important to hold to account "such people as furthered National Socialism in any way" (#182). Significantly enough, however, the most ardent opponents of the idea of denazification were the highly educated and the upper middle and upper socioeconomic groups.

Acceptance in principle did not imply acceptance in practice. The number of respondents satisfied with the way in which denazification was being carried out declined from roughly half in the winter of 1945-1946, when the idea was new and relatively untried, to about a third from October 1946 to the following September, to about a sixth in January 1949 (#7, 60, 182). The dissatisfied respondents (65%) were almost equal in number to those approving of the idea of denazification (66%).[23] And again the more socially mobilized groups within the population were the most likely to express criticism.

The most frequently heard objection to the denazification procedures was that they dealt too harshly with minor party members in comparison with the major ones (#7, 182). The second most persistent complaint was that the proceedings were too arbitrary and the judgments too inconsistent. Only from those who thought the program too easy did interviewers hear the view expressed that some punishments should be harsher.

Those directly affected by the proceedings, because of their past affiliation with the NSDAP, did not share this latter view. In contrast to respondents without such connections, only five per cent of whom had been dismissed from their jobs once or more times between January 1945 and September 1947, well over a third of the former members had suffered such a fate (#80). Over four in five reported that they were either much worse off (69%) or somewhat worse off (13%) in their current jobs than they were formerly. Half (51%) of the unaffected but as many as 78 per cent of those who claimed former membership in the NSDAP expressed dissatisfaction with the denazification proceedings. Asked what the most serious consequences of these proceedings were, former Nazi adherents most frequently named the lack of governmental and business experts, as well as the economic stress suffered by those removed from their jobs.

All this bitterness notwithstanding, few Germans were willing to take denazification entirely out of the hands of American occupation authorities. In March 1946 only one in eleven wanted primary German responsibility, a position held by every sixth respondent a year later (#7, 55). The reason most frequently given for this was the expectation that the Americans would be more impartial than Germans in meting out justice. But underlying this was the simple unwillingness to assume full responsibility for an unpopular program.

Summing up, the views on National Socialism, the Nuremberg trials, and the denazification proceedings uncovered by the OMGUS surveys point to a persistent pattern. On the one hand, there were relatively few wholehearted Nazis in the American Zone. Our impressionistic judgment, based on a review of all the surveys reported in this volume, is that roughly 15 to 18 percent of the adult population were unreconstructed Nazis in the immediate postwar period.[24] The bulk of Germans emphatically rejected the specifically Nazi aspects and leaders of their recent history. And it seemed unlikely, at least for the near future, that they would again follow a pied piper of Hitler's caliber — especially if he were garbed in explicitly Nazi robes.

On the other hand, however, AMZON Germans were far from unanimous in turning their backs on National Socialism. They increasingly expressed their view that National Socialism was basically a good idea, although carried out poorly (see Figure 5). Substantial numbers continued to subscribe to sentiments closely tied up with Nazi ideology (as well, of course, as with other racist and reactionary ideologies, such as shown in Figure 7). And not only did they refuse to accept responsibility for the crimes of the Nazi era, but they objected when denazification boards levied stiff penalties upon the lesser supporters of the NSDAP.

Even if the Nazi Party and its leaders were discredited, then, it was by no means certain that their underlying principles were. The eradication of the outward manifestations of Nazism seems not to have eliminated the potential for movements

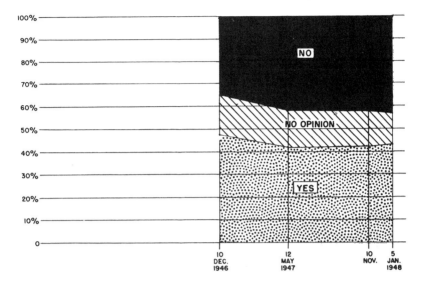

Fig. 7.   *Government and Racial Superiority*
   Question: "Do you think that some races of people are more fit to rule than others?"
   Source: OMGUS Report 100, March 1948, p. 9.

equally totalitarian in their aims although explicitly eschewing the "brown" past. But what about the more positive aspects of the American occupation policy – those seeking to change, or democratize, German political culture?

Re-education for Democracy

Crucial to any attempt to change German political culture was a determination of what, in fact, its chief characteristics were. Although this is a topic that has interested writers since the time of Tacitus, the possibility of investigating it in an objective, systematic manner did not really exist before World War II. The OMGUS surveys came at a time when social scientists were developing the necessary concepts and tools. It is not surprising, therefore, that these surveys sometimes seem naive to the modern scholar: The hypotheses are occasionally primitive, the questions used to test them often not very sophisticated and the conclusions rather overly simplified.

Moreover, given the preoccupation of American occupation authorities with the heinous interlude of Nazism, it is also not surprising that some of their research suffered from an underlying tendentiousness. These caveats notwithstanding, the surveys provided some material basic both to the occupiers trying to change the perspectives on which German politics rested as well as to subsequent investigators interested in the actual impact of the occupation upon Germany's political culture.[25]

German Political Culture. There are, of course, many aspects of German political culture that deserve mention. Of most importance here are the views of Germans on authority and democratic processes, no less than aspects of their political behavior.

"Two souls, alas, do dwell in my breast!" lamented Goethe's Faust. And roughly the same is true of the postwar German body politic (although not necessarily of individual Germans). Living amongst a sizable proportion of "democrats" was a goodly number of "authoritarians," conceivably susceptible to the sirens of yet another demagogue promising an ordered society.

As suggested earlier, it is not difficult to demonstrate the persistence in postwar Germany of perspectives closely associated with National Socialist ideology: 15 per cent of the AMZON Germans and West Berliners willing to suppress leftwing parties; 18 per cent agreeing on the importance of a dictator in creating a strong nation; 29 per cent amenable to censorship of publications critical of the government; 33 per cent feeling that Jews should not have the same rights as others (#19). Perhaps one in six could be said to have held explicitly Nazi orientations. In December 1946 the Opinion Survey Section classified 21 per cent of its AMZON respondents as anti-Semites, and another 18 per cent as intense anti-Semites — a total of 39 per cent (#49).

And yet to write off the mass of postwar Germans as authoritarians and racists would most surely be an injustice. Indeed, the main finding of the extensive survey cited in the previous paragraph is that most Germans had perspectives that were by and large democratic. An average of three in ten responded in a democratic direction on each of the eleven scales included in the survey; an additional third answered in a democratic direction on all but one question in each scale (#19). Similarly, the later survey on anti-Semitism found a fifth (20%) of the AMZON population to have little bias and another fifth (19%) to be nationalists but not racists – again a total of 39 per cent (#49).

Other signs of a predispositional duality in German society are scattered throughout the OMGUS surveys. Consider, for example, German views on the purpose and means of education. In January 1948, respondents considered the chief purpose of the schools to be a comprehensive education (37 per cent in West Berlin and 52 per cent in Stuttgart); the second most frequently mentioned purpose in West Berlin (28%) was discipline and, in Stuttgart (20%), job training; and only one in six opted for the response "to teach children to think for themselves" (#95). An earlier survey revealed that 65 per cent in the American Zone and 51 per cent in the American and British sectors of Berlin approved of granting teachers the right to whip or beat "very disobedient and very unruly children" (#66). (It must be added, however, that those opposing such a right were much more vehement in expressing their views than were those favoring it.)

Another example focuses upon the freedoms that Germans thought necessary. Asked whether they preferred a government offering "economic security and the possibility of a good income" or else one guaranteeing "free elections, freedom of speech, a free press and religious freedom," six out of ten persistently opted for economic security from February 1947 to January 1949, with half that number preferring guaranteed liberties (#175; see Figure 8). Asked in June 1947 which of a list of four freedoms they considered most important, a plurality (31%) selected commercial freedom. Of the remainder, 22 per cent chose religious freedom, 19 per cent free elections, and 14 per cent free speech (#82). Close to a third indicated that they would give up certain rights "if the state would

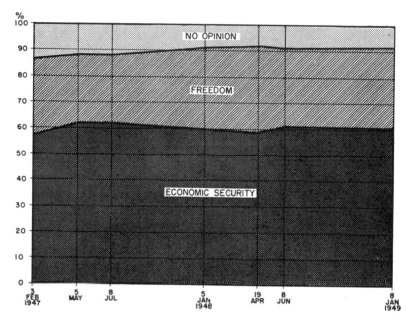

Fig. 8. *Economic Security vs. Guaranteed Freedoms*

Question: "Which of these types of government would you, personally, choose as better:
A. A government which offers the people economic security and the possibility of a good income,
B. A government which guarantees free elections, freedom of speech, a free press and religious freedom?"
Source: OMGUS Report 175, June 1949, p. 7.

thereby promise economic security" (#175). About half of those willing to give up some rights were willing to do without the right "to vote for the political party" of their choice; almost a third the right "to read all the books and magazines" they wished to read; almost a quarter the right "to work in the place" they liked; about a tenth the right "to express [their] opinion freely"; and roughly a twentieth the right "to bring up [their] children according to [their own] view." Regarding freedom of speech, although 77 per cent were willing to grant it to all Germans, only 55 per cent agreed that it should be applicable for communists (#48).

Still another area in which this duality appears in the survey data comprises German attitudes toward leadership. On the one hand, large majorities felt that the people should determine what direction the government should follow: In response to one question, 78 per cent of the AMZON residents thought that the people, rather than the politicians, (14%) should perform that task; in response to another question they expressed their preference for the people (70%) over the "experts" (23%) to perform it (#98).[26] On the other hand, in a situation close to them, AMZON youth displayed a different predisposition (#96, 99, 101). Two-fifths of those in youth clubs reported having appointed leaders rather than elected leaders (51%). Roughly the same percentages (41 and 58 percent, respectively), preferred the different modes of selection. In the event of a difference of opinion on the day on which their club should meet next, 43 per cent felt that they should meet on the day the leader wanted, and 56 per cent wanted to meet on the day chosen by the majority.

In evaluating these data, several points must be borne in mind. First, although they suggest a duality, this duality did not permeate all aspects of social life or politics. There were many areas which enjoyed high degrees of consensus. It nonetheless does seem that there was a sharp split in occupied Germany on some of the more crucial aspects of political life. Second, this dualism was not spread evenly throughout the areas of Germany under American control. Typically, the more democratic individuals were those living in large cities, respondents with 12 or more years of schooling, professionals rather than workers or employees, adherents of the Social Democratic Party, and middle income groups. Third, the data presented above say little about either the salience of the issues to the respondents or the likelihood that they would translate their perspectives into action. Finally, the data also tell us nothing about the middle groups — the sometimes substantial numbers of Germans hovering between democratic and authoritarian perspectives. In what circumstances, for instance, would they swing their support in one direction or another?

Political Participation. The first surveys conducted by the American military authorities revealed a fairly low interest in political activity: Only half felt themselves sufficiently informed about political events, and most of the remainder

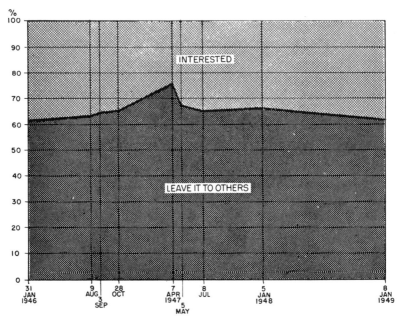

Fig. 9. *Interest in Politics*

> *Question:* "Are you yourself interested in political affairs or do you prefer to leave that to others?"
> *Source:* OMGUS Report 175, June 1949, p. 13.

indicated that they were making no effort to get more information (see Figure 9); over three-quarters were not and did not intend to become members of a political party; whereas seven in ten knew that political meetings were allowed, less than a third of these claimed to have attended one; and about two-thirds of those eligible to vote in elections held in January 1946 had in fact done so (#3). In April 1946, 76 per cent flatly said that, if they had a son leaving school, they would not like to see him choose politics as a profession (#10; see Figure 10). Typical of the comments made by those respondents were "politics is a dirty business" and "one is a politician for ten years and then lands in a concentration camp" (see also Figure 11). The percentage seeing politics as a worthy profession (14%) was considerably lower than that in England (25%) or the United States (21-25%). In September of the same year, just before referenda on the state constitutions and elections to the state parliaments, a series of questions demonstrated that only

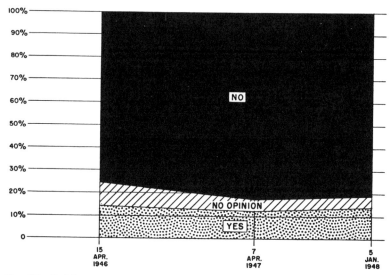

Fig. 10. *Politics as a Career*

Question: "If you had a son who had just finished school, would you like to see him take up politics as a career?"
Source: OMGUS Report 100, March 1949, p. 15.

one in five persons was sufficiently interested to have even the barest of information on the issues at stake (#26).

Similar findings emerged from surveys in the middle of 1947, more than two years after the beginning of the occupation. About two in five (42 per cent in May, 40 per cent in August) felt sufficiently well informed about current political events; of the remainder almost four in five either had not bothered to seek further information or did not care to (#72, 74). Levels of political information varied. Although 88 per cent knew the name of their town's mayor, only 47 per cent could name the minister president of their *Land* and 60 per cent could adequately define a secret ballot. Two-thirds (67 per cent in May, 64 per cent in August) preferred to leave politics to others rather than to concern themselves personally with it. And, indeed, few were active politically. In May, 90 per cent of the AMZON respondents indicated that they were personally doing everything possible to help rebuild Germany — but only seven per cent reported voluntarily helping with the census of October 1946, six per cent did any sort of volunteer work in

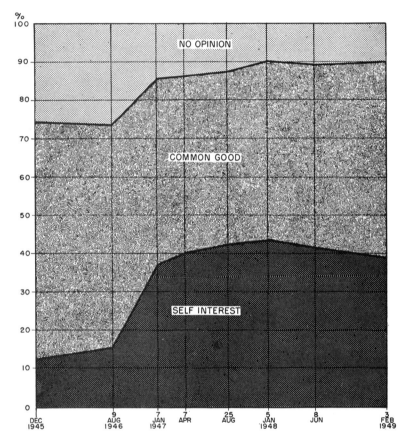

Fig. 11. *Trust in Local German Officials*

Question: "In general, do officials in the local German government work for the good of the community or are they primarily self-interested?"
Source: OMGUS Report 175, June 1949, p. 16.

their local community, and four per cent were members of a political party. As many as 40 per cent claimed no preference for any political party — a figure half again as great as for the occupation period as a whole (see Figure 12). More generally, they were inclined to see the responsibility for government lying with officials rather than with voters: Asked about poor government, 38 per cent held government officials responsible, 26 per cent the voting public, with 12 per cent assigning responsibility to both; regarding good government, 48 per cent were willing to give credit to government officials, 21 per cent to the voters, and 13 percent to both equally.

Two years later, on the eve of the promulgation of West Germany's Federal Republic, political participation continued at relatively low levels (#191). Few were well informed about politics: Less than one in six could venture a guess as to whether or not their state constitutions contained provisions for initiatives and referenda (and of these only somewhat over half gave the correct answer), 58 per cent could name the minister president of their *Land*, and as few as 39 per cent knew that the Parliamentary Assembly, which had met in Bonn since the fall of 1948, had drawn up a constitution for West Germany (but less than half of these could claim any familiarity with this constitution). Nor was interest in politics much greater. Two-thirds (67%) continued to prefer leaving politics to others (see Figure 9), only 38 per cent perceived any great interest in politics among their contemporaries, and, when asked the cause of low participation in the affairs of government, 61 per cent indicated a general lack of interest, 20 per cent a lack of opportunity. Whereas 76 per cent expressed a willingness to work an hour daily without pay for the economic reconstruction of Germany, only a third of that number (24%) were prepared, if asked to do so, to take a responsible position in the political life of their community.

These findings, taken together, reveal two key aspects of German political participation during the occupation period. First, it was not high. And yet, compared to other countries, as subsequent surveys have indicated, levels of political participation in Germany are not inordinately low. There is nonetheless an interesting stylistic difference in political behavior. In their survey of the late 1950s, Gabriel A. Almond and Sidney Verba found West Germans more interested in and knowledgeable about politics than citizens of four other democracies. The German sample ranked about midway between Americans and Englishmen on the one hand, and, on the other, Italians and Mexicans with respect to their belief that individuals should participate actively in the life of their community, their feeling that their activity could influence the course of political events,

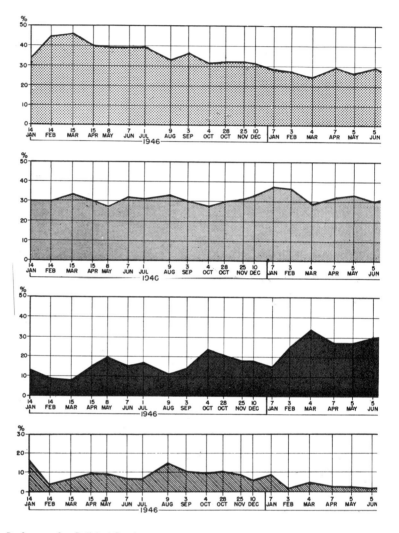

Fig. 12. *Preference for Political Parties*
   Question: "Which political party do you belong to or prefer?"

and their expectation that they would receive serious consideration both in a government office and from the police. Almond
and Verba concluded that, in West Germany "Awareness of
politics and political activity, though substantial, tend to be
passive and formal. Voting is frequent, but more informal
means of political involvement, particularly political discussion

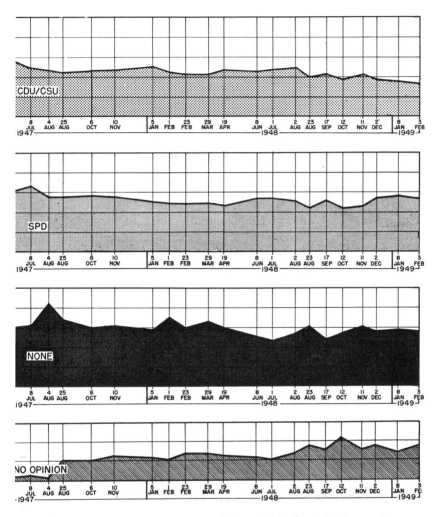

Source: OMGUS Report 175, June 1949, p. 18, 19. The following page in the same report gives preferences for the smaller parties as well as those responding "don't know."

and the forming of political groups, are more limited ... And norms favoring active political participation are not well developed. Many Germans assume that the act of voting is all that is required of a citizen." West Germans were satisfied enough with what their government was doing for them — but otherwise they felt no strong emotional ties to the West German political system.[27] The OMGUS data of the late 1940s suggest a similar detachment from politics. But whether this detachment is a long-standing characteristic of German political behavior, or whether it stemmed from a feeling that too much political activity in the past had led to too many burnt fingers, these data cannot tell us.

Second, the level of participation in the American-controlled areas remained fairly constant throughout the occupation years. (And, judging by data currently available, this level has not changed substantially in the two decades since the formation of the Federal Republic!) This finding raises a serious question about the overall effectiveness of the democratization program pursued by American occupation authorities – at least in terms of its measurable effects. Germans proved willing to go along with the destruction of Nazi symbols, including the last remnants of Nazi leadership. They were also agreeable to the principle of removing Nazi party members and sympathizers from important public and private jobs (provided, of course, that the denazification proceedings did not impinge upon their own families or circles of friends). But they did not adopt most of the new patterns of democratic behavior fostered by the military governments.

FROM DEMOCRATIZATION TO ANTICOMMUNISM: THE REORIENTATION OF AMERICAN POLICY

The total picture presented by the OMGUS surveys is therefore paradoxical – a population that was, potentially at least, pliable and yet did not change dramatically. Social psychologists tell us that the moods of entire publics are slow to change. The concatenation of traumatic experiences and official policy shifts, however, can shake all but the most deep-seated aspects of political culture.[28] For Germans, the physical and psychological destruction of the lost war was such a trauma; the policies enunciated by the Allies and the resurgence of voices suppressed during the Nazi period lent a tone to politics that Germans had not heard for well over a decade. Together, they could have meant a great watershed in the course of German history.

The existence of a population that was receptive to reorientation, if we are to judge from the available survey data, enhanced the Allies' opportunity to help shape German history. First of all, respondents in the American Zone were responsive to the occupiers: They recognized that the occupation would last for some time; they accepted American troops, without, however, ignoring their misdeeds; and they were not particularly hostile toward (although apparently few had great interest in) American information programs. Second, these respondents were by and large willing to cooperate with fundamental Allied policies aimed at eradicating remnants of the Nazi past — provided, of course, that these measures did not strike too close to home. And, third, the respondents reported finding conditions under the occupation tolerable. They seem to have expected much worse. Perhaps many of them had believed the all-too-credible Nazi propaganda about the Allied intention to implement the Morgenthau Plan, which would have reduced Germans to shepherds in a disarmed, de-industrialized, and dismembered land. This all-in-the-same-boat acceptance nonetheless changed as the occupation continued. The cumulation of shortages, the influx of refugees who taxed severely Germany's capacity to feed and clothe its citizens adequately, and possibly even the realization that the military government's bite was far less frightening than its bark led to rising grumbling despite the fact that the objective condition of the population (for example, in regard to caloric intake) was improving.

The four wartime Allies proved unable to realize this opportunity to test the extent to which they could actually change Germany's political culture. Although the Cold War surely did not originate in the years from 1945 to 1949, it was during this period that it blossomed. And the battleground was, to a very large measure, Germany. Disputes among the Allies about reparations, boundaries, transit rights, denazification, currency, economic and political reconstruction, and numerous smaller issues replaced interallied practices and institutions with bitterness and separate political systems. Here is not the place to assay the causes or history of the Cold War. Suffice it to say that, as early as the summer of 1945, Germans were feeling its effects.

The OMGUS surveys make clear the fact that these Germans saw what was happening to their country. They increasingly expressed alarm about the breakdown of East-West cooperation in Germany. They estimated a diminishing probability that the Allies would be able to work together to reconstruct the country in its 1937 or even its 1945 borders (see Figure 3). And they increasingly began to take sides. As Opinion Survey Section analysts wrote in August 1946 (#17): "It has been said that the world is becoming polarized toward either Russia or toward the United States, that these two countries are attracting a decision on the part of other people to line up with one or the other great nation. The data indicate that such a situation, if true, is further advanced in Germany than in countries such as France or Denmark." As the months rolled on, and particularly after the Soviet delegate walked out of the Allied Control Council meetings in March 1948 and the Soviet imposition of the Berlin blockade three months later, German hostility toward the USSR became even more pronounced.

Changes in American policy toward occupied Germany accompanied the deepening of the Cold War.[29] It became less interested in creating a new German society than in establishing Germany as a bulwark against communism. This had several practical implications. Of particular importance was the belief that revitalized economic and political institutions needed competent staffs (see Figure 13). But many of those whose training and abilities made them most desirable had records that were, according to current principles of denazification, dubious at best. The solution to this dilemma was a relaxation of the standards of personnel screening committees as well as the exoneration of Germans in wholesale lots from any implication in Nazi criminal activities. The changing policy also meant turning over more functions to German institutions. And it meant efforts to win over the German population.

Better living conditions and greater autonomy as instruments in the ideological battle over Germany were accompanied by heavy barrages of propaganda, aimed both at improving the image of the United States and sullying that of the Soviet

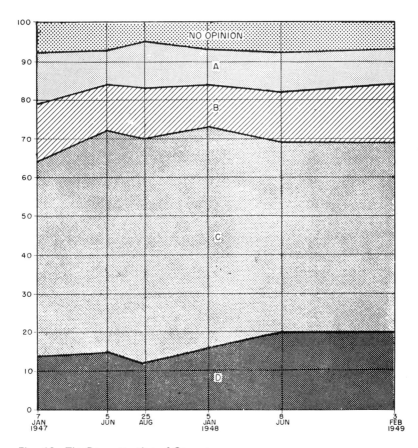

Fig. 13. *The Reconstruction of Germany*

Question: "Which of these statements comes closest to your opinion?
A. Germany herself should bear the responsibility for her reconstruction under the supervision of the Allies.
B. Germany should be occupied by the Allies until she is able to form a good democratic government.
C. The Americans should reconstruct Germany as soon as possible in order to avoid her becoming a prey to Communism.
D. The reconstruction of their country should be left to the Germans themselves without interference from the Allies."
Source: OMGUS Report 175, June 1949, p. 57.

Union. The "Voice of America," the information centers, and the American-controlled mass media saw to this latter task. And it is remarkable how receptive AMZON Germans were to publications decrying Soviet policies (e.g. #89 and 97). To some extent, interestingly enough, even the OMGUS surveys served in

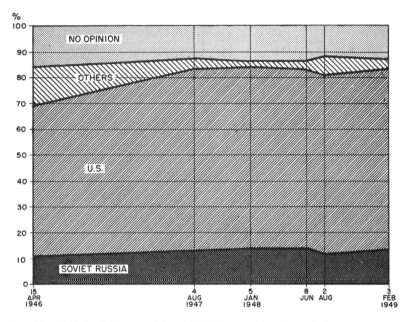

Fig. 14. *Relative Influence of the United States and the Soviet Union*

Question: "Which country will have the greatest influence on world affairs in the next ten years?"
Source: OMGUS Report 175, June 1949, p. 47.

the propaganda battle. In December 1947, for instance, interviewers asked a small panel of Berliners why the London Conference had broken up (#86). The report, after noting diminished morale because of "a feeling that events are occurring apart from the German people and in a direction over which they have no control," went on to make a policy recommendation:

It is suggested that interpretation of the London Conference should attempt to make clear to the public what the principles are which have guided American diplomats in their negotiations during the Conference. . . . These principles can be affirmed in such a way as to make room for the German people to associate themselves with the maintenance of such tenets. It might well be possible, thus to induce some Germans to consider that, instead of Allied disagreements bringing the Conference to an end, it was Russian refusal to accept principles (which everyone else

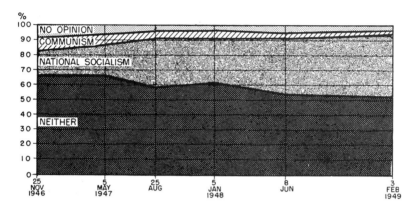

Fig. 15. *The Choice between National Socialism and Communism*

Question: "If you had to choose between Communism and National Socialism, under which government would you prefer to live?"
Source: OMGUS Report 175, June 1949, p. 9.

recognizes as necessary to maintain) which caused adjournment.

It was not difficult to follow this advice. By then Germans were quite receptive to anti-Soviet propaganda. A report in April 1948 (#113) noted that, although AMZON Germans "have very strong opinions about Russia and the Russians, their factual information about what country is in general at a fairly low level." Moreover, "when in doubt, they tend to select the 'fact' least favorable to Russia." It would seem, then, that Western interpretations of Soviet behavior merely activated a latent antibolshevism in the German population (see Figure 14).[30]

The all-out effort to enlist Germans on the side of the West in the Cold War, however successful, had its costs. Most immediately, as suggested earlier, it meant a partial abandonment of efforts to root out the remnants of Nazism. We do not mean to suggest that American occupation authorities were no longer concerned with this task. They were, both in their emotions and their behavior. It is merely that anti-Nazism had to take second place to anticommunism. It must have been with considerable ambivalence that these officers read reports showing that AMZON Germans, asked to choose between a National

Socialist and a communist form of government, increasingly. chose the former (#60, 175; see Figure 15). Were their efforts to discredit communism producing a "brown" reaction in postwar Germany?

The OMGUS surveys indicate that the danger of resurgent Nazism, viewed with alarm by some observers even today, was in fact highly overrated. The bulk of Germans had already rejected the National Socialist movement. The movement itself had had many faults, its leaders had proved themselves to be less than heroic, and both, moreover, had led Germany to disaster. Relatively few, perhaps a sixth, seemed to continue espousing a complete set of Nazi images and values.

More ominous was the possibility of recreating those conditions that had given rise to the Nazi version of extremism in the first place. Some of these were to be sure the consequence of external circumstances: resentment about provisions of the Versailles Treaty, the virtual withdrawal from world politics of the Soviet Union and the United States, and the world economic crisis that began in 1929. But other European countries, too, winners and losers alike, had felt the disastrous effects of World War I and subsequent changes in the international environment. The events themselves do not provide much of an explanation for domestic changes. More important were the perspectives of those who had to deal with these events – perspectives that found their roots in German political culture. Groups with different perspectives, after all, can interpret the same set of events and behavior as hostile or friendly, as threatening or nonthreatening. This suggests, then, that we must pay more attention to domestic conditions.

Several aspects of political culture are important in this regard. Some can be explored through surveying techniques. To the extent that we can project postwar German political perspectives backwards into an earlier era, it would seem that among the conditions prevailing when Nazi extremism emerged and seized power were an ethic of passive participation, reliance upon administrative rather than political procedures, the presence of authoritarians and democrats in the midst of the relatively uncommitted majority, a strong strain of anti-

Semitism and, more generally, a lack of tolerance of people and ideas that were different. Ralf Dahrendorf has pointed to still other aspects of pre-Nazi political culture in Germany: a high degree of industrial concentration, a low degree of social mobility, a social chasm between the elites and the masses, and principles of decision making that prevented basic conflicts from coming into public discussion.[31] Above all, a traditional political elite relied upon these popular orientations and the structural rigidity of German life to maintain themselves in power. Whatever its evils, and these should never be forgotten or underplayed, the Nazi regime under Hitler made great strides in destroying this traditional, relatively closed political culture.

Taking charge of a Germany with discredited pasts — the traditional political culture that had led to the breakdown of the Weimar Republic, as well as the revolutionary but unsuccessful politics of the National Socialists — presented the Allies with their unheard-of opportunity to help guide the nation in its choice of alternative futures. Coordinated persistence on the part of the Allies might have produced extensive cultural change. But there was neither coordination nor, in the Western zones at least, persistence. As the Cold War descended upon Europe, the Soviet Union devoted ever more of its attention to the establishment of a loyal satellite in its zone of occupation, and the West to the recreation of an anticommunist political system modelled upon the Weimar pattern.

In the American Zone in particular growing anticommunism got in the way of policies aimed at cultural change. AMZON residents were caught in the mill. Promised education for democracy, they ended up getting pushed off on another ideological crusade. Promised democratic procedures, they got an Allied occupation interested more in setting up bulwarks against communism than a clean sweep of the past, interested more in propaganda against the new enemy than in the critical self-appraisal and sometimes painful search for the truth that accompany democratic processes. Promised new democratic leadership, they got a reentrenchment of leaders from the discredited Weimar period, together with those too clever or lucky enough to avoid entanglement in the webs of either

Nazism or denazification. The OMGUS survey data summarized in this volume cannot, of course, demonstrate conclusively the accuracy of these assertions. They nonetheless show that the changes toward a more democratic public consciousness initially intended by the occupiers did not materialize: On the level of individual perspectives and behavior, there were few major changes to be noted; on the level of attitudes toward public events, a new set of frequently liberal perspectives merely replaced the old set.

Perhaps the restoration of practices and leaders ambivalent toward democracy, as well as the accompanying propagandistic distortions, were necessary to protect democracy against a communist threat. We do not deny it, although we also fail to see as much concrete evidence as was assumed at the time to exist. The point here is somewhat different: Having pounded anticommunism into receptive Germans, all the while giving impetus to the reemergence of illiberal predispositions, the United States and its allies prepared to leave the country to its own devices. What was left was for the United States and the rest of the world to reap the fruits of this restoration sown in the late 1940s.

NOTES

1. Cf. General Lucius D. Clay's stress on their importance in *Decision in Germany* (New York: Doubleday and Co., 1950), p. 283. The British, French, and Soviet military governments also sought to create organizations to conduct survey research, evidently not too successfully in the Soviet case. Cf. Henry Halpern, "Soviet Attitude Toward Public Opinion Research in Germany," *Public Opinion Quarterly*, 13:1 (Spring 1949), 117-118. The Soviet Military Government viewed American operations as espionage, subsequently infiltrating the Opinion Survey Section itself and turning over at least some of its findings to the press in East Berlin. On the occupation in the western zones, cf. also W. Friedmann, *The Allied Military Government of Germany* (London: Stevens and Sons, 1947); Hajo Holborn, *American Military Government: Its Organization and Policies* (Washington,

D.C.: Infantry Journal Press, 1947); Carl J. Friedrich et al., *American Experiences in Military Government in World War II* (New York: Rinehart and Co., 1948); Edward H. Litchfield et al., *Governing Postwar Germany* (Ithaca, N.Y.: Cornell University Press, 1953); John D. Montgomery, *Forced to Be Free: The Artificial Revolution in Germany and Japan* (Chicago: University of Chicago Press, 1957); Harold Zink, *The United States in Germany, 1944-1955* (Princeton, N.J.: D. Van Nostrand Co., 1957); W. Phillips Davison, *The Berlin Blockade: A Study in Cold War Politics* (Princeton, N.J.: Princeton University Press, 1958); Eugene Davidson, *The Death and Life of Germany: An Account of the American Occupation* (New York: Alfred A. Knopf, 1959); Raymond Ebsworth, *Restoring Democracy in Germany: The British Contribution* (London: Stevens and Sons; New York: Frederick A. Praeger, 1960); F. S. V. Donnison, *Civil Affairs and Military Government: North-West Europe, 1944-1946* (London: Her Majesty's Stationery Office, 1961); John Gimbel, *A German Community under American Occupation: Marburg, 1945-52* (Stanford, Calif.: Stanford University Press, 1962); Harry L. Coles and Albert K. Weinberg, *Civil Affairs: Soldiers Become Governors* (Washington, D.C.: Department of the Army, Office of the Chief of Military History, 1964); and John Gimbel, *The American Occupation of Germany: Politics and the Military, 1945-1949* (Stanford, Calif.: Stanford University Press, 1968). For a recent German view, see Caspar Schrenck-Notzing, *Charakterwaesche: Die amerikanische Besatzung in Deutschland und ihre Folgen* (Stuttgart: Seewald Verlag, 1965). Basic to an understanding of the occupation, of course, is some insight into the Nazi period itself. Perhaps the best brief introduction is Alan Bullock, *Hitler: A Study in Tyranny*, rev. ed. (New York: Harper and Row, 1964); in addition to numerous, more specific monographs, an excellent body of German documentation exists, as catalogued in Gerhard L. Weinberg and the War Documentation Project Staff, under the direction of Fritz T. Epstein, *Guide to Captured German Documents*, War Documentation Project, Study No. 1, Research Memorandum No. 2, Vol. 1 (Maxwell Air Force Base, Ala.: Air University, Human Resources Research Institute, December 1952); and the series initiated by the American Historical Association's Committee for the Study of War Documents, *Guides to German Records Microfilmed at Alexandria, Va.* (Washington, D.C.: The National Archives, National Archives and Records Services, General Services Administration, 1958-).

The reports summarized in this volume also include five on aspects of the American occupation of Austria, particularly Vienna. Since they deal primarily with mass communications media, we shall not analyze them in this brief introductory section.

2. For a compilation of the USIA data from France, West Germany, Italy, and the United Kingdom, covering the years from 1952 to 1963, as well as for a series of methodological and substantive articles using these data, see Richard L. Merritt and Donald J. Puchala, *Western European Perspectives on International Affairs: Public Opinion Studies and Evaluations* (New York: Frederick A. Praeger, 1968).

3. Inquiries should be addressed to: Archives Branch, Washington National Records Center, Washington, D.C., 20409. The files are in Box 233–3/5 and 233–5/5 (#1243) at the Washington National Records Center's office in Suitland, Maryland.

4. Elmo C. Wilson, "Report on ICD Opinion Surveys," memorandum prepared for Colonel Gordon E. Textor, Director, Information Control Division, Office of Military Government for Germany (U.S.), 4 August 1948 (dittoed), p. 9.

5. Leo P. Crespi, "The Influence of Military Government Sponsorship in German Opinion Polling," *International Journal of Opinion and Attitude Research*, 4:2 (Summer 1950), 167-168.

6. Ibid., pp. 168-169.

7. Cf. Aaron M. Bindman, "Interviewing in the Search for 'Truth'," *Sociological Quarterly*, 6:3 (Summer 1965), 281-288.

8. Inquiries should be addressed to: Archives Branch, Washington National Records Center, Washington, D.C., 20409. The cost is five cents per page on 35 mm. microfilm (positive or negative) or 20 cents per page for electrostatic (xeroxed) prints. The summaries contained in this volume show the number of pages in each report; the total number, excluding extraneous material, is about 2,081 pages.

9. Cf. Report No. 22, "A Study of Attitudes Toward the Reconstruction and Rehabilitation of Germany" (25 September 1946). Henceforward the numbers in parentheses, e.g. (#22), will refer to the reports summarized in the next section of this volume; report numbers prefaced by II refer to Series 2 (HICOG) of the American-sponsored surveys of German attitudes, summaries of which will be published in due course.

10. In June 1950, almost half (46%) of a nationwide sample reported that their experiences during the occupation had been unpleasant

(23%) or very unpleasant (23%); ten per cent recalled that their experiences were pleasant, and another 28 per cent did not remember noticing anything in particular (the remainder, 16 per cent, had not been in Germany). Broken down by occupation zones, those who had been in the British Zone were least negative (37 per cent unpleasant, 16 per cent pleasant, and 47 per cent not noticing), followed by residents of the American Zone (49, 15, and 36 per cent, respectively), the French Zone (65, 7, and 28 per cent, respectively), and the Soviet Zone (95, 1, and 4 per cent, respectively). Elisabeth Noelle and Erich Peter Neumann, editors, *Jahrbuch der oeffentlichen Meinung, 1947-1955* (Allensbach am Bodensee: Verlag fuer Demoskopie, 1956), p. 146.

11. Ibid., p. 74. Among radio listeners in the Federal Republic as a whole, the share listening regularly to VOA declined from 22 per cent in March 1950 to 14 per cent in March 1955, those listening occasionally from 33 to 27 per cent.

12. In July 1955, only a quarter (27%) of a nationwide sample felt that at the time of the currency reform seven years earlier they had been undernourished, and two-thirds (67%) denied this. The items they reported most often having to purchase on the black market were, first, bread, flour, and potatoes, and, second, fats, butter, and cooking oil, followed by clothing, meat, sugar, and eggs. Elisabeth Noelle and Erich Peter Neumann, editors, *Jahrbuch der oeffentlichen Meinung, 1957* (Allensbach am Bodensee: Verlag fuer Demoskopie, 1957), p. 226.

13. In February 1953, almost two-thirds (63%) of a nationwide sample felt that the refugees had adjusted satisfactorily to life in the Federal Republic (with 18 per cent taking the opposite position), but only 36 per cent felt that enough was currently being done for refugees from the German Democratic Republic (with 28 per cent saying that not enough was being done). Asked whether the Federal Republic should continue to accept refugees from the German Democratic Republic, 25 per cent were unconditionally positive in their response, 57 per cent specified conditions that should be met (such as proof that flight had resulted from political persecution), and 15 per cent responded negatively. Noelle and Neumann, editors, *Jahrbuch, 1947-1955*, pp. 199-200.

14. A decade later, in April 1959, 38 per cent of the expellees from the Oder-Neisse territories reported that they would definitely return if the area were restored to German control, 27 per cent that they

would perhaps return, and 30 per cent said that their return was out of the question. Elisabeth Noelle and Erich Peter Neumann, editors, *Jahrbuch der oeffentlichen Meinung, 1958-1964* (Allensbach and Bonn: Verlag fuer Demoskopie, 1965), p. 505.

15. Over the course of the next two decades, reunification and economic issues vied for top position in Germans' view of the most important problem facing their country. As economic prosperity overcame the country in the mid-1950s, the reunification question took first place with unprecedented consensus (45 per cent in Janaury 1959), but the economic crisis that began in 1965 again raised the issue of prosperity to first place (62 per cent in January 1967). Ibid., p. 482, Elisabeth Noelle and Erich Peter Neumann, editors, *Jahrbuch der oeffentlichen Meinung, 1965-1967* (Allensbach and Bonn: Verlag fuer Demoskopie, 1967), p. 387.

16. Cf. Richard L. Merritt, "West Berlin – Center or Periphery?" in *Comparing Nations: The Use of Quantitative Data in Cross-National Research*, eds. Richard L. Merritt and Stein Rokkan (New Haven, Conn.: Yale University Press, 1966), pp. 321-336.

17. Hitler's image suffered during succeeding years. In January 1950 as much as a tenth of a nationwide sample rated Hitler as the statesman who had done most for Germany, but in April-May 1967 only two per cent did so. In July 1952 a tenth agreed that Hitler was the greatest statesman of the century whose true greatness would be recognized only later, with another 22 per cent feeling that, although he had made a few mistakes, Hitler was nonetheless an excellent chief-of-state. The percentage claiming that, except for the war, Hitler would have been one of Germany's greatest statesmen declined from 48 per cent in May 1955 to 32 per cent in April-May 1967; the number denying this assertion rose from 36 to 52 per cent. The percentage reporting their willingness to vote again for a man such as Hitler dropped from 14 per cent in 1953 to 6 per cent in 1968 (although in 1965 and 1967 it had been still lower, at four per cent); interestingly enough, in 1968 34 per cent of the adherents of the new rightist National Democratic Party (NPD) indicated that, if the opportunity arose, they would vote for a man like Hitler. Noelle and Neumann, editors, *Jahrbuch, 1965-1967*, pp. 144-145; and EMNID-Institut, *Informationen* 20:8-9 (August-September 1968), p. A-18.

18. Of a nationwide sample of university students in July 1966, 44 per cent reported that they could think of something positive about Hitler and the Third Reich (with over three-fifths of these mentioning

the resolution of Germany's economic crisis of the early 1930s), and 38 per cent could find nothing good to say. Noelle and Neumann, editors, *Jahrbuch, 1965-1967*, p. 368.

19. Some of these data are from summary sheets not included in the OMGUS reports and hence differ slightly from data reported elsewhere (e.g. #16). This special collection is to be found in the Library of the University of Illinois under the title "Some Results of Public Opinion Polls of the German Republic" (q940.9343, G3125s).

20. Asked in September 1952 about five defendants still serving prison sentences, an average of 14 per cent of a nationwide sample thought it just that they were still there, with 52 per cent considering it unjust. Noelle and Neumann, editors, *Jahrbuch, 1947-1955*, p. 202. More generally, Germans have grown increasingly impatient with discussions of German war crimes: In 1966 well over half (58%) of a nationwide sample and 51 per cent of the university students questioned thought that the time had come to stop such discussions. Noelle and Neumann, editors, *Jahrbuch, 1965-1967* pp. 204, 368. An indication of the bitterness on this point came in November 1952, when 46 per cent reported liking a recent speech containing the sentence, "The real war criminals are those who made this unholy peace alone, who destroyed entire cities without military reasons, who dropped the bombs on Hiroshima, and who are producing new atomic bombs"; 29 per cent did not like the speech, and 25 per cent gave no response. Noelle and Neumann, editors, *Jahrbuch, 1947-1955*, p. 276.

21. Meanwhile, Soviet military authorities had removed 307,370 and excluded 83,108 Germans from jobs; the British had removed 186,692 and excluded 104,106; and the French had removed and excluded 69,068 Germans. Friedmann, *The Allied Military Government of Germany*, p. 332.

22. Gimbel, *The American Occupation of Germany*, pp. 101-110, 158-162, 246-252. Cf. Montgomery, *Forced to Be Free;* and John H. Herz, "The Fiasco of Denazification in Germany," *Political Science Quarterly*, 63:4 (December 1948), 569-594.

23. The independent Institut fuer Demoskopie found still greater opposition in August 1948: 14 per cent felt that denazification had accomplished its goals (17 per cent in November 1953), contrasted to 39 per cent who felt that the proceedings had been necessary but incorrectly conducted (63 per cent in 1953), and 40 per cent who expressed outright opposition (40 per cent in 1953). Asked in

September 1951 what the greatest mistake made by the occupiers was, denazification ranked seventh (having been mentioned by six per cent), right behind the war crimes trials (8%) and well behind the response "dismantling, destruction, and holding down of industry" (21%). Noelle and Neumann, editors, *Jahrbuch, 1947-1955*, pp. 142, 140.

24. Evidence summarized by Karl W. Deutsch and Lewis J. Edinger, *Germany Rejoins the Powers: Mass Opinion, Interest Groups, and Elites in Contemporary German Foreign Policy* (Stanford, Calif.: Stanford University Press, 1959), p. 40, suggests that, in the mid-1950s, about one in eight Germans was a hardcore Nazi or partial sympathizer. Public opinion data from the late 1960s indicate that this proportion has dropped by about half.

25. For a recent summary of some studies of German perspectives, see Sidney Verba, "Germany: The Remaking of Political Culture," in *Political Culture and Political Development*, eds. Lucian W. Pye and Sidney Verba (Princeton, N.J.: Princeton University Press, 1965), pp. 130-170. See also W. Phillips Davison, "Trends in West German Public Opinion, 1946-1956," in *West German Leadership and Foreign Policy*, eds. Hans Speier and W. Phillips Davison (Evanston, Ill., and White Plains, N.Y.: Row, Peterson and Co., 1957), pp. 282-304.

26. Surveys in the early 1950s nonetheless revealed that about a quarter of the population (33 per cent of the women and 21 per cent of the men), if given a choice, would have preferred a monarchy to any other form of government for Germany; Noelle and Neumann, editors, *Jahrbuch, 1947-1955*, p. 132. In the winter of 1962-1963, 18 per cent were in favor of having a monarch on the British or Swedish model; Noelle and Neumann, editors, *Jahrbuch, 1965-1967*, p. 137.

27. Gabriel A. Almond and Sidney Verba, *The Civic Culture: Political Attitudes and Democracy in Five Nations* (Princeton, N.J.: Princeton University Press, 1963), particularly pp. 428-429. Other cross-national surveys are to be found in William Buchanan and Hadley Cantril, *How Nations See Each Other: A Study in Public Opinion* (Urbana: University of Illinois Press, 1953), and Merritt and Puchala, *Western European Perspectives on International Affairs*.

28. See Karl W. Deutsch and Richard L. Merritt, "Effects of Events on National and International Images," in *International Behavior: A Social-Psychological Analysis,* ed. Herbert C. Kelman (New York: Holt, Rinehart and Winston, 1965), pp. 132-187.

29. More properly speaking, as Gimbel in *The American Occupation of*

Germany has pointed out, the conflict among American decision makers was resolved in favor of General Clay and others favoring a rapid rehabilitation of Germany; the effect from the point of view of the outside observer, however, was the same, since the American Military Government began to express views that sounded like policy changes.

30. For a graphic indication of the increasing polarity of German images of the United States and the Soviet Union, see Richard L. Merritt, "Visual Representation of Mutual Friendliness," in *Western European Perspectives on International Affairs,* eds. Merritt and Puchala, pp. 111-141, particularly p. 134.

31. See Ralf Dahrendorf, *Society and Democracy in Germany* (New York: Doubleday and Co., 1967), who stresses the antiliberal elements of Germany's pre-Nazi history. See also David Schoenbaum, *Hitler's Social Revolution. Class and Status in Nazi Germany, 1933-1939* (New York: Doubleday and Co., 1966).

PART II

THE OMGUS SURVEYS

RADIO LISTENING IN GERMANY, WINTER 1946

Sample: 964 households in the American Zone.
Interviewing dates: 21 January 1946. (21 pp.)

Fifty-six per cent of the population in the American Zone listened to the radio, either on their own or someone else's set. Only 42 per cent of the families interviewed had sets in working order. Nearly all sets picked up middle-wave lengths, and one-third also received short- and long-wave broadcasts.

Audience composition differed at different times of the day, with the median group listening to the radio about two hours daily. Among those most frequently tuning in one of the three American-sponsored stations, both Radio Munich and Radio Stuttgart had audiences that listened for rather long periods of time. An appreciable number (37%) restricted their daytime listening to save electricity. The largest audiences were during the evening hours from 6 to 10 p.m., but significant numbers were also at their radios at 7 a.m. and at noon. Listeners with above average-sized families seemed to use the radio socially, as the center of the evening at home. Listening habits varied with the size of the community: except in Bavaria, the larger the community, the more people who listened to the radio.

Most radio listening occurred among groups with the following characteristics: male; aged 18 to 29; twelve or more years of education; upper-middle-class status; former membership in the NSDAP; irregular churchgoing Catholics; professionals, government officials, or self-employed; and weekly income of 70 RM or more.

Listeners preferred the American-licensed station in their own *Land*, although they also listened to stations from other *Laender* in AMZON. For the Zone as a whole, Radio Leipzig and Radio Berlin ranked fourth and fifth respectively in the competition for listeners, behind Radio Munich, Stuttgart, and Frankfurt.

In regard to the type of program preferred, 65 per cent of the respondents listed musical programs. Second most popular were news programs (25%). Differences of taste for types of programs were related to sex, age, and education variables.

Among radio listeners, 65 per cent were confident that the radio presented the news more truthfully than did the newspapers. A majority of listeners, however, admitted that newspapers have the advantage of being able to present more complete news. Respondents seemed to feel that news broadcasting in English was more complete than that in German, but only 11 per cent claimed to listen to broadcasts in English. Radio listeners also indicated a preference for personalized news presentation.

Almost two-thirds (63%) of the listeners said that they listened to the "Voice of America." Fifty per cent said that they heard the program from German stations only; the remainder heard it sometimes on German stations, sometimes from London or New York. Among radio listeners, those who listened to the "Voice of America" were more likely to be male, Protestant, middle or upper class, and to have had only eight years of schooling rather than much more or less. Those who listened to the "Voice of America" on German stations were also those who most frequently listened to Radio Frankfurt or Radio Stuttgart.

Report No. 2 (March 1946)

WHO IN GERMANY HAS READ "MEIN KAMPF"?

Sample: 954 residents of the American Zone.
Interviewing dates: 14 February 1946. (3 pp.)

Almost a quarter (23%) of the adult population in the American Zone had read at least part of Hitler's *Mein Kampf*. Of this group, seven per cent had read the entire book. The largest percentage of readers were among the following groups: former NSDAP members (18 per cent completely, 28 per cent in part); upper social class (14 and 31 per cent, respectively); 12 or more years of education (31 and 41 per cent respectively); young people under the age of 30 (5 and 22 per cent, respectively); men (11 and 21 per cent, respectively); prisoners of war (12 and 24 per cent, respectively); and those preferring the Communist Party (13 and 18 per cent, respectively). Religious affiliation was not a significant variable for discriminating readers from nonreaders.

Report No. 3 (15 March 1946)

SOME POLITICAL ATTITUDES PROBED
ON RECENT SURVEYS

> *Sample:* from 364 to 996 American Zone residents.
> *Interviewing dates:* 14 surveys from 26 November 1945 to 15 March 1946. (9 pp.)

A third (33%) of the respondents polled in March 1946 preferred the SPD to other parties then in existence. Asked which party they would choose in the event of a merger between the SPD and the Communist Party, a third of these SPD adherents indicated support for the new party, but 37 per cent said that they would switch either to the CDU (19%) or the CSU (18%), and another three per cent thought that they would support one of the smaller, right-wing parties in that event.

Regarding political awareness, the number feeling that the Germans had learned in recent months how to govern themselves better varied from 61 per cent in January to 47 per cent in March. Roughly half felt themselves sufficiently informed about political affairs; and somewhat over a third of the remainder indicated that, although they were not sufficiently informed, they were making an effort to inform themselves. Only 15 per cent could name an outstanding German who, in their opinion, could hold an important position at the *Land* level.

Regarding political participation, in March only seven per cent claimed membership in a political party, although another 16 per cent indicated their intention to join one. About two-thirds (63%) in March wanted to exclude all but three or four political parties, and as many as 11 per cent wanted to exclude all but one. A solid majority, ranging from 60 per cent in November 1945 to 72 per cent in March 1946, felt that political meetings were desirable. By March as many as 25 per cent of the entire population said that they had attended such a meeting. Three in five respondents (60%) thought that some categories of individuals should not be permitted to enter politics, as opposed to another fifth (20%) favoring no such discrimination: Almost all of those opting for a discriminatory policy listed former NSDAP members or functionaries as the most undesirable. Support for the SPD grew and for the conservative parties (CDU, CSU, LDP) declined with the population size of the town. Of the former NSDAP members, somewhat over a quarter (28%) supported leftist parties (SPD, KPD) in early 1946, almost twice that number (52%) favored conservative parties.

Those least likely to vote in elections taking place in early 1946 were individuals without party affiliation (54%), former Nazi Party members (58%), men (36%), and persons under the age of 30 (45%). Most voters in the January elections were able to give a reason for having voted. Vaguely defined issues were alluded to by a majority, while a sizable minority said that they had voted merely out of a sense of civic duty (35%) or just to express an opinion once again (4%). Issues referred to indirectly included leadership (23%), reconstruction (12%), interparty rivalry (10%), voting against the Communist Party (5%), and political reorientation (7%).

Report No. 4 (25 March 1946)

INCOME AND EXPENDITURES OF GERMAN FAMILIES IN THE AMERICAN ZONE, WINTER 1946

Sample: 2,448 families in 70 communities in the American Zone.
Interviewing dates: second week in January 1946. (10 pp.)

In the American Zone, the absolute labor force was at least twice as large as the percentage of those actually working. While 28 per cent of family members interviewed were working, an additional 30 per cent were adults capable of working but holding no income-producing jobs; another ten per cent were incapable of working. Almost two-thirds (63%) of the labor force were male. People with jobs were, on the average, almost as likely to be over 40 as younger. Most of the workers (77%) had no more than 8 years of education.

The average income of families in the Zone was about 35 RM per week. Almost all of this income came from wages or salaries. Nearly 15 per cent of all families interviewed said they had no income. Their standard of living, however, approximated that of the average German family. This group was most likely temporarily dislocated and was living on its savings. Over a third (35%) of all families were drawing on savings for necessary living expenditures. Although 85 per cent of those with no income were using savings for current expenses, this percentage decreased as income rose.

Lowest incomes were reported in small towns and Baden-Werttemberg (median family income of 35 RM). Catholics were slightly better paid than Protestants (41 RM as opposed to 38 RM). Home owners (40 RM) and the better educated (92 RM) received more income than renters (36 RM) or those with only 7 years of education (46 RM). Former NSDAP members (45 RM) were relatively well paid compared with those who had no Party affiliations (36 RM). The difference in income between men and women was not great, nor was it consistently greater for men. Workers between the ages of 30 and 39 tended to receive more income (42 RM) than younger (29 RM) or older people (39 RM for those aged 40-49, 38 RM for those over 50 years of age).

On the average, incomes were higher than expenditures. Respondents reported making expenditures only for necessities. Even the best paid spent very little for education, entertainment, or luxuries. The greater the income, the more money spent. The greatest difference between income groups was in the amount spent for food; families earning 10-29 RM weekly paid about 8 RM for food, whereas those earning 80 RM or more weekly spent about 18 RM for food. Rents had hardly increased since May 1945 for those in the average renting brackets, and were stable for those paying high rents. Home owners, who made up 46 per cent of the population, expected to spend large sums in 1946 for the repair of their homes.

Report No. 5 (1 April 1946)

SPECIAL POLITICAL SURVEY, WINTER 1946

Sample: 162 community leaders in the American Zone.
Interviewing dates: end of February 1946. (17 pp.)

The 162 persons questioned in this survey were all community leaders – politically alert and sophisticated – living in villages and cities throughout AMZON. The majority were over 50 and mostly of higher socioeconomic groups. The overwhelming majority preferred to be personally involved in politics rather than leaving politics to others. The dominant impression given by the respondents was nonetheless a general disillusionment with party politics.

Those who admitted the need for democratic methods and democracy in general regarded them only as preparation for the mere function of voting without any reference to or indication of their appreciation of democratic social attitudes or democracy's functioning within a community. When asked what the fundamentals of a democratic form of state were, most answered from a classical point of view, giving short definitions. A large percentage mentioned equality as a fundamental requirement, but only two specified racial equality among other forms named. About two in five (43%) of the 162 respondents felt it was generally possible to establish democracy in Germany based on western democratic principles, a third (34%) felt it was generally not possible to do so, and 23 per cent were uncertain. Many respondents, fearing a political situation in which there would be a number of parties, felt democracy would encourage this situation. Accordingly, many felt the number of political parties should be limited, especially during the period of reconstruction. Many felt the British system should be emulated, but with a president rather than a monarch.

When asked if the Military Government could do anything to foster democracy, respondents most frequently demanded unification, the immediate abolition of the Zone system, and the reestablishment of economic prosperity. The next most frequent demand was for a humane execution of denazification. Many stressed that the occupation itself should be an example of democracy. All favored the gradual trend by the Military Government to give more power to the Germans themselves; almost all, however, felt that the Military Government should retain final control and decision.

Of the 162 respondents, 67 preferred the CSU or the CDU, 47 the SPD, nine the KPD, seven the LDP and two the *Deutsche Arbeiterpartei* which exists in the British Zone. Most of the former Nazi Party members preferred the CDU or the CSU. Continuity in pre-1933 and postwar political allegiance was noticeable mainly among the Social Democrats and, to a lesser extent, the Communists. Sixty per cent of those who preferred the CSU or the CDU were former members of the Center Party, the Bavarian People's Party, or the German National People's Party.

When questioned about responsibility for the Nazi rise to power, 90 per cent concentrated on the factors which in their view had lead to dictatorship; only about ten per cent gave opinions as to what positive steps could have been taken to prevent the Nazi rise to power. Replies to this question, the question of collective guilt of the German people, and the responsibility of the individual to obey his government divided sharply according to the party preferences of the respondents.

These community leaders were sharply divided on the possibility that the Nazis or some similar group might emerge and attempt to seize power. Nearly all respondents thought that such a seizure could not happen while the occupation lasted. But the conditions that might favor a Nazi resurgence included material difficulties and misery, unjust and harsh occupation policy, nationalist reaction, together with division of Germany, licensing of reactionary parties, and the problem of homeless refugees and unemployed former prisoners of war. Conditions hindering such a resurgence included the presence of occupation troops, the fact that the Nazi regime and the war taught a lesson to everyone, the existence of strong leftist parties, and stricter international interdependence and surveillance in the framework of the new international organization.

If the Nazis or some similar group attempted to seize power, the majority of the respondents felt that civil war would follow. A majority also thought that, after the Nazi experience, the democratic parties would prevent any development which might lead to such a coup. At least half the respondents believed that the Allies would immediately intervene, and an appreciable minority thought that it would be the duty of an international organization to act. About five per cent hoped that United States forces would not leave until, in the respondents' words, "democracy is safely established."

When questioned about the main duties of the state toward its citizens and what the respondent expected from his government, about 75 per cent said that the satisfaction of essentially material needs is the first duty of the state. Only about 25 per cent mentioned individual freedom of conscience, of expression, of religion, and freedom from secret police. Respondents expected Germany to rebuild its cities, renew its export trade, provide raw materials, more homes, and better health services. A large percentage of respondents named the establishment of friendly international relations as the chief demand of the people on their government. On the one hand, many felt that the government should not intervene in social and economic life; on the other hand, many expected comprehensive social services from cradle to the grave.

Report No. 6 (20 April 1946)

LAW NO. 3

Sample: unspecified (c. 985) in American Zone.
Interviewing dates: third week in February 1946. (4 pp.)

Over three-quarters of the sample (76%) had heard of Law No. 3, which obliged workers to register at the local labor office. Approval of the law was almost unanimous: 87 per cent of the entire population approved of the law and thought that it would facilitate reconstruction, as opposed to only two per cent who disapproved of the law or thought that it would hinder reconstruction. A firm majority (62%) approved and a quarter (25%) disapproved of the provision that workers could not leave their presently-held jobs.

Attitudinal differences among groups within the population indicated that areas where conditions were more difficult were also more discontented with the regulation. Bavarians, who were best off of all people in the American Zone, were more in agreement than those in the other *Laender*. In the large cities of Frankfurt, Stuttgart, and Munich there was a relatively lower degree of approval than in other city-sized communities. Towns with populations between 10,000 and 100,000 gave the highest degree (70%) of approval of the law.

Seventy per cent of those interviewed allowed that many

people who could work did not do so because they could not find appropriate positions. Indications of particular group worries were found in the fact that more young people (81%) than middle-aged (70%) said that many people were looking for suitable jobs, and that more residents of the three large cities (88%) than those of smaller cities (69%) also thought that many were seeking work cut to their interests.

Among all those working, however, a solid majority was definitely well (63%) or fairly well (23%) satisfied with their jobs and only ten per cent expressed dissatisfaction. The middle-aged were more satisfied (83%) than were people under the age of 30 (73%). Dissatisfaction stemmed largely from the fact that respondents were engaged in work for which they had not been trained. Some white-collar workers, for instance, pointed out that circumstances forced them to accept ordinary labor tasks. Others complained that their work was too hard, and former Nazi Party members, particularly, said that their work was frequently humiliating. Still another complaint was that income was too low in view of the high taxes.

Those who did not work gave various reasons for their lack of steady employment. Nearly half (44%) were housewives who did not contemplate seeking any job. A quarter (24%) of the unemployed reported that they were either unable to work because of their age or the state of their health or did not have to work because they were already pensioned. One in ten (9%) nonworkers said that denazificiation had led to refusals of jobs. About the same number (12%) asserted that there was no work to be found in their area or that the work they sought could not be found.

A substantial minority (31%) of workers considered that they were not working as hard as they had during the war. About half (51%) of all those who had worked during the war and were still working reported no change in the pressure of their work. About a fifth (18%) claimed that the times and special hardships encountered made their work more difficult than had previously been the case.

Report No. 7 (11 May 1946)

REACTIONS TO RECENT REVISIONS IN THE DENAZIFICATION PROGRAM

Sample: 992 residents of the American Zone.
Interviewing dates: 15 March 1946. (6 pp.)

Although 59 per cent of those interviewed in AMZON had heard of the changes in the denazification program made just prior to the survey, only 28 per cent had a reasonable idea of what the changes were. Recognition of the provisions of the new law was more widespread than recall of the changes instituted, yet only 35 per cent were able to recognize these changes.

Only four per cent of those who had heard of the new law felt the changes to be for the worse. Over a third (36%) said that the law would allow for a better implementation of denazification, since it would permit individual treatment and punishment. Others viewed the new law with misgivings. Criticism from both those satisfied and dissatisfied with the denazification program centered about suggestions for more discrimination in judgments imposed and regarding each case on its individual merits.

Over half (54%) of the population could give a comparative estimate of the way denazification was being carried out in all four zones. Of the 26 per cent who perceived a difference, 13 per cent said denazification was best carried out in the American Zone, 12 per cent felt it was most rigorous in the American Zone. An appreciable minority felt denazification to be harshest in the Soviet Zone.

Well over half (57%) of the adult population said they were satisfied with the manner in which denazification was being carried out. This figure indicated an increase in satisfaction over the level expressed in previous surveys. Three in four of those who preferred to have the Americans handle the program without *any* German help expected that this situation would produce justice and impartiality. Those who would like to see some German assistance while still leaving the main job in the hands of the Americans argued that, despite the need for cooperation, the responsibility and supervision should be American (28%), or that the Germans could not be trusted to do a fair and impartial job (22%). Another fifth (20%) frankly admitted that the Americans were more just and impartial.

Satisfaction of former NSDAP members with the new program or with denazification generally did not differ markedly from that of the general population. Respondents with relatives who were former Party members, however, criticized the denazification program more sharply.

Report No. 8 (1 June 1946)

REACTIONS TO THE NEW TAX LAWS

Sample: 991 residents of 80 communities in the American Zone.
Interviewing dates: 1 March 1946. (5 pp.)

Of the 68 per cent of those interviewed in the American Zone who had heard of the new tax law, almost all thought that its effect would be to raise taxes. There was evidence of a lack of knowledge about the new law. More than two in five (43%) were unable to guess any amount when asked to estimate their taxes. Lower income groups made up a higher percentage of those who were uninformed than did higher income groups. Income groups varied little in the percentages which agreed that the new taxes would make it impossible to meet necessary expenses. When grouped by social class, however, there was appreciable variation.

A plurality (43%) cited reparations when asked to account for the increase in taxation. Almost three-quarters (72%) saw a justification for the higher taxes. Reasons for favoring the new tax law were the prevention of inflation (56%) and the economic reconstruction of Germany (61%).

In commenting on the abolition of the social bonuses paid under National Socialism to parents with many children, 62 per cent expressed their opposition to the Nazi bonus plan and only 22 per cent endorsed it. More than half (55%) felt that the new law abrogating the bonus system would actually prevent people from having as many children as they might have had. As many as a third (33%) felt this was the purpose of the new law. Those who denied this intent to the law (47%) said, rather, that the law was designed to raise money for Germany's reconstruction (24%), to give equity to small families (7%), to raise money for reparations (4%), or to help prevent inflation (3%).

Report No. 9 (7 June 1946)

ATTITUDES TOWARD RELIGION AND THE CHURCH AS POLITICAL FACTORS IN GERMAN LIFE

Sample: 996 persons in the American Zone.
Interviewing dates: 8 March 1946. (11 pp.)

The survey focuses upon the attitudes of four major groups in the AMZON population: regular churchgoing Catholics and Protestants, and irregular churchgoing Catholics and Protestants. Some of the characteristics of these groups are important in that they shed light on the attitudinal patterns of their representatives. Among Catholics, 65 per cent said they attended church regularly. Fifty per cent of the Protestants claimed regular attendance. Seventy-one per cent of the regular churchgoing Catholics preferred the CSU or the CDU. Among regular churchgoing Protestants, 38 per cent supported the SPD; 40 per cent, the two Christian parties (CDU and CSU). The irregular churchgoing members of both faiths were predominately SPD supporters. Sixty-three per cent of the LDP supporters were irregular churchgoers. More of those who regularly attended church (74%) took part in the previous elections than nonchurchgoers (59%).

Former Nazis tended to be nonchurchgoers. Of the regular churchgoers interviewed, 12 per cent formerly belonged to the NSDAP; 17 per cent of the nonchurchgoers were former members. Hence, former NSDAP members, who were not allowed to vote, increased disproportionately the size of the nonvoting groups reported. Forty-nine per cent of regular churchgoing Catholics had seven or less years of education. About one-fourth of the other groups were similarly educated. Twenty per cent of the regular churchgoers of both faiths had attended nine or more years of school, while 28 per cent of the irregular churchgoers had been similarly educated.

Members of each of the two major religious faiths generally refrained from criticism of the other church's lack of opposition to the Nazis. Criticism that did develop stemmed mostly from irregular churchgoers of both faiths. While 70 per cent of the regular churchgoing Catholics stated that the Church had done its utmost to offer resistance to the National Socialists during their regime, only 47 per cent of regular churchgoing Protestants made a similar claim. Only among regular churchgoing Catholics did a majority believe that the clergy had warned them of the dangers of voting for National Socialism. Among irregular churchgoing Catholics a plurality (35%) stated that there were still Nazis among the clergy. Most members of the other three groups denied this fact. It appears that a fairly large percentage of respondents replied in a prejudiced fashion in an attempt to stem criticism of their own church.

Important groups in the population felt that religion was a real force in the reconstruction of Germany. But support of religion as a moral force in life was distinguished from support of the church when it plays a political role. A plurality (43%) of the entire population believed that the church was taking part in political affairs at that time. Seventy per cent, however, felt that the church should be less interested in political affairs. Major opposition was also expressed to instruction by the clergy in regard to voting in an election or support for particular political parties. Support for the reconstitution of another *Zentrum* party was found among 32 per cent of regular churchgoing Catholics. As many Catholic women favored as opposed the suggested move. But all other characteristic groups expressed strong opposition. Underscoring the minimal inter-church rivalry found, more members of all groups studied thought that Catholics and Protestants would be able to cooperate successfully in a "Christian" political party than denied this possibility.

A large majority of the general population felt that the military government had given sufficient and appropriate support to the church.

Report No. 10 (21 June 1946)

ATTITUDES TOWARD POLITICS AS A CAREER FOR THE COMING GENERATION IN GERMANY

Sample: 1,515 adults in the American Zone and the American Sector of Berlin.
Interviewing dates: 15 April 1946. (9 pp.)

A very large majority (76%) of the German public thought of politics as no career for their sons. Two important variations in these attitudes occurred within the class structure of the society. The very uppercrust was relatively more disposed, and the upper-middle class relatively less disposed, toward such a career than was the average German. Disillusionment with politics was apparent not only among those who participated in the Nazi government but also among those groups that closely identified themselves with National Socialist aims and ideals.

The most important of these latter groups were the returned prisoners of war, and the young men and women under 30 years of age. Significantly greater respect for politics as a worthy profession existed among supporters of left-wing political parties and among trade union members.

Important differences were recorded among residents of various sized communities. Farmers least favored (5% favored) a political career for their sons. Residents of the large cities of Frankfurt, Stuttgart, and Munich, and of the American Sector of Berlin, seem to have overcome political apathy to an appreciable degree.

Comments made by interviewees exemplified the patterns of public thinking on this subject. Those not favoring a political career for their sons remarked on the crooked nature of politics, the belief that it is not a profession, and its demand for maturity. Many respondents indicated horror and repugnance at the thought of their sons taking up politics. Reasons for favoring a political career included taking care of the needs of the people, making things better, the need for greater attention to politics, working for peace, freedom from militarism and fascism, and becoming good democrats.

In contrast to the AMZON population, only 14 per cent of which would favor politics as a career for their sons (76% against), cross-samples of the American population revealed 21 per cent in favor and 68 per cent against in January 1945, and 25 per cent in favor and 65 per cent against in the spring of 1946. Among the British population in January 1945, 25 per cent favored and 48 per cent opposed such a career for their sons. In the United States the lower class was more inclined than the upper class to be favorable; in England the reverse was true.

Report No. 11 (27 June 1946)

GERMAN ATTITUDES TOWARD TRADE UNIONS

Sample: 1,600 adults in the American Zone and in the American Sector of Berlin.
Interviewing dates: 15 April 1946. (11 pp.)

The general public was divided on whether the Nazis' denial of collective bargaining and the right to strike was good or not. Thirty-five per cent of the respondents viewed positively the Nazi labor policy, asserting that strikes were bad and the standard of living had been good. Thirty-eight per cent opposed the Nazi policy on the grounds that the workers had lost all their rights under the Nazi system. Opinion was also split on the German Labor Front's record. Thirty-seven per cent said that the DAF did an unsatisfactory job of representing workers' interests, while 22 per cent thought it had done a good job representing these interests. Some were willing to recognize the DAF's policies on social benefits even though they did not think that the DAF satisfactorily represented the workers. More people (42%) opposed the reestablishment of collective bargaining after the occupation than favored it (34%). Most people (71%) favored an advisory voice for workers in management, such as the Workers Councils (approved by 66 per cent) recently authorized by the Allied Control Council provide. Fifty-five per cent favored the Military Government's wage fixing policy; 24 per cent opposed it.

Unionists in the American Zone were oriented toward the Western democracies rather than toward the Soviet Union. The bulk of leftist sentiment among unionists favored the SPD rather than the KPD. Certain authoritarian features of a government-controlled economy attracted a surprisingly large minority of unionists. Pre-1933 unionists (68%) and current unionists (74%) were nonetheless more democratic than the population as a whole (49%) in favoring free trade unions with collective bargaining rights.

Nazism made some inroads among the pre-1933 unionists, but the compromised unionists tended to remain outside the free trade unions now being organized. The new trade unions attracted the more democratic of the pre-1933 unionists (for example, 56 per cent of pre-1933 unionists active in 1946 thought the Nazi wage control policy bad). The new generation of unionists without pre-1933 experience was not appreciably less democratic than the old generation of pre-1933 unionists who resumed their union activity.

Report No. 12 (28 June 1946)

ATTITUDES OF SOME BAVARIAN SCHOOLCHILDREN

Sample: 250 schoolchildren between the ages of 12 and 18 in Regensburg, Welheim, Pirkensee, and Burglengenfeld. *Interviewing dates:* not specified. (6 pp.)

Although 88 per cent of the children had belonged to Nazi youth organizations, only 12 per cent were members of a new youth organization. Thirty-seven per cent of their parents had belonged to the NSDAP, a figure about average for the American Zone. Eighty-four per cent of the youth were Catholic. Most (48%) would vote for the CSU if they were old enough, 18 per cent for the SPD, and three per cent for the KPD. Almost a third (29%), however, said they would not vote even if they could.

Their principal concern was obtaining food. Thirty per cent said that the type of aid Germany most needed was food, and 26 per cent reported that their greatest wish was for more food. They also desired peace and freedom for their brothers who were prisoners of war. Their secondary concern were jobs, clothing, and shoes. The children seemed to be in good health. Reading, sports, and handicrafts provided recreation.

Almost all the children (98%) claimed to like school. Most (66%) thought themselves to be average students. About one-third considered themselves to be good students. Only a few (3%) admitted that they were bad students. Although they were interested in a wide variety of subjects, they liked best mathematics, German, geography, history, biology, and English. Seventy-four per cent preferred to learn English rather than some other foreign language.

The employment aspirations of the youth were generally low. The girls wanted to be saleswomen, dressmakers, clerks, teachers, and hairdressers. The boys wished to be bakers, electricians, or carpenters. None of the boys wanted to teach. More girls (7%) than boys (3%) hoped to become physicians or dentists.

The most common reason given (36%) for Germany's loss of the war was the overpowering strength of the enemy. Second (30%) was Germany's lack of material. When asked to name the three greatest Germans, about ten per cent named Hitler, a quarter mentioned monarchs, and a third poets. When questioned as to what the respondent would do if he alone knew the secret of the atom bomb, the most common answer given (36%) was to keep it a secret. Democracy to these youths meant freedom for the people (23%) and government by the people (10%). Forty-eight per cent, however, had no opinion when asked what democracy meant.

Almost as many (35%) liked the American soldier as disliked him (39%). More than half of those who disliked the American soldier mentioned his general behavior as a reason.

Most of the youth expected a good, lasting, or just or wise peace from the Allies. Fifty-nine per cent did not expect another war soon. Of the 41 per cent who did expect war, most thought it would be with the Soviet Union.

Report No. 13 (28 June 1946)

A PRELIMINARY STUDY OF BOOK READING
IN GERMANY

Sample: approximately 1,000 adult Germans in the American Zone.
Interviewing dates: late February 1946. (5 pp.)

Over half the sample population (55%) stated that they did not read books at all. The remaining 43 per cent read for various amounts of time. Eleven per cent read up to two hours a week; 14 per cent between two and six hours per week. Most readers had recently been reading for amusement and diversion. *Kitsch*, sentimental love stories, novels, mysteries, and detective stories were most popular.

Although book readers came from widely diverse backgrounds, they were most likely to be from better educated circles, the younger adult age groups, and from middle-sized cities rather than from very small communities (under 2,000 inhabitants) or very large cities (over 300,000 inhabitants). Almost as many women read as men; men, however, tended to read many more hours per week than women. Former Nazis read a great deal more than those who had not been Nazis. Twenty-two per cent of the readers who were former Nazis read eight hours or more weekly, while only eight per cent of those who had not been Nazis read this amount.

Only a very small number (five per cent of the total adult population, nine per cent of all book readers) used local libraries. Many books were personal loans. The opportunity to purchase new books was still very limited.

Novels, fiction, and short stories were by far the most popular, both with groups that read up to four hours per week (71%) and with those who read over four hours per week. Book readers felt that forthcoming books on Germany's problems should deal with reconstruction, the future of Germany, and Europe. When asked what types of books and authors they would like to see on sale as soon as possible, book readers expressed greatest interest in books and authors forbidden during the Nazi regime. Second choice comprised new books by German writers living in Germany.

Report No. 14 (6 July 1946)

MAIL TO "STIMME AMERIKAS," FEBRUARY AND MARCH 1946

Sample: 3,466 pieces of mail written to the "Voice of America."
Interviewing dates: 29 January 1946 through 1 April 1946. (10 pp.)

Over half the mail to the "Voice of America" came from the American Zone (52 per cent in February; 54 per cent in March). Within AMZON there was an increase in the mail from the Bavarian audience (17 per cent in February; 21 per cent in March). Proportionate to the population of the three *Laender* in the American Zone, more listeners living in Hesse wrote to VOA than listeners in the other two *Laender*. During the period of this survey, nearly 85 per cent of the population lived in towns or villages with fewer than 100,000 inhabitants. At the beginning of the survey, 70 per cent of the mail came from communities of this size. In later weeks, this percentage dropped to about 60 per cent. Although 60 per cent of the inhabitants of AMZON were women, well over half of the letters written to the "Voice of America" came from men. More letters were mailed to VOA on Monday (20%) than on any other day of the week. This percentage declined as the week progressed, falling to 6 per cent on Sunday.

In the period considered, a smaller percentage of letters raised considerations of personal problems abroad, such as requests for aid in returning prisoners of war from the United States, than in earlier periods. A large percentage of the mail concerned personal problems in Germany (45 per cent in February; 38 per cent in March). About an eighth of the mail (11 per cent in February; 13 per cent in March) contained denials of the war guilt of all the German people or pointed out the guilt of specific segments of the population, such as Hitler or the SS. About half that number (six per cent in February; seven per cent in March) criticized the denazification program. In March, there was a sharp increase in mail containing references to the reconstruction of Germany (eight per cent in February; 17 per cent in March). About a tenth (11 per cent in February; nine per cent in March) of the letters requested information about leaving Germany.

The letters contained very few critical remarks. Such criticism as there was concerned the commentators, the time at which broadcasts took place, and a dislike for the jazz music broadcast. The commentators remained the most popular feature mentioned. in this period. Second most popular were discussions and speeches. About two per cent requested more material about life in the United States or reported liking VOA for its presentation of various aspects of American life.

Report No. 14A (8 July 1946)

GERMAN ATTITUDES TOWARD THE EXPULSION OF GERMAN NATIONALS FROM NEIGHBORING COUNTRIES

Sample: 964 persons in the American Zone (nine per cent of whom identified themselves as evacuees).
Interviewing dates: 11 March 1946. (16 pp.)

Although 60 per cent of the evacuees expected to get along with the resident German population, only 50 per cent of the resident population had a similar expectation. Even this group made reservations. For example, the resident Germans thought that the evacuees would get along if they were decent, or if they did their part and cooperated. A quarter (25%) of both the evacuees and the resident Germans did not expect to get along. More members of the higher social classes had met with evacuees than had members of the lower social classes. More former NSDAP members (48%) had developed conversational contacts with evacuees than nonmembers of the Party (32%).

The population of the American Zone was basically unaware of the mass migrational character of the movement of evacuees. Only 34 per cent thought that at least one million evacuees would come to the American Zone, and 42 per cent were unable to suggest any number at all.

Most people projected responsibility for the move upon groups other than the general German population. One-half (51%) blamed the Allies for a policy of hatred and revenge; 29 per cent blamed the Nazis and their misdeeds; and 25 per cent of those questioned were unable to judge who or what was responsible for the evacuations. More people (48%) felt the Allies should be held fully, or at least partly, responsible for the care of the evacuees than accepted the problem as a responsibility of the German nation or communities (40%). Almost half (46%) of the residents of Hesse were ready to accept the responsibility for the evacuees themselves. In the other two *Laender*, there were more who wanted to escape the responsibility (45%) than were willing to accept it (37%). In general, Protestants, the better educated, former NSDAP members, the higher social classes, and residents of the largest cities demonstrated a greater sense of responsibility for the evacuees. There was greatest resistance to German efforts to care for evacuees in cities of between 100,000 and 250,000 population. Four-fifths (81%) were ready to give economic equality to the evacuees, but only 74 per cent were willing to give political equality. Primary opposition to giving political equality stemmed from supporters of the CSU. A solid majority of all those questioned despaired of finding a solution for the lack of food (71%) and housing (64%), but only a third (35%) thought the matter of jobs to be insoluble.

A large majority (72%) felt that the evacuations were not justified. Those most likely to support the policy (14 per cent of the whole population) were SPD supporters (18%), irregular churchgoers (18%), nonmembers of the NSDAP (16%), the lower classes (17%), residents of the larger cities (25%), and inhabitants of Hesse (19%).

Report No. 15 (27 July 1946)

RELATIVE EFFECTS OF FOOD SCARCITY IN TWO COUNTRIES

Sample: a representative sample of 992 (March), 1,515 (April), and 1,698 (May) adults in the American Zone and, in May only, in the American Sector of Berlin.
Interviewing dates: 15 March 1946; 15 April 1946; and 8 May 1946. (3 pp.)

In the American Zone, 61 per cent of the respondents stated in March 1946 that they were not getting enough food to be able to work efficiently. There was a cut in rations which took effect in AMZON on 1 April 1946. After this cut, 72 per cent of the population reported insufficient food. In May 1946, 70 per cent reported insufficient food. Eighty-eight per cent of the Berlin respondents, questioned for the first time in May, reported food scarcity. Within the American Zone, an even larger percentage (93%) of the residents of towns between 100,000 and 250,000 reported such hardship. Eighty-five per cent complained of scarcity in towns between 50,000 and 100,000 population and in the large cities of Frankfurt, Stuttgart, and Munich. The percentage reporting scarcity declined to 75 per cent in communities from 2,000 to 50,000 and to 60 per cent in villages under 2,000 population.

In England, a survey in late November 1945 and another in March 1946 produced identical results: Exactly half the people questioned said that they felt they were not getting enough food to be able to work efficiently; and almost as many (47%) said that they were procuring sufficient food.

Report No. 16 (7 August 1946)

GERMAN ATTITUDES TOWARD THE NUREMBERG TRIALS

Sample: summary of eight surveys, with sample sizes ranging from 331 in November 1945 to 2,969 in August 1946. *Interviewing dates:* not specified; relevant surveys from 26 October 1945 to 9 August 1946. (6 pp.)

The results of a survey shortly after the International Military Tribunal convened in November 1945 revealed that, in the intervening few weeks, 65 per cent of the German people had learned something from the proceedings. In later polls the percentage of people having gained some information rose to 87 per cent. When asked at the time of the survey what they had learned, 29 per cent reported first learning about the concentration camps. At the time of the second survey, 57 per cent reported first learning of the concentration camps. In this second survey, 30 per cent of the respondents said they first learned of the annihilation of the Jews from the Trials. No one on the first survey reported having gained this knowledge.

The number of respondents believing that the Nazis would receive a fair trial never dropped below 75 per cent. The average for the eight surveys showed the belief by 80 per cent that the Nazi leaders would receive a fair trial; four per cent thought that the trial would not be fair, and 16 per cent held no opinion.

A majority of the population felt that the war leaders on trial were guilty. Seventy per cent thought all to be guilty. Among the nine per cent who named someone they considered to be not guilty, Hess was mentioned most frequently. Sixty per cent of the respondents felt that the indictment of whole organizations – such as the Reich Cabinet, the leadership corps of the Nazi Party, the SS, the SA, the Gestapo, and the General Staff and High Command of the Army – was justified. A quarter (25%) saw no justification for such an indictment.

Nearly half the respondents believed that the accused would receive the death sentence. The sampled group split sharply on the question of whether all defendants would receive the same punishment. Over a third (37%) thought that they would; and nearly all of these thought that the punishment would be death. Almost half (46%) felt that the punishment would vary according to the individual defendant.

Seventy per cent thought that there were others guilty of war crimes in addition to the 21 then on trial. Respondents most frequently named Nazi Party members and lesser leaders as being guilty. Almost 60 per cent felt that those guilty should be charged after the Nuremberg Trials, but a similar percentage did not know which of these groups would be charged. And although they expected further trials to be held at the conclusion of the trial of the 21 major defendants, 82 per cent of the people did not know that the political leaders then in prison camps were expected to be tried.

The series of surveys showed that a majority of the readers found newspaper reports of the Trials to be complete and trustworthy.

Report No. 17 (8 August 1946)

ATTITUDES TOWARD INTERNATIONAL LEADERSHIP IN GERMANY COMPARED WITH ATTITUDES IN SEVEN OTHER COUNTRIES

Sample: 1,515 residents of the American Zone.
Interviewing dates: 15 April 1946. (5 pp.)

A solid majority (58%) thought that the United States would chiefly influence world history in the coming decade. About one in 20 more (60%) was ready to assume that the United States and Britain would act together as one power. Only about one in ten AMZON Germans (11%) looked to the Soviet Union as the most important country in the ten years to come, but a small group (6%) could not distinguish between the relative strengths of the United States and Russia. Only a very tiny proportion (2%) held that Britain was the country which would influence future world decisions. About one in seven respondents (15%) was unable to express a judgment on this matter.

The reasons given in support of the replies emphasized the fundamental distinction made by Germans when they thought of the future reorganization of their own country under the direction of the Allies. Practically half of those thinking that America would dominate the world scene, for instance, held that its great economic strength, rich resources, and great stocks of food would place America in the supreme position. About one in five thought that its political ideology and leadership directed toward peaceful ends would carry America forward in a dominant role. Only about one in seven referred to the military might of the United States – its army and navy, and the atomic bomb.

By way of contrast, nearly six in ten of those who thought that the Soviet Union would occupy the leadership position referred to the revolutionary drive of Bolshevism. Another one in seven spoke respectfully about the ideological leadership and need for peace which would determine Soviet behavior in the future.

Britain's force, said most people who chose this nation, lay in her political strength. Some also mentioned Britain's naval and military power as well as the overseas economic resources of the British Empire.

The rankings by eight countries seeing the United States exerting future leadership were: the United States (63%), AMZON Germany (58%), Austria (50%), Sweden (50%), Great Britain (48%), France (43%), Canada (36%), and Denmark (21%). The rank orders for countries envisioning future Soviet leadership were: France (41%), Great Britain (31%), Austria (26%), the United States (24%), Canada (24%), Sweden (21%), Denmark (19%), and AMZON Germany (11%). Only Austrians and Canadians (19%) saw the future importance of Britain to be high, followed by the British (14%), Danes (9%), Swedes (8%), Americans (5%), French (4%), and AMZON Germans (2%).

Report No. 18 (14 August 1946)

A STUDY OF FOOD CONSUMPTION AND ATTITUDES TOWARD RATIONING AND GENERAL HEALTH OF THE GERMAN POPULATION

Sample: 1,698 interviews (1,504 in the American Zone and 194 in the British and American Sectors of Berlin) plus 526 additional cases to build up the sample to permit more detailed breakdowns, making a total of 2,224 respondents.
Interviewing dates: 8 May 1946. (53 pp.)

Two-fifths (41%) of the AMZON respondents and a fifth (22%) of the Berliners believed that food rations were largest in the American Zone; 29 per cent of the AMZON Germans and 16 per cent of the Berliners felt rations to be largest in the British Zone. A fifth (22%) of the AMZON sample and a third (32%) of the Berliners saw residents of the Soviet Zone getting the smallest rations. Almost nine in ten (89%) of the respondents in the American Zone, but only 37 per cent of the Berliners, said that the food rationcard system was fair. Respondents in Berlin aimed their complaints about the rationcard system at those who they thought obtained more food than they deserved rather than at actual food shortages. Respondents in both AMZON (41%) and Berlin (31%) nonetheless blamed an actual shortage of food for the food reduction of 1 April 1946. A majority of the Berliners (61%) but only a minority of the AMZON residents (37%) felt that the food situation would improve. More generally, not a single Berliner and only 12 per cent of the AMZON respondents indicated satisfaction with the food ration, although 21 per cent in Berlin and 24 per cent in the American Zone reported that their rations were adequate.

AMZON residents, on the whole, ate much better than did Berliners. Bread and potatoes led the list of foods eaten in the American Zone in the 24 hours immediately preceding the interview, while most Berliners had had cereal and bread. Greater food scarcity in Berlin was demonstrated by the fact that Berliners (25%) received substitutes for unavailable rationed food items more frequently than did residents of AMZON (12%), whereas more of the latter (25%) than of the Berliners (5%) had received special food rations in the week preceding the interview.

To supplement their food ration, 40 per cent of the AMZON respondents had homemade preserves as did only 11 per cent of the Berlin respondents. Over half (53%) of the Berlin respondents and 21 per cent of those in AMZON said that they were able to obtain food in addition to the rationed items purchased at the store. In Berlin, 15 per cent said they obtained their supplementary food on the black market. The median interval at which both Berliners and residents of AMZON obtained supplementary food is, for the majority, one meal for one person per week. About a sixth (18 per cent in

AMZON; 15 per cent in Berlin) went to the country to obtain supplemental food. Only 11 per cent of the AMZON and 12 per cent of the Berliners ate in restaurants. Eight per cent in AMZON and ten per cent in Berlin indicated that they gave food away, most often to members of the immediate family or relatives. Considering all additional sources, 80 per cent of those interviewed in the American Zone and 90 per cent of the Berlin sample were able to obtain some food in addition to the authorized ration.

Every respondent interviewed in Berlin said that a black market existed in that city. In the American Zone, 43 per cent of the respondents reported the existence of a black market in their community, 29 per cent said that there was no black market in their community, and 28 per cent did not know whether or not a black market existed. Substantial majorities (56 per cent in AMZON, 82 per cent in Berlin) blamed the black market for shortages in food, clothing, shoes, and tobacco as well as other items. Even larger majorities (67 per cent in AMZON; 91 per cent in Berlin) believed that the black market exerted an unfavorable influence on economic conditions. The respondents directed their complaints particularly at farmers who, they felt, were keeping their produce from the open market. Over three in five (63 per cent in AMZON; 62 per cent in Berlin) perceived the authorities to be doing everything possible to eliminate the black market.

Regarding general health, 66 per cent of the AMZON respondents and 76 per cent of the Berlin respondents reported having lost weight between January 1946 and the time of the interview. In the American Zone, the median number of kilograms lost was four to five; in Berlin, six to ten. Seven-tenths (71%) of the AMZON respondents and 88 per cent of the Berliners said that they did not get enough food to work efficiently. Over a quarter (30 per cent in AMZON; 26 per cent in Berlin) had suffered at least one cold in the month prior to the time of the interview.

Regarding prospective supplementary food sources, 50 per cent of the AMZON and 31 per cent of the Berlin respondents expected to make preserves during the coming summer. Sixty per cent in AMZON and 24 per cent in Berlin planned to have a garden that summer. Most respondents (92 per cent in AMZON; 91 per cent in Berlin) did not expect to receive food parcels from friends or relatives outside Germany.

Report No. 19 (19 August 1946)

BASIC ATTITUDES EXPLORED BY THE "GERMAN ATTITUDE SCALE"

Sample: 1,470 persons in the American Zone, 182 in the American Sector of Berlin, 295 youths aged 17 to 27 in Wuerttemberg-Baden, 84 political prisoners to be detained in camp, 95 political prisoners to be released, and 214 Marburg University students.
Interviewing dates: not specified. (55 pp.)

The questionnaire used in this survey comprised eight sets of questions (with a total of 110 items), each of which probed attitudes in a generally defined area. Eleven scales focused on: family, women, and children; ethics and justice (social responsibility); anti-Semitism; projection of guilt; future of Germany (supervised responsibility); flattery (questions to which respondents could give answers flattering to the occupation powers; replies providing a test of the sincerity of the individual's responses); war and militarism; and four aspects of government, democracy, authority – the necessity of political information and interest, independent thinking as a value, the fallibility of leadership, and independence and rights of others.

On the average, about three in ten AMZON Germans replied in the democratic direction on all eleven scales. An additional third answered in a democratic direction on all but one question within each scale. Those most likely to give democratic responses were Hessians, residents of cities over 100,000 in population, those with more than 12 years of schooling, those between 50 and 59 years of age, men, married persons, SPD supporters, those who had a professional occupation, middle income groups, political prisoners, and the Marburg students. Those who were usually undemocratic were residents of towns under 10,000 in population, those with less than seven years of schooling, those who had a former member of the NSDAP in the family, those under the age of 20, women, the widowed, those with no party preference, farmers, low income groups, and youth in Wuerttemberg-Baden.

Report No. 20 (27 August 1946)

PRELIMINARY STUDY OF MOTION PICTURE ATTENDANCE AND ATTITUDES

Sample: in the American Zone, 331 respondents in November 1945, 414 in December, 964 and 993 in January 1946, and 985 in February 1946.
Interviewing dates: 19 November 1945, 1 December 1945, 21 January 1946, 31 January 1946, 21 February 1946. (28 pp.)

In the period covered by this series of surveys, between 23 and 45 per cent of the respondents reported attending the movies. When asked in February 1946 how often they had been to the movies since the beginning of the occupation, most (17%) had been to the movies from one to five times. Most (16%) walked to the movies. The respondents who did not attend the movies were also asked in February what their reasons were: Most (26%) said that there were no movies in their town; 20 per cent indicated that they had no time; and 13 per cent had no interest in the movies.

Of the 23 per cent who attended movies at the time of the February 1946 survey, about half (12%) felt that the films were good or very good. Seven per cent gave answers ranging from "all right" to "awful." Among moviegoers in the February survey, 94 per cent stated they would like to see an old German film again, as did 55 per cent of the nonmoviegoers. The two main reasons for wanting to see an old German film were: a preference for films emphasizing things German, that is, German films made more sense, were more beautiful, or were more personal; and because of the language, and particularly a dislike of subtitles.

Of the 23 per cent who went to the movies at the time of the February 1946 survey, 18 per cent had seen the newsreel *Die Welt im Film* (*The World in Film*). Most (11%) thought the newsreel good, all right, or interesting. Most (10%) gave as the main reason for liking the film the fact that it brought news from the outside.

Only 12 per cent of the 31 January 1946 respondents in Bavaria (less than one third of the moviegoers in this *Land*) had seen the concentration camp film *Todesmuehlen* (*Mills of Death*). Nineteen per cent of all Bavarians interviewed (70 per cent of the Bavarian moviegoers who had not seen the film) said they would not have been deterred from going to the movies if they had known ahead of time that a concentration camp film was to be shown. Twelve per cent in Bavaria would not go to the movies if they knew that such a film was being shown. Most of those who saw the film (11%) thought the film an accurate account of conditions in concentration camps; and most (9%) said they had learned something from the film.

Of the American films seen by Germans, they liked *Madame Curie* best and *Todesmuehlen* least. The old German film which respondents would most like to see again was *Die Goldene Stadt* (*The Golden City*).

Report No. 21 (25 September 1946)

ATTITUDES TOWARD LICENSED NEWSPAPERS IN SOME AMERICAN OCCUPIED AREAS

Sample: 8,029 adults in the American Zone and West Berlin.
Interviewing dates: last three weeks of June 1946. (13 pp.)

This survey examined the attitudes toward 33 American-licensed newspapers on the part of residents in the cities where the newspapers were published; appendices appear in Report No. 34 of 28 December 1946.

The more education a person had, the more likely he was to read newspapers: In Bavaria, 27 per cent of those with less than seven years of schooling said that they did not read papers and 15 per cent of this group in Wuerttemberg-Baden were in the same category; only four per cent of those with 12 or more years of schooling, however, said that they did not read newspapers. Very few men (5%) did not do so, whereas nearly three times as many women did not. Those able to name a political party that they preferred were more likely to read newspapers than were those who could not choose a party. Those under 20 and those over 70 had the least number of readers in their ranks, although in Hesse it was only the very old who were nonreaders; Hessians under the age of 20 claimed to read papers as frequently as their parents.

An average of 49 per cent felt that their local paper was either "very good" or "good." Greatest dissatisfaction was shown by the residents of Hesse, usually a fairly critical population on any issue. There was only a slight positive correlation between disapproval of the German press and the feeling that it was hampered by American censorship. There was some indication that dissatisfaction rested upon the fact that the newspapers did not contain all that the readers were interested in, although many indicated recognition of shortages in newsprint, equipment, and personnel. The tetrachoric correlations between proportions liking the paper and approving of the local government administration showed a positive coefficient in every instance except West Berlin and Fulda, which showed no relationship between the two variables. In Bavaria there was a strong relationship between the charges that a paper propagandized and that it gave preference to a political party; this tendency was less strong in the other two *Laender*.

A large majority (77%) of newspaper readers preferred papers with no political party domination. Bavarian feelings were above average on this issue, with 80 per cent saying that they were opposed to party papers; these data may have reflected the overrepresentation of SPD editors in Bavaria, considering the relative strength of this party in the *Land*.

Based on a weighted scale of replies to questions concerning news coverage, the combined sources of all readers in AMZON suggested that 34 per cent rated their own paper as "good," 27 per cent rated it "fair," 21 per cent rated it "poor," and about the same proportion (18%) rated it "very good."

Report No. 22 (25 September 1946)

A STUDY OF ATTITUDES TOWARD THE RECONSTRUCTION AND REHABILITATION OF GERMANY

> *Sample:* 1,192 interviews – 993 in the American Zone and 199 in the American Sector of Berlin.
> *Interviewing dates:* first half of April 1946. (57 pp.)

Of those who could estimate how long the Americans would continue to occupy Germany (62 per cent in AMZON; 90 per cent in Berlin), the majority (37 per cent in AMZON; 55 per cent in Berlin) expected it to last ten years or more. Most respondents (22 per cent in AMZON; 26 per cent in Berlin) estimated that the reconstruction of Germany would take from 20 to 30 years; an almost equally large number (20 per cent in AMZON; 22 per cent in Berlin) thought that it would take 50 years or more. The bulk (72%) of the West Berlin respondents reported that the reconstruction in the American Zone had gone more quickly than they had expected. Respondents in the American Zone were divided; 41 per cent said that reconstruction had gone more quickly than they had expected as opposed to 40 per cent who thought that it had gone more slowly. The majority of respondents in both the American Zone and Berlin (56 and 73 per cent, respectively) were optimistic about the possibility of reconstruction being accomplished with some degree of speed and energy. Two-fifths (42%) of the AMZON respondents and a third (34%) in Berlin had heard disturbing rumors: Disturbing them most (34 per cent in AMZON; 20 per cent in Berlin) was the rumor that there would be another war.

Seventy per cent of the AMZON respondents and 83 per cent of the Berlin respondents believed that reconstruction could best be accomplished through "hard work." Most (56 per cent in AMZON; 62 per cent in Berlin) saw the greatest handicap to reconstruction to be the lack of building and raw materials. Over a third (35%) of the respondents in the American Zone and 42 per cent in Berlin thought the SPD to be the party best able to carry out the reconstruction of Germany.

Most respondents (60 per cent in AMZON; 90 per cent in Berlin) thought that the Americans had furthered the recovery and reconstruction of Germany. Over six in ten (63%) of the respondents in Berlin said that the main way in which the Americans had helped the recovery of Germany was by bringing in food and improving food conditions. AMZON respondents were more likely to stress American interest and aid in general (23%) than food (11%). About half (49 per cent in AMZON; 55 per cent in Berlin), looking toward the future, said that the Americans could help Germany most by bringing in food; large numbers of respondents (49 per cent in AMZON; 47 per cent in Berlin) also mentioned supplying materials and equipment.

Most respondents in both the American Zone and Berlin

(48 per cent and 60 per cent, respectively) did not expect the four occupying powers to cooperate successfully in the reconstruction of Germany. A quarter (24%) of the AMZON residents and almost twice as many Berliners (44%) perceived the Soviet Union as uncooperative; 13 per cent in the American Zone and five per cent in Berlin mentioned both the Soviet Union and France. Around two-thirds (59 per cent in AMZON; 70 per cent in Berlin) did not feel that occupation by foreign powers was a national humiliation for Germany. Whereas 60 per cent of the respondents in the American Zone and 77 per cent in Berlin felt it was just that the Allies first help the Allied nations, an appreciable minority (25 per cent in AMZON; 20 per cent in Berlin) thought Germany should be aided first.

Three-quarters (74%) of the AMZON respondents and 70 per cent in Berlin denied that all Germans were responsible for the war. Most (56 per cent in AMZON; 59 per cent in Berlin) said that the Nazi regime had begun the war and hence had to bear the responsibility for it. As many as 41 per cent of the respondents in the American Zone and 47 per cent in Berlin denied their own guilt by such statements as "We couldn't do anything about it; The little people had no say; What could we do; The leaders are the guilty ones." A majority (53 per cent in AMZON; 65 per cent in Berlin) did not think that the individual should always obey without question the orders of his state; many (40 per cent in AMZON; 35 per cent in Berlin), however, did approve of such obedience.

Roughly half (55 per cent in AMZON; 44 per cent in Berlin) felt that National Socialism was a good idea badly carried out. Almost all (87 per cent in AMZON; 91 per cent in Berlin) indicated that they stopped trusting Hitler by the end of the war; most of these (35 per cent in AMZON; 51 per cent in Berlin) reported never having had any faith in Hitler. Over a third (36%) of AMZON residents and 28 per cent of the Berliners reported having accepted the prewar view that territories with considerable German minorities should be reincorporated into Germany. A minority (14 per cent in AMZON; three per cent in Berlin) coninued to agree with the prewar statement that international Jewry alone would profit from the war. About an eighth (14 per cent in AMZON; 12 per cent in Berlin) still felt the Nordic race to be superior to all others.

Report No. 23 (22 October 1946)

THE VIENNESE NEWSPAPERS: AN OPINION RESEARCH STUDY

> *Sample:* about 500 persons in the American Sector of Vienna.
> *Interviewing dates:* first days of September 1946. (16 pp.)

The poll showed that Vienna was very largely (85%) a Catholic city. It was also a two party community, with the SPOe (*Sozialistische Partei Oesterreichs*) and the OeVP (*Oesterreichische Volkspartei*) amassing the support of a very large proportion (93%) of voters with stated preferences.

More than nine in ten (92%) Viennese living in the American Sector reported reading newspapers, with readership being broadly defined as having read at least one paper during the previous two weeks. The most widely read paper was the United States sponsored *Wiener Kurier* (73%) and a solid majority (60%) also liked it best of all the available newspapers. Only 42 per cent of the readers of *Neues Oesterreich* liked that paper the best, and only the *Weltpresse* approached the *Wiener Kurier* in popularity. Among the five most popular newspapers, no paper was strongly disliked by an appreciable proportion of the population.

There were no significant differences between those who thought National Socialism a bad idea and those who thought it a good idea badly carried out in relation to their preference for the *Wiener Kurier*. As for group differences, Protestants were slightly more apt to like it than Catholics, there were no age differentiations, and, as might be expected, laborers and apprentices preferred the *Arbeiter Zeitung*; there was little distinction to be made along social class lines, again suggesting its broad general appeal.

In a multiple factor rating scale designed to show readers' opinions on coverage of 11 different types of news items in the five most popular newspapers, it became clear that the *Wiener Kurier* was publicly recognized as emphasizing news about the Americans and the United States rather than the new responsibilities of the Austrians. According to the same scale, the *Weltpresse* satisfied its readers, more than others satisfied theirs, in the coverage given foreign affairs.

Report No. 24 (22 October 1946)

MANNHEIM ATTITUDES TOWARD NEGRO TROOPS

Sample: 226 Mannheim adults (over 18 years of age).
Interviewing dates: 27 September 1946. (7 pp.)

Nearly two-thirds (64%) of the respondents reported having no personal relations with American soldiers. A fifth (20%) reported some relationship with white soldiers, eight per cent with Negro soldiers, and eight per cent with both. Although eight per cent said that they or some member of their family had had a pleasant experience with a Negro, 13 per cent reported an unpleasant experience; and a few (2%) told of both pleasant and unpleasant experiences. When asked about the behavior of Negro soldiers, a substantial number (36%) said that the Negroes were friendlier toward the German populace than white troops and only 16 per cent said they were less friendly.

Most respondents (45%) reported that they were definitely not afraid of the Negroes in Mannheim, as opposed to 15 per cent who expressed fears. When asked if the Negroes were inferior to the white race, 38 per cent of those who responded positively were also afraid of the Negroes, whereas only 21 per cent of those who answered negatively were afraid of them.

The bulk (70%) of the respondents felt that the conduct of the Negro had been good. Of these, however, almost half (33 per cent of the total sample) noted exceptions; and an additional 17 per cent of the sample thought the Negroes' behavior to be improper. As many as four in five of those noting exceptions or improper behavior could point to specific examples: The most common complaints were murder, rape, mistreatment of citizens, mishandling women and girls (24%); and drunken irresponsibility (13%). More young people under 30 (68%) reported the behavior of Negroes not always decent than did those over 30 (46%).

Report No. 25 (8 November 1946)

GERMAN KNOWLEDGE ABOUT AND ATTITUDES TOWARD INFLATION

Sample: summaries of six surveys from 14 January to 7 June 1946; in the American Zone, 972 respondents in January, 954 in February, 991 in March, 1,501 in April, 1,504 in May, and 1,486 in June; in West Berlin, 199 in April, 194 in May, and 196 in June.
Interviewing dates: 14 January, 14 February, 1 March, 5 April, 8 May, and 7 June 1946. (47 pp.)

In AMZON, the percentage believing prices would go up increased from 30 per cent in January 1946 to 56 per cent in February, dropped to 40 per cent in May, and increased to 50 per cent in June. In Berlin, 25 per cent in both May and June 1946 felt that prices would go up; and 27 per cent in May and 41 per cent in June thought that prices would go down.

Only in April did a majority (54%) of AMZON respondents think that the *Reichsmark* would be worth as much in six months as it was at the time of the interview. In Berlin, however, a substantial majority in each survey (75 per cent in April, 58 per cent in May, 63 per cent in June) expected no such inflation.

In June, only 27 per cent of the AMZON respondents were able to select the correct statement, given a choice of three, defining the cause of inflation; even fewer in Berlin (14%) selected the correct statement. In June, 36 per cent in the American Zone and 41 per cent in Berlin believed there was a possibility of inflation. At that time 85 per cent of the respondents in the American Zone and 93 per cent in Berlin said that the American and German authorities really wanted to prevent inflation, and 79 per cent in the American Zone and 94 per cent in Berlin thought them able to do so. A substantial majority (54 per cent in AMZON; 72 per cent in Berlin) indicated that the Military Government and the Civil Administration were in the position to keep prices stable. An even greater majority (82 per cent in AMZON; 91 per cent in Berlin) was confident that the Military and Civil Governments would actually do their best to hold prices at the existing level.

Report No. 26 (13 November 1946)

INFORMATION ABOUT THE LAND CONSTITUTIONS AND THE INTENTION TO VOTE IN THE CONSTITUTIONAL ELECTIONS

Sample: 2,987 persons in the American Zone.
Interviewing dates: first two weeks in September 1946. (6 pp.)

Only 19 per cent of the respondents knew that a *Landtag* election or a constitutional vote was to be held late in the fall. About a quarter (22%) knew that constitutional assemblies were meeting at the time of the interview; and not many more (27%) knew what the task of the constitutional assemblies was. Among respondents who reported an interest in politics, 50 per cent could state what the purpose of the coming elections was. Of those who expected to vote in the coming elections, 28 per cent were aware of the purpose of the election, whereas among those who did not expect to vote, only 18 per cent knew their purpose.

Almost eight in ten (78%) of the general population expected to vote in the coming elections, including 86 per cent of those who expressed an interest in politics. The highest percentage of those expecting to vote were those with no association with the NSDAP, either through personal membership or membership in the family (82%); seven or less years of education (83%); upper socioeconomic status (84%); and those belonging to a political party (97%). The KPD had the highest percentage of expected voters (89%), followed by the CSU (88%), CDU (87%), LDP (86%), and SPD (85%). Place of residence seemed to have slight effect on expectations of voting. Sex did not make a significant difference in voting expectations, except that incapacitated women (73%) were less likely to express an expectation to vote than were women capable of working (78%).

Report No. 27 (13 November 1946)

GERMAN-AMERICAN RELATIONS IN GERMANY:
FREQUENCIES OF GROUP CONTACTS

Sample: 2,987 persons in the American Zone; 404 persons in the American and British Sectors of Berlin.
Interviewing dates: first two weeks in September 1946. (8 pp.)

Two-thirds (66%) in the American Zone had no relations with the American forces. A fifth (20%) reported having talked with an American and 14 per cent had come to know an American "well" or "fairly well." In West Berlin, 80 per cent had no relationship, 13 per cent said they had talked with an American, and seven per cent claimed a closer relationship. Persons most likely to have had contacts with American soldiers were professionals (66%), LDP supporters (48%), those having a telephone (47%), former NSDAP members (45%), those expressing an interest in politics (45%), and former soldiers (44%).

Perhaps the most important variable determining interaction between Germans and Americans was socioeconomic status. The higher the socioeconomic status of the respondent, the greater the likelihood that he had established a relationship with an American. Over half (55%) of upper-class respondents had contacts with Americans, as did only 15 per cent of those living on government relief. Over half (54%) of those with 12 or more years of education had contacts with an American, as did only 29 per cent of those with seven or less years of education. Professionals (66%), businessmen (46%), and white-collar workers (52%) were more likely to have contacts with Americans than were other occupational groups.

More men (42%) than women (32%) had developed some relationship with an American. The younger people were more likely to have had contact with an American: Almost three men in five (59%) under 20 had contact with an American – a percentage that decreased steadily with age. Women showed the same basic pattern, except that among the youngest women (those 20 or less) 30 per cent had contact with an American whereas 43 per cent of women in their twenties had such contact.

Rural-urban and regional differences probably indicated the distribution of troops, as well as variant activity by area. Hessians reported the most contacts (42%), followed by Bavarians (36%), and residents of Wuerttemberg-Baden (28%). Residents in small and medium-sized towns had a greater level of contacts than did residents of larger towns.

The difference between churchgoing and nonchurchgoing persons was far greater than the difference between Catholics and Protestants. A third (34%) of regular churchgoing Catholics and 29 per cent of regular churchgoing Protestants reported contacts with Americans; 41 per cent of Catholics and 38 per cent of Protestants who were not regular churchgoers reported such relationships.

Report No. 28 (14 November 1946)

AN INVESTIGATION TO DETERMINE ANY
CHANGES IN ATTITUDES OF NATIVE GERMANS
TOWARD THE EXPELLEES IN WUERTTEMBERG-BADEN

Sample: 624 persons (8.5 per cent of whom had lived in Wuerttemberg-Baden for less than one year, 9.5 per cent for a period not exceeding four years, 82 per cent for more than five years).
Interviewing dates: 13 September 1946. (10 pp.)

From the point of view of the expellees, there was a decrease from 75 per cent in March 1946 to 60 per cent in September in the number expressing satisfaction with their reception in Wuerttemberg-Baden (Cf. Report No. 14A of 8 July 1946). Two-fifths of those who were dissatisfied with their reception stated that, instead of regarding them as Germans, the natives considered them to be human beings of inferior value, foreigners, or even beggars. As many as seven in ten expressed a desire to return to their original homes. Asked about the greatest problem that they had faced since coming to the American Zone, 35 per cent mentioned housing, 20 per cent the lack of work, and another 20 per cent clothing. Asked what problems they anticipated in view of the fact that winter was approaching, nearly half (43%) mentioned housing, 39 per cent clothing and shoes, 31 per cent work, and 24 per cent food. (Native residents shared this ranking of problems, with 61 per cent pointing to housing, 50 per cent to food and clothing, and a smaller percentage to the lack of work.)

From the point of view of the native residents of Wuerttemberg-Baden, opinions on the expellees were divided. The population was generally convinced that Czechoslovakia and Hungary were not justified in expelling these people (75 per cent in March, 84 per cent in September). Indeed, in September, 28 per cent of the sample considered the expellees to be foreigners, as opposed to 49 per cent willing to recognize them as German citizens. (Among those with more than eight years of education, the share viewing the expellees as foreigners rose to 42 per cent; and 38 per cent of the middle-class respondents held the same view.) Majorities (83 per cent in March, 74 per cent in September) were nonetheless willing to grant the expellees full participation in politics, although the more highly educated and better off citizens were somewhat more inclined to limit these rights. Two-fifths (40%) of the 17 per cent of the total sample who, in September, expressed a desire for limitations of the expellees' political rights also indicated that the expellees were not Germans and did not think as Germans.

The residents of Wuerttemberg-Baden were increasingly unwilling to assume responsibility for the care of the expellees: The number stating that Germans alone should care for them dropped from 39 per cent in March to 27 per cent in September; those giving responsibility to the countries which expelled them rose from seven to 36 per cent; the number mentioning international organizations remained roughly constant (15 per cent in March, 16 per cent in September); and the share mentioning the Americans or the Western Allies, with or without a German contribution, dropped from 23 to six per cent. Those with the highest level of education were least likely to assign responsibility to Germany. Three-quarters of the native residents (73%) and five-sixths of the expellees (83%) felt that the American authorities were doing all they could to assist German officials who were trying to solve the expellee problem. Again, the highly educated and those of middle class status or above were most inclined to disagree. Almost four in five of the natives (78%) felt that the expellees were a burden on the financial and economic status of the American Zone – an attitude stronger among the well educated and the middle and upper classes – as opposed to only 13 per cent who saw the expellees exerting a favorable influence on the AMZON economy.

Report No. 29 (21 November 1946)

THE TREND OF CARES AND WORRIES IN GERMANY

Sample: summary of seven surveys in the American Zone between May and October 1946, with sample sizes of 1,427 in May, 1,485 and 1,524 in June, 1,536 in July, 2,969 in August, 2,985 in September, and 2,983 in October.

Interviewing dates: 8 May, 7 June, late June, 1 July, 9 August, early September, and 4 October 1946. (8 pp.)

Between May 1946 and October 1946 there was a shift toward greater material distress among the concerns of the general population. The concerns mentioned in May in order of frequency were lack of food (34%), anxiety over prisoners of war and missing persons (18%), and general insecurity (9%). The concerns mentioned in October in order of frequency were lack of food (36%), lack of clothing and shoes (23%), unemployment (22%), anxiety over prisoners of war and missing persons (15%), housing and furnishing problems (9%), and lack of implements of production (7%).

Comparing the three *Laender*, residents of Wuerttemberg-Baden reported difficulties, particularly regarding food, more frequently than did residents of Bavaria or Hesse. Even rural areas (under 2,000 population) in Wuerttemberg-Baden reported greater concern over food than rural areas in Bavaria and Hesse, but, in all three *Laender*, lack of food was mentioned by increasing percentages of the population as the size of the community increased. More people in smaller villages and towns reported lack of clothing and shoes than in larger cities. Worry about missing prisoners of war and other missing people was centered in the rural areas. Lack of housing and furnishings was more widespread in the large cities than in towns and villages.

Report No. 30 (14 December 1946)

RADIO LISTENING IN VIENNA

Sample: 1,496 persons living in the British and American Sectors of Vienna.
Interviewing dates: not specified. (16 pp.)

A large majority of the population (73%) listened to the radio. Radio listeners were likely to be men, better educated, younger, from upper and middle classes, and from higher occupational status positions.

Among listeners, 46 per cent said radio was their chief source of news, as opposed to 51 per cent who cited newspapers. More radio listeners (85%) read newspapers than did nonlisteners (77%). Although about as many listeners (42%) considered radio more accurate than newspapers as believed the opposite (43%), a large majority of listeners (67%) felt that newspapers gave more complete news. A majority of listeners (56%) did not think that radio programs contained too much propaganda; a large majority (64%), however, felt that radio was censored. The largest percentages of those who felt both that radio was censored and contained too much propaganda were those with 12 or more years of education (28%) or under 30 (28%), as well as owners of a radio in good condition (23%).

The median number of listeners per radio was 2.15. Whereas 57 per cent of those with less than seven years of schooling and 49 per cent of those in the lower social classes listened in groups of one or two other people, only 40 per cent of those with college education and 33 per cent of those in the upper-middle class listened in groups of this size. Within the upper class, listening was an individual function or an activity of a rather large group. Larger listening groups were found among young people.

Radio listening was well dispersed throughout the week days. Sixty per cent of the listening audience listened two or more hours a day, and 26 per cent listened from one to two hours a day. Those who listened two or more hours were more likely to have nine or more years of education (61%), to be under 30 (70%), and women (64%). Three-quarters (74%) said that they did not restrict their listening to save electricity.

As many (44%) would like to hear more American programs if they could be well received as would not like to hear these programs. A majority of those with 12 or more years of education (59%), of upper-middle (71%) and upper (62%) classes, half of those under 30, half of those with nine to 11 years of education, and almost half (48%) of the men, however, would like to hear more programs from America.

A quarter (23%) reported hearing the "Voice of America." A majority (60%) of the VOA listeners felt that the program offered just the right amount of political news, and 17 per cent thought it offered too little news. Most (32%) liked best the news portion of VOA.

Report No. 31 (14 December 1946)

THE STANDARD OF LIVING

Sample: 1,485 persons in the American Zone.
Interviewing dates: 7 June 1946. (7 pp.)

Although 36 per cent knew that the four powers had announced plans for the allocation of German industry, 53 per cent were not aware of it and as many as 11 per cent stated that there had been no announcement. Seven in ten (71%) stated that Germany's industry was being reduced to do away with war industries. Close to an absolute majority (49%) felt that the limits were more severe than they should be, as opposed to seven per cent who thought them not severe enough and 44 per cent who expressed no opinion. A substantial number (44%) felt that the Allies were not justified in placing these limits on German industry, in contrast to 29 per cent who felt the limits justified.

Almost half (45%) of all the respondents and 59 per cent of the informed respondents felt that under the new plan the German people would have a worse living standard than the average European country (excluding England and the Soviet Union). Almost half (48%) saw no justification for the reduction in standard of living, as opposed to 30 per cent who felt it just and 22 per cent who withheld judgment. A quarter (26%) of all the respondents (over half of those who felt that the reduced living standard was not justified) saw such inhumanity to man as a frightful thing. A smaller group, 18 per cent of the total number of respondents, felt the reductions unfair because they were personally innocent.

Whereas 64 per cent of those who thought the limitation of industry unjust and 61 per cent of those who thought the reduction in the standard of living unjust also felt that the German civil government was in some way to blame for the food situation in Germany, 41 per cent and 46 per cent, respectively, saw the German civil government in no way responsible for it. Slightly larger percentages – 69 per cent of those perceiving unjust industrial limitations and 67 per cent perceiving unjust reductions in the standard of living — attached some blame to the Military Government for the food situation, an appreciable minority (36 and 41 per cent, respectively) did not. Half (52%) of both dissatisfied groups felt that National Socialism was a good idea but badly carried out. Half (50%) of those who felt the limitations just and 44 per cent of those who felt the reductions just also saw some truth to the statement that the German people were responsible for the war because they allowed a government to come to power which intended to bring war upon the world.

When asked about the probable duration of the Allied industrial program, 41 per cent could give time estimates: Most of these (17%) foresaw a period from four to eleven years, but almost as many (15%) expected a shorter duration. Half (53%) stated various factors that might influence the duration of the plans, of which the most frequently named (16%) was that the restrictions would last "until the economic situation is better; until work and food for all men are available; until trade is reestablished in the world; until the world situation is cleared up." As many as 30 per cent of the sample had no idea how long the Allied industrial program would remain in effect.

Report No. 32 (10 December 1946)

INCOME, EXPENDITURES, AND CURRENCY HOLDINGS OF THE GERMAN POPULATION AND ATTITUDES TOWARD GENERAL ECONOMIC PROBLEMS

Sample: 1,524 respondents in the American Zone, 198 in West Berlin.
Interviewing dates: 1 July 1946. (70 pp.)

About three-quarters (69 per cent in AMZON; 74 per cent in West Berlin) reported having at least one bank account. In West Berlin, however, 63 per cent of the respondents reported their bank accounts to be frozen, as did only .2 per cent in the American Zone. Savings accounts outnumbered checking accounts by a ratio of almost four to one in the American Zone and five to one in West Berlin. Half (53%) of the AMZON Germans and eight per cent in West Berlin had at least RM 1,000 in their checking accounts: The median account holdings were RM 2,575 in the American Zone and RM 2,325 in West Berlin. Between January and July 1946 there had been a slight increase (.3%) in total number of accounts in the American Zone and an increase of almost three per cent in Berlin. The median holdings, however, decreased in AMZON (from RM 2,725 to RM 2,575) while rising in West Berlin (from RM 1,700 to RM 2,325). Those whose accounts decreased generally gave living expenses as the reason.

About three-quarters (78 per cent in AMZON; 72 per cent in West Berlin) reported having at least RM 50 cash in addition to their funds in bank accounts. The median amount on hand was RM 160 in the American Zone and RM 165 in West Berlin.

The median monthly income from all sources was RM 170 in AMZON (on the basis of reports by 86 per cent of the respondents) and RM 251 in West Berlin (with 93 per cent reporting). Reported median income rose as the size of the city increased — from RM 137 in communities with less than 2,000 inhabitants to RM 266 in cities with a population of a quarter of a million or more.

The median family expenditure per month was RM 152 in the American Zone and RM 267 in West Berlin. Most income was spent for food, followed by building repairs, rent, clothing, utilities, insurance premiums, and fuel. Median family expenditures increased with city size, from RM 117 in the smallest (under 2,000) to RM 220 in the largest (over 250,000). About a third (32 per cent in AMZON; 39 per cent in West Berlin) said that their family's total income was not high enough to cover necessary living expenses; a quarter (23%) of the AMZON respondents reported having to make up the difference from their savings.

Only minorities (39 per cent in AMZON; 25 per cent in

West Berlin) had life insurance policies. Most of the policy holders (34 per cent in AMZON; 18 per cent in West Berlin) had their premiums paid up. The median amount for which respondents were insured in the American Zone was RM 2,700; in West Berlin, RM 1,180.

Almost all respondents (88 per cent in AMZON; 97 per cent in West Berlin) saw the black market influencing the economic situation. The bulk (66 per cent in AMZON; 83 per cent in West Berlin) held black market dealers responsible for the increase in the volume of money in circulation.

Only minorities of 36 per cent in the American Zone and 40 per cent in West Berlin felt that a new currency was needed. Those who did not see a need for currency reform (52 per cent in AMZON; 40 per cent in West Berlin) were questioned about freezing bank accounts as a means of reform. Most (28 per cent in AMZON; 32 per cent in West Berlin) advocated freezing bank accounts over a certain amount, but an appreciable minority (4 and 10 per cent, respectively) disapproved of such a move. On the question of timing most (44 per cent in AMZON; 45 per cent in West Berlin) thought that the monetary adjustment should take place immediately.

Most (46%) of the AMZON respondents and a majority (51%) in West Berlin would have preferred to have any money reserve in the form of goods. Second and third choices in the American Zone were bank accounts (29%) and cash (8%), and, in West Berlin, cash (25%) and bank accounts (20%).

Substantial numbers (38 per cent in AMZON; 72 per cent in West Berlin) had claims against the former Reich government but, of those with such claims, 29 and 43 per cent, respectively, expected no compensation. The most frequent claim was for war damages and bombing (23 per cent in AMZON; 43 per cent in West Berlin), the median of which were RM 4,900 in the American Zone and RM 6,300 in West Berlin. (In addition, 39 per cent of the West Berliners had claims for frozen bank accounts, the median being RM 2,700.) Although 40 per cent in the American Zone and 81 per cent in West Berlin had suffered property damage during the war, three and 16 per cent, respectively, wanted no compensation; and only six and eight per cent, respectively, felt that they should be compensated for all war damage.

Seven in ten (72%) of the AMZON respondents felt that those who had not suffered war losses should be asked to help those who had. Almost all respondents (95 per cent in AMZON; 90 per cent in West Berlin) said that people who had an average income during the war or were in a position to save substantially should be asked to help those less fortunate. Two-thirds (63%) of the AMZON respondents and 43 per cent in West Berlin mentioned war casualties as the group which should receive such aid, followed by those who were bombed out, refugees, expellees, dependents of war casualties, political persecutees, and Jews. A quarter (24%) in AMZON and 31 per cent in West Berlin said all of these groups should receive aid.

Report No. 33 (18 December 1946)

THE TREND OF PUBLIC REACTIONS TO THE NUREMBERG TRIALS

Sample: 2,983 respondents in the American Zone.
Interviewing dates: 4 October 1946. (5 pp.)

There was a decline in interest in the trials beginning in late February 1946 and continuing through March and into April. Readership interest in newspaper accounts of the trials increased when it was announced in August 1946 that the trials would soon be completed. After the sentencing, public interest in the trials was almost as great as when the trials were getting under way: Ninety-three per cent of the population claimed to have heard what the verdicts were.

Most people were satisfied that the news reports of the trials had been complete and trustworthy. Those who were not satisfied criticized the news for its incompleteness rather than for inaccuracy.

There was widespread feeling that the defendants were receiving a fair and orderly trial. When the verdicts were announced in October 1946, just as many agreed that the trial was fair and orderly as had anticipated a year previously that the defendants would receive a fair trial.

Seven in ten (71%) felt that the current defendants were not the only guilty ones. After the verdicts, just as many (43%) thought that lesser leaders should be brought to trial as thought it was sufficient to have the higher leaders punished. Three in four (77%) felt that a heavier burden of guilt for the Hitler regime lay on NSDAP officeholders than on those who did not hold office. One-third thought pre-1937 Party members carried greater guilt for Party actions. Only 18 per cent felt post-1937 joiners more blameworthy. One-third held there was no difference in degree of guilt between the two groups.

The bulk of AMZON Germans (92%) rejected the idea of collective war guilt. A majority (51%), however, felt that the Germans, because of their support of Hitler's government, were at least partly responsible for its actions.

In August 1946 only about half felt all defendants to be guilty, whereas in December 1945 and in March 1946, 70 per cent had said this. After the sentences were announced, 60 per cent reported feeling none of the verdicts to be too harsh.

Majorities (57 per cent in November 1945; 60 per cent in January 1946; and 59 per cent in October 1946) favored the indictment of whole organizations, such as the SA, SS, and the General Staff. Although a considerable minority opposed indicting these organizations, few opposed indicting the Gestapo, the Reich cabinet, and the leadership corps of the NSDAP.

After the verdicts were announced, when asked what they had learned from the trial, 30 per cent pointed out the dangers of dictatorship and one-sided politics, and said caution was needed in the election of future statesmen. A quarter (25%) said that the lesson of the trials was to maintain peace. Only a few (6%) spoke in negative terms: that there is no justice, that only

Germans get punished, that human rights were violated, that politics should be avoided. And over a third (34%) gave no articulate reply as to the lesson of the trials. Half (50%) said they had become more aware of the inhumanity of the concentration camps.

Report No. 34 (28 December 1946)

ATTITUDES TOWARD LICENSED NEWSPAPERS IN SOME AMERICAN OCCUPIED AREAS

Sample: 8,029 persons.
Interviewing dates: last three weeks in June 1946. (11 pp.)

This report consists solely of appendices to Report No. 21 of 25 September 1946.

Report No. 35 (5 January 1947)

ATTITUDES OF TRADE UNION MEMBERS

Sample: 527 members of trade unions in the American Zone and British and American Sectors of Berlin.
Interviewing dates: not specified (c. first two weeks of November 1946). (14 pp.)

This survey is primarily concerned with three groups of trade union members: rejoiners, that is, those who had been members of unions before 1933 and had since rejoined (37%); new-comers, those who did not belong to a trade union before 1933 but had recently become members (27%); and abstainers, those who were members of a trade union before 1933 but had not renewed their membership (36%). The group of newcomers, when compared with others, was both younger and better educated, and more likely to be women, Catholics, and Bavarians. Despite the fact that the newcomers were more conservative than the rejoiners, 59 per cent of them favored leftist political parties. The newcomers' primary reason for joining a union was inducement by fellow workers (48%), followed by the desire to obtain better wages and working conditions (39%).

Almost all (94 per cent of the rejoiners; 84 per cent of the newcomers; 91 per cent of the abstainers) favored extending the base of union activities throughout all of Germany. About 80 per cent found nothing strongly objectionable to a central organization of trade unions in Germany. Most favored broadly based vertical unions. Most (69 per cent of the rejoiners; 75 per cent of the newcomers; 70 per cent of the abstainers) favored a single common union rather than industrial unions. Whereas a majority (55%) suggested democratic procedures for settling differences of opinion on how a union should be organized, 45 per cent could not explain or express democratic procedures. On only one of three questions – the form of organization which is permissible – concerning basic information about union rights in Germany did a majority answer correctly (61 per cent of the newcomers; 62 per cent of the rejoiners; 44 per cent of the abstainers).

Most (49 per cent of respondents) felt that collective bargaining to secure higher wages and better living conditions for workers was the most important activity of a trade union. Second most important (16%) was preventing rearmament, followed closely by securing workers' representation in the management of business and industry (15%), and educating union members and youth on a democratic basis (14%). A majority (58%) thought that the establishment of free bargaining for wages and hours would greatly help the unions. A somewhat smaller percentage (33%) stressed the establishment by law of certain standards for wages and hours as a means to help the unions.

Only among the rejoiners did a majority (56%) feel that the leaders of the local unions did a good job, as opposed to a fairly good or a bad job. While most (41%) of the newcomers felt the local leaders did a good job, 30 per cent felt they did a fairly good job and 28 per cent had no opinion. A majority (62%) of the abstainers had no opinion.

A majority (68 per cent of the rejoiners; 58 per cent of the newcomers; 62 per cent of the abstainers) felt that the actions of the Military Government had helped the growth of trade unions. Almost two-thirds (64%) of all groups also thought that attendance by local Military Government officials at union meetings would substantially help the unions. Eight in ten (81%) felt that the church should not exert an influence in union affairs, as did 72 per cent with regard to political parties.

Report No. 36 (11 January 1947)

THE GERMAN PEOPLE AND SOCIAL CLASSES

Sample: 1,485 persons in the American Zone.
Interviewing dates: 7 June 1946. (5 pp.)

Respondents classified themselves as belonging to one of four classes: upper (2%), middle (45%), working (51%), and lower (2%). Interviewers then ranked the respondents according to a socioeconomic scale: upper (1%), middle (41%), working (55%), and lower (3%). At the lower end of the scale there was high correspondence between interviewers' ratings and self-classification. Only 30 per cent of those who said they were upper class were also ranked "upper" by the interviewer, however, and 60 per cent of the self-reported "middle class" received such a rating from the interviewers. Nearly all the remainder were downgraded in the interviewers' ratings.

Those self-perceived members of the middle class whom the interviewers downgraded (16%) differed markedly in some aspects from those seen by themselves and the interviewers as middle class (27%). The former group contained more women and more Bavarians than did the latter. Members of the former group more frequently were employed at skilled or semi-skilled jobs, and many were unemployed. The latter group were largely white-collar workers, professionals, independent businessmen, and government employees. This group was better educated. It also contained more former members of the NSDAP. Among the attitudinal differences between the two groups, the sharpest was in regard to political interest: Whereas 11 per cent of those who were ranked lower by the interviewer were interested in politics, 26 per cent of those who were ranked middle by the interviewer were interested in politics. The former group was more inclined to blame the German civil government and the Military Government for food shortages, to perceive denazification as too harsh, to deny any collective guilt on the part of the German people for the Nazi accession to power, and to think that the Allied imposition on controls of German industry was justified.

Report No. 37 (13 January 1947)

OPINIONS OF NEWSPAPER READERS

> *Sample:* 3,423 persons in the American Zone and the American and British sectors of Berlin.
> *Interviewing dates:* first two weeks of November 1946. (3 pp.)

Although West Berliners were more frequently newspaper readers (91%) than were residents of the three *Laender* in the American Zone, they did not differ greatly from residents of large cities in the American Zone. Wuerttemberg-Baden had the highest percentage (85%) of newspaper readers of the three *Laender*, followed by 83 per cent in Bavaria and 79 per cent in Hesse. Even in the smaller towns and villages of Wuerttemberg-

Baden there were more who read newspapers (in villages under 1,000, 14 per cent nonreaders; and in towns from 2,000 to 5,000, 18 per cent nonreaders; in Hesse, 30 and 30 per cent, respectively; in Bavaria, 20 and 19 per cent respectively).

Almost half (48%) of the AMZON respondents (51 per cent in Bavaria; 45 per cent in Wuerttemberg-Baden; 38 per cent in Hesse) and a majority (71%) in West Berlin rated their newspapers "good" or "very good." In cities from 10,000 to 100,000 in population, respondents tended to consider their newspapers only "fair."

A large majority (77%) in West Berlin did not feel that the local government influenced their newspapers. In the three *Laender*, 48 per cent in Wuerttemberg-Baden, 54 percent in Hesse, and 60 percent in Bavaria made a similar claim. In contrast, only 11 per cent in West Berlin, 14 per cent in Bavaria, 17 per cent in Hesse, and 21 per cent in Wuerttemberg-Baden felt that the local government did influence the newspapers. Almost three in ten (29%) of those who rated their newspapers "poor" saw them as politically dominated. Of those who complained about the political domination of the press, about half thought that the newspapers were not sufficiently critical of the local government.

Report No. 38 (14 January 1947)

A PRELIMINARY STUDY OF CHANGES IN JOB STATUS

Sample: 2,860 respondents in the American Zone and 406 in West Berlin.
Interviewing dates: 14 October 1946. (18 pp.)

With few exceptions, changes in occupational status have been in a downward direction. Those strata of society which cater to its fundamental needs (such as for food, housing, and clothing) were relatively unaffected by the defeat or the occupation.

Such crises hit more severely those groups catering to the more specialized demands of society.

Recovery from the downgrading experienced by the more specialized occupational groups was perceived to be dependent upon the length of stay of the Allies in Germany, the amelioration of the denazification program, the energy of any future government of Germany, the reconstruction of basic and consumer goods industries, and so forth.

In only one occupational classification, that of former government officials, did more than half change their occupation in the postwar period: In the American Zone, only 40 per cent remained in their former occupation as did only 29 per cent in West Berlin; as many as a quarter of the former officials of the American Zone had become unskilled workers (19%) or clerks (7%). Levels of stability over time were considerably higher in other AMZON occupational groups: farmers (86%); independent businessmen (77%); unskilled workers (74%); independent craftsmen (70%); clerks (59%); semiskilled workers (54%); professionals (53%); and skilled workers (50%).

Report No. 39 (14 January 1947)

REACTIONS TO AND PENETRATION OF INFORMATION MEDIA IN VIENNA

Sample: 1,499 persons in the American and British Sectors of Vienna.
Interviewing dates: latter part of November 1946. (9 pp.)

Most of the respondents paid attention to one or another of the information media. Four-fifths (80%) listened to the radio. The same proportion reported reading a newspaper regularly, and an additional 17 per cent said they read a paper occasionally. The most widely read paper (52%) was the *Wiener Kurier.* Well over half (57%) said that they went to the movies. And almost half (45%) had heard the Vienna Philharmonic within the past year: 39 per cent on the radio; 11 per cent at a concert; and five per cent did both.

When questioned about denazification of films and of the Vienna Philharmonic, 52 per cent thought that films should be shown even though the actors appearing in them were former members of the NSDAP or allied organizations. Almost the same 52 percent also supported the continuation of former NSDAP members in the Vienna Philharmonic.

Practically the entire adult population (99%) of Vienna could be reached through the combined impact of newspaper reading, listening to the radio, attendance at movies and at concerts. The most popular single activity was newspaper reading. Eleven per cent reported reading newspapers regularly but doing nothing else. When two media activities were enjoyed, they were usually radio listening and newspaper reading (27%). The most popular combination of three media was radio-movies-newspaper (41%). Only six per cent participated in all four activities.

Different groups exhibited different characteristics regarding media participation. Whereas 44 per cent of the men listened to the radio, read a paper, and went to the movies, only 38 per cent of the women did all three. Over a quarter (28%) of those high in socioeconomic status participated in all four activities or in combinations of any three except the paper-movie-radio grouping. The better educated and the younger groups participated in more media activities than did the poorly educated or older groups. Older but better educated people, however, participated in more media activities than did the young but poorly educated.

Media participation was also related to attitudinal characteristics. Seven in ten (70%) of those who participated in all four media activities or attended concerts in addition to participating in two of the other three activities opposed most strenuously denazification of the Vienna Philharmonic and 64 per cent approved most strongly the showing of films in which former NSDAP members appeared. These groups consisted largely of the upper class, the better educated, and the young. Eight in ten (79%) of this group who had an opinion said that the Allies had hindered Austrian reconstruction.

Report No. 40 (21 January 1947)

AUSTRIAN ECONOMIC DIFFICULTIES AND ATTITUDES TOWARD ECONOMIC PROBLEMS

Sample: 1,499 persons in the American and British Sectors of Vienna.
Interviewing dates: latter part of November 1946. (12 pp.)

Responses to an initial question concerning the person's greatest care and worry indicated that the Viennese were not much better off than Germans with respect to the number of problems facing them. Only one in a hundred Viennese said that he had no problems; for 54 per cent food was the greatest problem. Significant minorities were concerned primarily about former NSDAP membership (25%), fuel (19%), clothing and shoes (18%), unemployment (11%), and housing (10%), etc. Although food was a major concern, a large majority (67%) felt that the rationcard system was being handled fairly, and nearly everybody (88%) said that the stores usually had the things they came for when they had the necessary coupons; the largest problem was getting potatoes. The margin of adequate winter clothing was very slim for over half the population. A bare majority said that they had enough such clothing and about the same number claimed to have only one pair of shoes, which in many cases were not heavy enough to withstand the rigors of the winter months. Those most frequently saying that they had enough clothing for the winter were craftsmen (73%), independent businessmen (72%), and managers and officials (63%). At the bottom of the list were semi-skilled workers (37%).

Not a single respondent denied the existence of a black market and 83 per cent said that it was widespread and serious.

People who thought that the authorities were not doing everything possible to eliminate the black market also believed strongly that it was widespread and serious, or was responsible for shortages of goods, or adversely affected the economy. In contrast, those who felt that the authorities were doing all they could tended to take a more sanguine view of the entire black market situation.

In response to a question concerning trade, a greater number of people (61%) spoke of the importance of imports than mentioned exports (51%). Although political party affiliation did not seem to affect a respondent's views on these matters, other group differences were evident. A solid majority (61%) of the college educated said that both imports and exports were very important but only 22 per cent of those with seven years or less schooling did so. More of the upper classes (67%) maintained the great importance of both aspects of trade than did members of the poorest groups (37%); the poorer elements in the population spoke more insistently for imports than for exports.

Almost everyone (98%) had heard of the Vienna Fair, and a very large proportion of these (86%) thought that it was a good idea. Most of the objections to the Fair centered on the complaint that it was all for foreign trade and not for purchases by private Viennese citizens.

Report No. 41 (15 January 1947)

ATTITUDES TOWARD GENERAL ECONOMIC CONDITIONS

Sample: 3,022 respondents in the American Zone and 401 in the American and British Sectors of Berlin.
Interviewing dates: first part of November 1946. (25 pp.)

From July 1946 to November 1946 monthly family incomes declined RM 20 in the American Zone and RM 30 in West Berlin. In November 1946 the median family monthly income was RM 129 in the American Zone and RM 199 in Berlin. Of the three *Laender* in the American Zone, Wuerttemberg-Baden reported the highest median monthly income (RM 150), followed by Bavaria (RM 123) and Hesse (RM 120). Highest monthly incomes were reported by professionals and business-men (RM 287), residents of cities of 250,000 or more in population (RM 188), those with more than 11 years of education (RM 177), men (RM 153), and those between 40 and 49 (RM 148).

In November 1946, 39 per cent of the respondents in the American Zone said that their family's total income was not sufficient to cover necessary living expenses, as did 48 per cent in West Berlin. These percentages were the highest recorded since surveying began in November 1945. Among the three *Laender* of the American Zone, more respondents in Hesse (41%) reported insufficient income than in Bavaria (39%) or Wuerttemberg-Baden (37%). The highest percentages reporting insufficient income were residents of cities between 100,000 and 249,999 in population (46%), unskilled laborers (53%), those with 12 or more years of education (46%), women (41%), those between 30 and 39 (48%), and those with no income (86%).

A substantial number (26%) of AMZON respondents relied on their savings to meet necessary expenses. Many West Berliners (18%) relied on barter and the sale of personal property, and only ten per cent fell back upon their savings. It should be noted, however, that an increasing percentage said that they could not buy everything they needed (seven per cent in AMZON; 13 per cent in West Berlin).

Half (52%) of the respondents in both the American Zone and West Berlin felt that there were some taxes which should be lowered or which were not fairly apportioned. In general, the higher the income, the greater was the objection to current taxes, except among the three *Laender* of the American Zone. Half (52%) of the respondents in Bavaria, where incomes tended to be lower, said taxes were not fairly apportioned or should be lowered, in contrast to 49 per cent of the respondents in

Wuerttemberg-Baden and 44 per cent in Hesse who made a similar claim. Respondents in the American Zone objected most to taxes on tobacco (25%) and alcohol and luxury items (16%). Respondents in West Berlin objected most to taxes on wages and community taxes (23%) and to income and personal property taxes (14%).

Confidence in the continued value of the *Reichsmark* had declined since April 1946. A substantial portion (43%) of the AMZON and West Berlin respondents did not think the *Reichsmark* would be worth as much six months later as it was in November 1946. Half (50%) of the respondents in West Berlin, however, expected no such inflationary trend. As far as confidence in the *Reichsmark* as compared to Allied military money was concerned, most people (55 per cent in AMZON; 46 per cent in West Berlin) found no difference between the two currencies.

The respondents were optimistic about economic conditions in the next six months: 45 per cent of the AMZON respondents and 51 per cent in West Berlin felt that economic conditions would improve in the next six months; 22 and 18 per cent, respectively, expected no change, and 24 and 13 per cent, respectively, expected a deterioration of economic conditions.

Report No. 42 (5 February 1947)

THE TREND OF RUMORS

Sample: trend results from four surveys in 1946, with 954 respondents in the American Zone in February, 964 in the American and British Sectors of Berlin in March, and 3,022 persons in the American Zone and 401 in the American and British Sectors of Berlin in November.
Interviewing dates: 14 February, 22 March, 29 March, and early November 1946. (13 pp.)

There was a fluctuation in the percentages hearing disturbing rumors during 1946. In February, 33 per cent heard disturbing rumors; in March, 38 per cent; in April, 43 per cent, and in November, 25 per cent. Among the three *Laender* of the American Zone, the percentages hearing rumors in Hesse were consistently lower than those in Bavaria or Wuerttemberg-Baden. There was also considerable and inconsistent variation in the incidence of rumors among different-sized communities.

Perhaps the most significant rumor was that of a war between the United States and the Soviet Union. In the American Zone, in February, 30 per cent of the reported rumors concerned war (reported by 10 per cent of the population). In March, 85 per cent and in April, 80 per cent of the reported rumors concerned war (reported by 33 and 34 per cent, respectively, of the population). By November 1946, only 55 per cent of the reported rumors concerned war. In West Berlin, however, these percentages increased between April and November 1946. In April, 60 per cent of the reported rumors concerned war and in November, 65 per cent (reported by 20 per cent of the population).

A persistent rumor throughout 1946 in the American Zone was that the Soviet Union would take over more of Germany. In November this rumor took the form that the Soviet Union would move into the American Zone. At its height in November

1946, it accounted for eight per cent of the reported rumors and was reported by two per cent of the AMZON population.

Other common rumors were that the *Reichsmark* would be revalued; there would be smaller food rations; there would be a housing shortage caused by American requisitions; and there would be housing shortages caused by the influx of evacuees.

According to the November 1946 survey, different groups in the AMZON population were more likely to hear rumors. The likelihood of hearing a rumor increased if the respondent was under the age of 40 (27%), in a professional or academic occupation (37%), highly educated (43%), and a newspaper reader (27%) rather than a nonreader (16%), or if he had an interest in politics (36%) and felt himself sufficiently informed about politics (32%).

Report No. 43 (5 February 1947)

READERSHIP OF "HEUTE," "AMERIKANISCHE RUND-SCHAU," AND "NEUE AUSLESE"

Sample: 3,022 respondents in the American Zone and 401 in the American and British Sectors of Berlin.
Interviewing dates: first two weeks of November 1946. (10 pp.)

The total readership of *Heute, Amerikanische Rundschau,* and *Neue Auslese* constituted more than half of all magazine readers at the time of the survey. One-seventh (14%) of the respondents were magazine readers. The combined readership of the three American-sponsored magazines was nine per cent of this 14 per cent. The total readership of each in the American Zone was as follows: *Heute,* eight per cent; *Neue Auslese,* four per cent; and *Amerikanische Rundschau,* three per cent. Higher socio-economic status and better educated groups were more likely to read one of the three magazines. Of those who reported thinking about politics, 74 per cent read one of these magazines. Eight in ten (81%) of the readers felt themselves sufficiently informed about present day affairs.

Group differences, however, existed among readers of the three magazines. *Heute* had a broader based readership. Those with seven years of education or less (11%), the less well to do, that is, with a monthly income between RM 90 and RM 190 (24%), Bavarians (40%), and women (35%) read *Heute*. *Amerikanische Rundschau* readers, by way of contrast, comprised a greater share of those with 12 or more years of education (38%), of those with a monthly income of RM 390 or more (28%), and of respondents aged 50 and older (25%). *Neue Auslese* had the highest portion of readers with 12 or more years of education (42%), professionals, businessmen, officials, and white-collar workers (78%), and those with a monthly income of RM 390 or more (30%).

Circulation figures alone do not give the complete picture of the coverage of the magazine, since more than two people read each copy (*Heute*, 2.9; *Rundschau*, 2.3; *Auslese*, 2.5). A majority bought the magazine at newsstands. A majority also felt the price of the magazine was fair.

When asked about the quality of the magazines, most reported finding them good (*Heute*, 56 per cent; *Rundschau*, 61 per cent; *Auslese*, 48 per cent). Half (49%) were unable either to point to any inadequacies of the magazines or to voice a specific criticism. Of those who did specify needed improvements, the largest number (13%) wanted more articles about conditions in the United States. When asked directly, 32 per cent did not think that the magazines presented enough detailed articles about the United States to enable the reader to form an objective picture of conditions there. A majority of readers, however, did feel enough coverage was given to American affairs (*Heute*, 66 per cent; *Rundschau*, 64 per cent; *Auslese*, 58 per cent).

The majority of the readers (68%) approved the "tone" of the three magazines. When questioned directly, most readers (*Heute*, 41 per cent; *Rundschau*, 51 per cent; *Auslese*, 52 per cent) nonetheless felt that the point of view taken in the magazine was foreign.

Only a minority (20%) thought that the magazines should be under German control. A larger proportion (36%) advocated publication by the occupation forces, and almost as many (34%) sought joint United States-German publication.

Report No. 44 (6 February 1947)

OPINIONS OF GERMAN COMMUNITY LEADERS ON INTERNATIONAL AFFAIRS

Sample: 188 persons in the American Zone and West Berlin.
Interviewing dates: first two weeks of November 1946. (8 pp.)

The 188 persons who were selected and interviewed as community leaders exhibited the following characteristics: Almost all (185) were men. Half (51%) were Catholics; 42 per cent, Protestants. Half were between 44 and 59 years of age, the median being 49 years. Four in ten (41%) had college training but a large minority (29%) had seven or less years of education. Over half (56%) were employers; 12 per cent were farmers; and a quarter (27%) worked for the German government. As a group, these leaders had shifted rather sharply away from some former occupation for which they had been trained to other positions.

Less than half (45%) reported membership in a political party; the remainder (55%) said that they did not belong to a party. Of those who were members, 55 per cent preferred parties of the right and center; 45 per cent, parties of the left. A fifth of those who claimed no party membership said that they wanted nothing to do with politics anymore. These individuals tended to be older than the group as a whole, the median age being 54; more of them were well educated and professionally trained than the entire group of community leaders; and nearly two-thirds lived in Bavaria.

A large percentage of all the community leaders defended the German people as a whole from the charge that large numbers of Germans wanted Germany to rule the world in 1938. As many as three-fourths said that less than 25 per cent of the German people had such desires; and half said ten per cent or less. Two-thirds (66%) of the community leaders said that those few who had desires for German supremacy had learned their lesson from the war. Almost a third (31%), however, thought that those who desired supremacy would try again.

When asked to recall the two most important events which had occurred since the end of the war, 40 per cent named the Nuremberg Trials and 30 per cent named Secretary of State James Byrnes' speech of 4 September 1946 in Stuttgart. Although nine in ten (91%) said that the Nuremberg Trials had, as one of its most important results, set up an international legal basis for trying those who commit crimes against humanity or against peace, 30 per cent also pointed out that aggressors in other countries were not being charged under the laws applied at Nuremberg. Asked what steps they felt were necessary immediately and in the long run to implement Secretary Byrnes' ennunciated policy of a lasting peace, 55 per cent of the immediate proposals were economic in nature, and 33 per cent said that what was most needed was increased cooperation among the Allies; for the long run, the response most frequently given (29%) was that such cooperation was a basic necessity.

Almost half (45%) of the community leaders reported no change in their attitude toward the United States in the past year; over a third (37%), however, reported a friendlier attitude, and 17 per cent reported a less friendly attitude. Most (64%) also reported no change in their attitude toward Great Britain, with 28 per cent saying their attitude was more, and six per cent less, friendly. France and the Soviet Union were less well regarded than they had been. Almost half (45%) reported no change in their attitude toward France, but 39 per cent said that they felt less friendly as opposed to 11 per cent who were friendlier. Most (54%) felt less friendly toward the Soviet Union; only three per cent reported more friendliness and 37 per cent no change. The community leaders were evenly split on the question of whether there would be another war within the next 25-30 years (47 per cent on each side, and the remaining 6 per cent undecided).

Three-quarters expected the United States to occupy Germany for ten years if not more, a fourth for 20 years or longer. Whatever their guesses, however, 76 per cent felt that the United States *should* stay that length of time. A majority (55%) felt the United States would have the greatest influence upon world affairs in the next ten years as opposed to 15 per cent who mentioned the Soviet Union and 21 per cent who mentioned both. Three-quarters (77%) considered economic unification more important than political as a first step toward achieving complete unification of the Zones.

Very large majorities favored central government for all European countries (82%) and active participation by Germany in world affairs (85%). As a first step in the direction of a united Europe, the response most frequently given (24%) stated that Germany should ally herself with western European countries. Of those who mentioned specific countries, most (33%) named France, followed by Great Britain (20%), Belgium (16%), the Netherlands (16%), Austria (13%), and Switzerland (10%).

Report No. 45 (17 February 1947)

RADIO LISTENING IN THE AMERICAN ZONE AND IN BERLIN

Sample: 2,861 respondents in the American Zone and 407 in the American and British Sectors of Berlin.
Interviewing dates: 14 October 1946. (13 pp.)

Over half (51%) of the adult population in the American Zone and 67 per cent in West Berlin were radio listeners. More men (56 per cent in AMZON; 76 per cent in West Berlin) than women (44 and 66 per cent, respectively) were listeners. Listening increased with educational level: Whereas 46 per cent of those with seven or less years of education in the American Zone and 60 per cent in West Berlin were listeners, 66 and 79 per cent, respectively, of those with 12 or more years of education were listeners. The percentage of listeners also increased with community size. Four in ten residents of AMZON communities with less than 2,000 in population were listeners; 72 per cent listened in communities of 250,000 or more. Fewer older people listened. The lowest percentages of listeners were found in those 60 and over in the American Zone (43%) and in those between 50 and 59 in West Berlin (60%). Among occupational groups in AMZON, farmers listened least (33%), and more employers (69%) than employees (55%) listened. In West Berlin, more employees (70%) listened than employers (67%).

Half (50%) of the listeners claimed to have no favorite day for listening. Among listeners who did prefer certain days, AMZON listeners named Sunday (42%) and Saturday (22%) most frequently, as did West Berliners. The most popular time for listening was 8:00 p.m.: 70 per cent in the American Zone and in West Berlin listened at that hour.

The government of each *Land* controls its own radio station and there are no independently owned stations. In each *Land* the most frequently heard station was that of the *Land's* major metropolis: In Bavaria, 79 per cent listened to Munich; in

Hesse, 70 per cent listened to Frankfurt; in Wuerttemberg-Baden, 93 per cent listened to Stuttgart. Nine in ten listeners in each *Land* listened to these stations because of their good reception. In West Berlin, 67 per cent listened to the Soviet station, again largely because of clearer reception. Of all the *Laender* stations, Stuttgart had the largest audience outside the territory of its own *Land*. Of stations outside the American Zone, Leipzig was the only one with a significant secondary audience: 22 per cent in Bavaria, 15 per cent in Hesse, and eight per cent in Wuerttemberg-Baden sometimes tuned in Leipzig.

Laender residents tended to consider their local station best: 62 per cent in Wuerttemberg-Baden liked Stuttgart best; 57 per cent in Bavaria, Munich; 41 per cent in Hesse, Frankfurt; 40 per cent in West Berlin, (Soviet) Berlin. Most of the radio audience (75 per cent in Bavaria and Hesse; 87 per cent in Wuerttemberg-Baden; 62 per cent in West Berlin) found it difficult to name the station they liked least. When asked directly what station in the American Zone had the best programs, respondents in Wuerttemberg-Baden (79%) and Bavaria (70%) favored their local *Land* station. In Hesse, a relatively large number (27%) was unable to decide, while 38 per cent said Frankfurt had the best programs. Almost three-quarters (72%) in the American Zone and 85 per cent in West Berlin preferred musical programs. Large majorities in the American Zone (86%) and West Berlin (87%) wanted half or more of all radio time devoted to music.

Whereas a majority (51%) in the American Zone preferred factual news reporting, the majority in West Berlin (61%) preferred news commentaries. In the American Zone, slightly more (41%) favored impersonal than personalized reporting (37%); in West Berlin, the majority (51%) favored personalized reporting. Radio listeners (55%) tended to think that radio gave the most accurate news, but that newspapers gave more complete news. In the American Zone, 66 per cent did not think that radio programs contained too much propaganda; in West Berlin, however, 58 per cent thought the opposite. A majority in both the American Zone (64%) and West Berlin (72%) felt that there was radio censorship.

Three-quarters (75%) in the American Zone heard *Stimme Amerikas* ("Voice of America"), but only a third (33%) heard it in West Berlin. In the American Zone, most (26%) liked VOA's news best. Second most popular (24%) were the commentaries. In West Berlin, most (16%) liked the commentaries best while 11 per cent preferred the news on VOA.

Report No. 46 (19 February 1947)

ARMY AID TO GERMAN YOUTH ACTIVITIES EVALUATED BY GERMAN ADULTS

Sample: 3,008 adults (those over 18) in the American Zone and 399 in the American and British Sectors of Berlin.
Interviewing dates: 25 November 1946. (15 pp.)

A majority (55%) of the general population reported having heard of the United States Army Youth Program. Certain groups of the population, however, were more likely to have heard about the program than others: those with 12 or more years of education (84%), men (67%), residents of the four largest cities of the American Zone (68%), and those with children (57%). Although a majority in each *Land* knew about the program, more Bavarians (58%) claimed such knowledge than residents of Hesse (51%) or Wuerttemberg-Baden (52%).

Reported participation in the Army Youth Program was not widespread. Only seven per cent of all parents and 11 per cent of parents who knew about the program said that their children had taken part in these activities. Areas with highest participation were towns with between 5,000 and 10,000 in population (14%); 13 per cent in West Berlin reported participation by their children.

Although few parents said that their children were taking part in the Army program, parents generally did not object to participation. Almost all (94%) of the parents who had heard of the program and who thought that the program was designed to teach the American way of life, and 88 per cent of the parents who had heard of the program but thought that their main purpose was to keep children off the streets would have permitted their children to participate. Even among parents whose children had not yet participated in the program, 84 per cent said they would give permission to participate.

Those who knew about the Army program most often approved the program. Among those who had not heard of the program, only 37 per cent approved, while 68 per cent of those who had heard of the program approved of it. Three-quarters (77%) of those parents whose children had participated approved of the Army Youth Program.

Respondents had varied images of the program's goals: The largest number (37%) spoke of a democratic education for youth, 12 per cent about understanding other peoples, 11 per cent of freeing the youth from Nazi spirit and political education, and 11 per cent of the development of friendship and trust for Americans and the occupation troops. Among parents whose children had participated in the Army sponsored program, 43 per cent felt the goal of the program to be democratic education.

Asked directly what they thought the most important part of the program was – teaching youth about the American way of life, giving them something to do in their spare time, or keeping them off the streets – the largest number (41%) said that keeping the youth off the streets was most important, 26 per cent teaching the American way of life, and 19 per cent occupation in spare time. Responses in West Berlin were 56, 20, and 15 per cent, respectively.

Report No. 47 (20 February 1947)

OPINIONS ON THE EXPELLEE PROBLEM

Sample: 3,417 persons in the American Zone and the American and British Sectors of Berlin.
Interviewing dates: last two weeks in November 1946. (8 pp.)

Among those interviewed in the American Zone, seven per cent were expellees (5 per cent from Czechoslovakia, 1 per cent from Hungary, 1 per cent from Poland). Almost all (89%) of these expellees, except the Hungarians, considered themselves to be Germans, 84 per cent of them nonetheless wanted to return to their homeland, 64 per cent emphatically. Although a majority of the expellees (72%) in November 1946 were satisfied with the treatment they had received from the native AMZON population, this percentage had declined from March 1946 (78%). A majority (53%) also felt that the *Laender* governments were not doing all they could to ease the expellees' problems.

In November 1946, 50 per cent of the native AMZON population thought the expellees would get along with the native Germans, as opposed to 36 per cent who expected no such cooperation. (Both figures had increased since March 1946.) Six in ten native Germans thought that the *Laender* governments were handling the expellee problem satisfactorily. Even though a majority of the native Germans (55 per cent in AMZON; 65 per cent in West Berlin) considered the expellees German citizens, these figures were considerably below the 88 per cent of the expellees who considered themselves Germans. Nine in ten (91%) of the native Germans expected the expellees to return to their homelands when and if given a chance to do so.

A large majority of both the native Germans (90%) and the expellees (97%) saw no justification for the expulsion from Czechoslovakia and Hungary. A substantial majority (59%) of the expellees and minorities of the native Germans (46 per cent in AMZON; 31 per cent in West Berlin) thought that the state expelling these people should be responsible for their care. In contrast, 20 per cent of the expellees, 28 per cent of the native AMZON Germans, and 48 per cent of the West Berliners felt the German government to be responsible for caring for the expellees. A ninth (11%) of the expellees, 14 per cent of the native AMZON Germans, and 19 per cent of the West Berliners thought that the responsibility lay with the Allies.

Report No. 48 (5 March 1947))

GERMAN ATTITUDES TOWARD FREEDOM OF SPEECH

Sample: 3,008 persons in the American Zone and 399 in the American and British Sectors of Berlin.
Interviewing dates: 25 November to 10 December 1946 (21 pp.)

To test attitudes toward freedom of speech, respondents were asked three questions: Should the German people have complete freedom of speech? Should trade union members be permitted to speak on the radio? Should members of the Communist Party be permitted to speak on radio? A majority of AMZON respondents answered the questions affirmatively (77, 71, and 55 per cent, respectively). Relatively large percentages denied complete freedom of speech for the German people and access to the radio for members of the Communist Party (14 and 26 per cent, respectively), but only six per cent said that union leaders should not be permitted to speak on radio.

Among various population groups, men were more affirmative, as were members of the KPD in AMZON and the SPD and SED in West Berlin, members of the upper and middle classes in AMZON and of the lower class in West Berlin, former members of the NSDAP, the well educated, AMZON Protestants and West Berlin Protestants, and younger people. There were also differences among the three *Laender*: In Bavaria, 76 per cent favored complete freedom of speech, 72 per cent radio access for union leaders, and 54 per cent radio access for communists; in Hesse the percentages were 78, 71, and 61 per cent, respectively; and in Wuerttemberg-Baden, 77, 68, and 52 per cent respectively.

Report No. 49 (3 March 1947)

ANTI-SEMITISM IN THE AMERICAN ZONE

Sample: 3,006 persons in the American Zone and 409 in West Berlin.
Interviewing dates: last two weeks in December 1946. (19 pp.)

Nationalistic sentiment and racism had been shown in earlier surveys to provide a convenient base for anti-Semitism. With an increase in nationalistic feeling and racism, there was more anti-Semitic expression in the American Zone. This survey used a Guttmann scale, based on eight questions bearing directly or indirectly on attitudes toward Jews. It distinguished among five groups: those with little bias (20%), nationalists (19%), racists (22%), anti-Semites (21%), and intense anti-Semites (18%).

Different population groups exhibited different amounts of bias. West Berlin was comparatively less biased, with 45 per cent classified as racists, anti-Semites, and intense anti-Semites. Among the *Laender*, Bavaria had fewest in this biased category (59%), followed by Hesse (63%), and Wuerttemberg-Baden (65%). When examined by party preference, those supporting the KPD were least likely to be in the three biased groups (43%). Bias decreased as education increased: 63 per cent of those with seven years of education, compared to 48 per cent of those with 12 years or more of education fell into the biased groups. Those of upper middle or higher socioeconomic status (53%) were less biased than other groups. Professionals were less biased (48%) than other occupational groups. Catholics (61%) were less biased than Protestants (69%); those of both faiths who attended church irregularly (60 per cent Catholics, 57 per cent Protestants), however, were less biased than regular churchgoers. Women were markedly more biased than men: Considering only men and women able to work, 50 per cent of the former and 67 per cent of the latter were classified as racists, anti-Semites, and intense anti-Semites.

Frustration did not seem to play a role in bias. The most intensely anti-Semitic groups were not more seriously troubled by day-to-day difficulties than was the least biased group. A certain amount of apathy did characterize more biased groups. Only 12 per cent of the intense anti-Semites read magazines and less than half (46%) listened to the radio. As the level of bias increased, the proportion of those who knew how denazification was being carried out declined (from 66 per cent among those with little bias to 42 per cent among the intense anti-Semites), as did those who agreed that research had shown that the Germans tortured and murdered millions of helpless Europeans (from 72 to 41 per cent, respectively).

Criticism of the Allies also increased with the level of bias. On the question of Allied limitations on the number and types of industries that Germany could have in the future, the percentage thinking the policy just declined (from 17 per cent among those with little bias to 5 per cent among the intense anti-Semites), although the percentage declaring it unjust remained roughly constant (72 and 74 per cent, respectively). The percentage satisfied with the way in which denazification was being carried out declined from 35 to 28 per cent, respectively.

Differences were more marked on questions of general orientation. The percentage saying that National Socialism was a bad idea rather than a good idea badly carried out declined from 51 per cent among the least biased to 27 per cent among the intense anti-Semites. Similarly, the proportion denying that it was a national humiliation for Germany to be occupied by foreign powers declined from 67 per cent among the least biased to 43 per cent among the intense anti-Semites.

Report No. 50 (20 March 1947)

A PILOT STUDY ON DISPLACED PERSONS

Sample: 298 displaced persons in Hesse and Bavaria.
Interviewing dates: not specified. (6 pp.)

Nine per cent of the displaced persons claimed to be stateless or uncertain of their country of origin. The remainder represented 25 nationalities of which the largest single group (12%) was Polish. Most were men (62%) and under 30 years of age (48%); 40 per cent reported having gone to Germany in 1944 or later. When asked why they had come to Germany, the most frequent response was "deported" (19%), followed by "forced to come" (16%) and "brought to Germany by German government" or its agencies (14%). Three in five (61%) did not plan on remaining in Germany, but only 34 per cent of these people intended to return to their homelands, and 53 per cent hoped to move to another country (most particularly, the United States). Most of those who did not plan to return to their homelands were from eastern Europe: Almost half (49%) of the displaced persons mentioned that Soviet occupation of their homeland was the reason for not returning. The largest single group (38%) was comprised of skilled workers; 15 per cent were professional people. When questioned about making their living in the future, 47 per cent said they planned to work in the occupation for which they were trained; 30 per cent said they would be workers, do anything, or work where needed.

Report No. 51 (2 April 1947)

ATTITUDES TOWARD COLLECTIVE GUILT IN THE AMERICAN ZONE OF GERMANY

*Sample:*3,005 persons in the American Zone.
Interviewing dates: last two weeks of December 1946. (16 pp.)

Respondents in the American Zone were asked seven questions to ascertain their acceptance or rejection of collective guilt for the events of the Nazi era. Scores were computed by totaling the percentages rejecting each of the seven questions. Those scoring zero accepted responsibility on all seven questions; those scoring seven rejected collective responsibility on all seven questions. The median score for the total AMZON population was 3.8. On the whole, there were only slight variations among population groups in their acceptance or rejection of collective guilt. Those most likely to reject guilt were residents of Wuerttemberg-Baden (3.82), the less well-educated (3.83), those aged 30 to 39 (3.85) or 60 years of age or older (3.92), women (3.96), Protestants (3.88), the lowest socioeconomic (3.85) and income (3.90) groups. Intensely anti-Semitic respondents were particularly likely to reject any collective guilt.

On specific questions: 63 per cent felt that the German people were at least partly to blame for acts of the Hitler regime because they had supported that regime; 28 per cent felt that the Germans were to blame for the outbreak of World War II; 68 per cent stated that the harshness of the Versailles Treaty did not give the German people the right to start another war, but 52 per cent said the Versailles Treaty was a cause of the war; 46 per cent denied that Germany had attacked Poland to protect Germans living there; 56 per cent felt that Germany often found itself in a difficult situation because other people had no understanding of Germany; 83 per cent believed that both sides in World War II committed many crimes against humanity and peace; and 59 per cent agreed that Germany had tortured and murdered millions of helpless Europeans.

Report No. 52 (27 March 1947)

ATTITUDES TOWARD FOOD, FUEL, AND BUILDING MATERIALS CONDITIONS

Sample: 3,022 respondents in the American Zone and 401 in the British and American Sectors of West Berlin in the survey of October-November 1946; in the November-December 1946 survey, 3,008 respondents in the American Zone and 399 in the British and American Sectors of Berlin; and, in January 1947, 3,011 in the American Zone and about 400 in West Berlin.
Interviewing dates: 28 October to 15 November 1946 (or building materials); 28 November to 10 December 1946 (on food and fuel); and January 1946. (45 pp.)

With the increase in the food ration from 1,250 to 1,550 calories per day came improvements in the reported health and morale of the German population: Two-fifths (42%) of AMZON Germans said that they felt "somewhat" better; 46 per cent in the American Zone and 20 per cent in West Berlin in November 1946 reported having sufficient food to do good work (compared to 28 and nine per cent, respectively, in May 1946).

There was still considerable complaint. Residents in large cities felt that equalizing the ration of all people regardless of whether they lived in a small town or in a large city was unfair: Two-thirds (68%) of the West Berliners disapproved of the equalization, whereas, in the American Zone as a whole, 66 per cent approved; in AMZON cities with between 100,000 and 249,999, however, 47 per cent disapproved.

The food situation in West Berlin and Wuerttemberg-Baden was more critical than anywhere else in the American-controlled areas: Four-fifths (81%) in West Berlin and 57 per cent in Wuerttemberg-Baden said that they got along only "poorly" with the food ration; 48 per cent in Wuerttemberg-Baden reported not feeling any better since the food ration was increased; and 78 per cent in West Berlin and 62 per cent in Wuerttemberg-Baden claimed not to have enough food to enable them to do good work.

Farmers, being the source of supply, offered few complaints and indicated the highest degree of satisfaction with the food ration. A third (34%) of the farmers said that they got by "well" with the food ration and 56 per cent said they "managed to get by." In contrast, only eight and 29 per cent, respectively, of those in professional or business occupations made the same claim. Almost two-thirds (63%) of this group said they got by "poorly" whereas only ten per cent of the farmers gave this answer. Following farmers in degree of satisfaction with the food rations were artisans and master craftsmen: Nine per cent of this group got along "well" and 42 per cent "managed to get by."

Fuel did not appear to offer as great a problem as food at the time of the study, even though it was the height of winter. In November 1946, only six per cent of the AMZON population said that fuel was their greatest care or worry; in January 1947, only 12 per cent reported fuel to be of major concern. Fuel was a more important problem in Berlin: In January 1947 as many as 36 per cent mentioned it as their major concern, as contrasted to 18 per cent in November-December 1946.

Respondents felt nearly unanimously (87 per cent in AMZON; 94 per cent in West Berlin) that it was more urgent to repair buildings then in use than to allocate available building materials for the reconstruction of heavily bombed cities. Large percentages (39 per cent in AMZON; 62 per cent in West Berlin) felt that the distribution of available building materials was unjustly handled. When asked why they believed it unjust, 23 and 17 per cent, respectively, said that materials could be obtained only in return for other goods and that, therefore, those in a position to barter got everything; in West Berlin, 27 per cent felt that there was unnecessary building and repairing of churches and businesses. Of the 33 per cent in the American Zone and 13 per cent Berlin who owned property, 13 and six per cent, respectively, said that they had not been able to get through legal channels the materials necessary to keep their buildings in repair or to rebuild them.

Report No. 53 (8 April 1947)

MAGAZINE READING IN THE AMERICAN ZONE

Sample: 3,005 interviews in the American Zone and 409 in the British and American Sectors of Berlin.
Interviewing dates: last two weeks in December 1946. (14 pp.)

A minority (18%) in the American Zone read magazines. In Berlin more (42%) read magazines. About half (44 per cent in AMZON; 57 per cent in West Berlin) said that they did not read because they had no interest or time. An equal percentage of AMZON Germans (44%) said they had no opportunity to get magazines; 37 per cent in West Berlin said they could not afford magazines. About three-quarters (70 per cent in AMZON; 75 per cent in West Berlin) felt that magazines were better at the time of the survey than they had been in the preceding 12 years.

The combined readership of the American-sponsored magazines *Heute, Neue Auslese,* and *Amerikanishe Rundschau* in both the American Zone and West Berlin was nine per cent. In the American Zone, 15 per cent read one of these three magazines; in West Berlin, however, more (22%) read the Soviet-licensed *Neue Illustrierte Zeitung* and only 13 per cent read the American-licensed *Sie.* AMZON Germans with more education, Catholics, older people, and those of higher socio-economic status were more likely than others to read American-licensed magazines. *Amerikanische Rundschau* tended to appeal to an upper-middle class, older, and more highly educated audience; *Neue Auslese* more to middle than to lower socioeconomic status groups; and *Heute,* although it had a more general appeal, to women, Catholics, and lower middle or lower socioeconomic status groups.

Report No. 54 (8 April 1947)

VIENNESE REACTIONS TO NEW DENAZIFICATION LAWS

Sample: 1,502 persons in the American and British Sectors of Vienna.
Interviewing dates: December 1946. (7 pp.)

This survey was taken shortly after the publication of new denazification regulations. Almost all (85%) of the respondents had heard of the changes. Of these informed respondents, a plurality (44 per cent of the entire sample) could not say whether or not they liked the law in its new form. Of those with opinions, most (24 per cent of the entire sample) disapproved of it, 14 per cent approved, and three per cent agreed partly with it. Of those who answered that they either agreed or partly agreed, most (56 per cent and 82 per cent of the respective subsamples) stated that the harsher punishment of those seriously charged was what they liked about the change in the law. Most of those who answered that they did not like the new law or only partly liked it (27 per cent and 80 per cent of the respective subsamples) gave as their reason the belief that the punishment for lesser charges was too harsh. The groups most disapproving of the newly defined denazification law were the better educated, middle and upper classes, upper-income groups, men, and supporters of the Austrian Communist Party. About three-quarters (74%) of those who thought that National Socialism was a good idea badly carried out also disapproved of the new form.

Report No. 55 (15 April 1947)

PUBLIC ATTITUDES TOWARD DENAZIFICATION

Sample: 3,005 adults in the American Zone and 409 in West Berlin.

Interviewing dates: ten-day periods in the months of December 1946, January and February 1947. (10 pp.)

Educational background, and perhaps even more importantly, direct interest in the proceedings affected knowledge about the denazification program. Those in higher socioeconomic groups (64%), the better educated (73%), as well as former NSDAP members (62%) were much more likely than others to know about how denazification was carried out, and much more likely to have heard or read about General Lucius Clay's speech to the *Laenderrat* criticizing the way in which denazification was being carried out. A fifth (21%) were so uninterested or so unaffected by denazification that they held no discernible attitude toward denazification. The general public favored, by a small plurality (36%), the then-current plan, in which Germans carried out denazification under American scrutiny. Nearly as many (30%), however, would have liked to see the Americans assume full responsibility for the program.

Nearly half (47%) of the people had heard or read about General Clay's speech to the *Laenderrat*. Probably because the speech was given in Stuttgart, residents of Wuerttemberg-Baden (56%) were more likely to have heard about it than were Bavarians (45%), Hessians (45%), or West Berliners (37%). Most (72%) of those who had heard about General Clay's speech thought the remarks justified; but few (13%) had observed any change in denazification methods in the first weeks following the speech.

Results of ten separate samplings since November 1945 showed that the percentage satisfied with denazification had declined about 15 per cent, whereas the percentage dissatisfied or expressing no opinion had increased in size. About as many (34%) said in December 1946 that they were satisfied with the way denazification was being carried out as were dissatisfied (32%). About 14 per cent thought the *Spruchkammer* rulings too lenient. A quarter (25%) would have differentiated more clearly between Activists and Followers, between guilty and not guilty. A seventh (14%) would have punished Activists more strictly.

In the American Zone, a majority (62%) opposed both noting former NSDAP membership on identification cards and keeping former NSDAP members from their former jobs. Former NSDAP members were all but unanimous in opposing these measures.

Report No. 56 (26 April 1947)

GERMAN CHILDREN APPRAISE THE YOUTH PROGRAM

Sample: 1,021 boys and girls ranging in age from ten to 18 years living in Frankfurt, Kassel, Heidelberg, and Munich.
Interviewing dates: early March 1947. (16 pp.)

Large proportions of the youth (an average of 45 per cent in the four cities) stated that they had not heard anything about the American Youth Program. Only a small percentage (12%) claimed to have heard a great deal about the program. Few (11%) said that they had actually taken part in the program, and most of those who had attended not only had attended infrequently but also stated that the meetings were either fairly well or very well led (10%).

Of those children who had an opinion (48%), most (30%) felt the program to be a very good idea. When asked what their main reason for taking part in the program was, the most frequent response (40%) was "to get candy and food." This was followed by "a chance for sports and games" (26%), "to show our former enemies what Germans really are" (23%), and "to learn English" (17%). Twenty-seven per cent stated their belief that German boys and girls attended because they really enjoyed the program rather than because they had nothing else to do or to keep warm (7%). Respondents tended to think that it was a good idea for boys and girls to take part in the program (41%), as opposed to nine per cent who categorically rejected this idea.

The children who participated showed greater interest in sports, hiking and trips offered by the Youth Program than in more sedentary or "educational" activities. When asked about improvements in the program, there were major differences among the cities: Most who had an opinion in Frankfurt (37%) suggested helping youth get more food, clothing and shoes; in Heidelberg 47 per cent suggested more sports opportunities and obtaining more sports equipment. To ascertain whether the respondents were aware of some of the broader purposes of the program, they were asked to rate the need for the program in certain specific areas: social development, education, vocational choice, religion, music and art, sports and games, democratic experiences, and German and world problems. Except for religion, the children rated the program "very necessary" in each of these areas.

Most of the youth who had an opinion on the subject (22%) stated they received either a little better or a much better idea of democracy from the youth activities; only four per cent denied this. A large majority of those with opinions believed that the Youth Program contributed fairly much (17%) or very much (17%) to the preservation of peace; only 12 per cent thought that it contributed little or nothing. A majority expected that German youth would learn a great deal (32%) or something (24%) about the United States and its aims through this Youth Program.

Asked what Americans gained through participation in the program, 33 per cent mentioned a chance to learn the problems and needs of Germany, and 28 per cent responded with the opportunity to "learn really to know Germans." Of those with opinions (46%) half (23%) thought that the Americans who participated did so because they enjoyed it and only four per cent thought that the Americans had been ordered to participate; the remainder gave both responses. The bulk of the respondents believed that German boys and girls would get to know American soldiers either well (31%) or somewhat better (23%) through the program. Most of these young people clearly had a very good (23%) or fairly good (39%) opinion of American soldiers, and a very good (30%) or fairly good (47%) opinion of the American people. Only a minority knew some Americans in Germany very well (16%), or fairly well (12%); the bulk either knew none but had spoken with some (29%) or had never spoken with Americans (37%).

Report No. 57 (29 April 1947)

READERSHIP AND POPULARITY OF THE FRANKFURT NEWSPAPERS

Sample: 300 adult Frankfurt residents.
Interviewing dates: third week in April 1947. (9 pp.)

More Frankfurt residents read the *Frankfurter Rundschau* (35%) than the *Neue Presse* (17%). Readers of the *Neue Presse* were better educated than *Rundschau* readers, had a higher income, were more likely to have been associated with the Nazi Party, and less likely to belong to a postwar political party. There was a slight tendency for more *Neue Presse* readers (16%) to say they would not read the *Rundschau* than *Rundschau* readers (6%) to say they would not read the *Neue Presse*. Half of the *Neue Presse* readers (8%) who objected to reading the *Rundschau* stated that they felt the *Rundschau* too biased or politically distasteful. *Rundschau* readers were aware of the bias of their paper, criticizing it particularly for its political bias and lack of coverage of cultural affairs. When asked which topics they would like to see more about in their papers, more *Neue Presse* readers (24%) than *Rundschau* readers (18%) wanted more news of Frankfurt; in contrast, more *Rundschau* readers (37%) than *Neue Presse* readers (32%) wanted more news of Germany.

Report No. 58 (1 May 1947)

CONFIDENCE IN NEWS IN PRESENT-DAY GERMANY

Sample: 3,400 adults in the American Zone and the American and British Sectors of Berlin.
Interviewing dates: unspecified. (9 pp.)

A large majority in both the American Zone (74%) and in West Berlin (85%) considered the news at the time of the survey to be more trustworthy than news during the war. The more one was inclined to suspect the postwar news, the greater the sympathy for the idea of National Socialism: Of the four per cent who thought postwar news was less accurate, 89 per cent thought National Socialism was a good idea badly carried out, as did only 51 per cent of those reporting postwar news to be more accurate. When questioned as to the accuracy of the postwar news, 46 per cent said that all or most of it was truthful, 27 per cent thought about half of it truthful, and nine per cent said that little of the postwar news was truthful. A majority (55%) felt that little of the wartime news was truthful. Those holding wartime news to be more accurate than or just as accurate as postwar news contained proportionately larger numbers of young, well-educated, and prosperous people.

Comparing the radio and newspapers, 37 per cent of AMZON Germans thought them equal in bringing the most trustworthy news; 24 per cent were more inclined to rely on the radio and eight per cent the newspapers. In West Berlin, however, most (32%) considered newspapers more trustworthy, with 26 per cent relying more on the radio and 19 per cent finding them equally trustworthy. Most in both the American Zone (43%) and West Berlin (59%) said newspapers brought more complete news.

Report No. 59 (10 May 1947)

EXPECTATIONS REGARDING REPARATIONS

Sample: 2,998 persons living in the American Zone and 401 in the American and British Sectors of Berlin.
Interviewing dates: February 1947. (6 pp.)

There were almost no discernible population differences concerning reparations, although West Berliners, as usual, displayed more sophistication and had a heightened degree of awareness of various facets of the problem as compared with AMZON residents. In addition, West Berliners tended to be somewhat more optimistic regarding Germany's future while at the same time appreciating even more fully than the people in AMZON that the Russians were prepared to insist on stiff reparations.

Almost all people (82%) believed that a higher reparations bill would be submitted to the German people following World War II than had been submitted after World War I. A large majority also expected that it would take a very long time to pay off these reparations: Only 13 per cent in West Berlin and ten per cent in AMZON estimated a period under 20 years. Large majorities estimated that the payments would generally be accomplished by means of goods or through production (30 per cent in AMZON; 48 per cent in West Berlin). Fewer believed that they would be paid by the removal of factories and machines (14 and 13 per cent, respectively). A plurality of AMZON respondents (44 per cent as opposed to 33 per cent in West Berlin) considered that both types of payments would be made.

Nearly all Germans (74 per cent in AMZON; 84 per cent in West Berlin) thought that the Soviet Union would demand the heaviest reparations; half the AMZON Germans (50%) and 39 per cent of the West Berliners thought that France would make the highest demands (multiple responses were permitted). Although in an earlier survey (January 1947) 71 per cent of the AMZON Germans indicated optimism regarding their personal future, a solid majority of 56 per cent said in February that an improvement in the standard of living was not possible while Germany was paying off the reparations.

Report No. 60 (April 1947)

TRENDS IN GERMAN PUBLIC OPINION

Sample: the number of respondents varied from 365 in the first survey to 3,500 interviewed in April 1947; the total number of persons interviewed was more than 75,000 in the American Zone and in the American and British Sectors of Berlin.
Interviewing dates: from 26 October 1945 to 7 April 1947 during which time forty complete studies of the American Zone were made as well as an additional 23 surveys of smaller size and in limited areas. (43 pp.)

This report summarizes in graphic form major trends of German opinion in the American occupied areas, covering seven major issues: economic affairs, food, the occupation, Nuremberg Trials, media, politics, and reorientation.

Economic Affairs. The proportion of the population who said that their incomes were adequate remained constant between November 1945 and July 1946 but then began to decline. General opinion that prices would rise increased sharply between January and June 1946; half the population believed that anti-inflationary measures would not succeed. In December 1945 nearly eight in ten people thought that conditions would improve within six months whereas in April 1947 only 45 per cent held this view. Confidence in the continued value of the *Reichsmark* suffered a constant decline after April 1946, when 54 per cent had such confidence; by October 1946, 43 per cent thought that its value would drop. Confidence in both Allied money and the German *Reichsmark* declined between April and October 1946, with over half saying that they saw no difference between the two.

Food. Although there was extensive complaining about the rationing of food, almost everyone agreed that the ration card system was being handled justly, with only a slight decrease between November 1945 and May 1946 from 93 to 88 per cent. Belief that the food ration was larger in some zones than in others gained less support in May 1946 (47%) than it did in March (60%). Between November 1945 and April 1947 people spoke of being worried about food more than about any other matter. Urban residents were three times as likely to mention it as were rural people; the latter, in turn, were twice as likely to complain about the lack of clothing and shoes as were city dwellers.

The Occupation. In November 1945, 70 per cent of those interviewed in AMZON said that the American occupation forces had furthered the reconstruction of Germany; by September 1946 this proportion had shrunk to 44 per cent of the population. At the same time there was a steady increase in the size of the group without an opinion on the issue and, in the last two surveys, there was a sharp increase in the proportion saying that the Americans were hindering that reconstruction.

Nuremberg Trials. A heavy majority of about eight in ten persons felt that the trials were conducted justly. Readership of newspaper reports concerning the trials declined from a high of eight in ten persons in January 1946 to 65 per cent in March 1946, and then rose once again to the original figure on the day following publication of the verdicts. As the trials progressed, waning confidence in the completeness and trustworthiness in the newspaper reports was displayed; nonetheless, even at the lowest point, seven in ten people were satisfied with the integrity and detail of the reports.

Media. The number of regular newspaper readers among AMZON residents declined 13 percentage points between January and October 1946, when it reached 63 per cent. Three surveys conducted between January and December 1946 revealed that slightly more than one-half of the population were radio listeners.

Politics. Claimed political interest rose gradually between October 1945 and June 1946 and then dropped off sharply, following the conclusion of general elections. The proportion of people considering political meetings to be worthwhile rose from 60 to 72 per cent between November 1945 and March 1946. In AMZON, until mid-summer 1946, the CDU/CSU enjoyed about 40 per cent plurality of membership or preference over other parties, with the SPD in second place, favored by about 30 per cent. Later studies revealed that while the SPD did not make any substantial gain, the CDU/CSU suffered a loss of about ten per cent of its following, with most of the defectors saying that they no longer favored any party. Less than one in ten supported the LDP/DVP and between two and three per cent favored the KPD. In Bavaria, the CSU was the foremost party (about 40 per cent); the SPD was second with about three in ten; about one-fourth of the people preferred no party; the KPD and the LDP each held about five per cent of the population; and the WAV claimed three to four per cent. In Berlin, from a low point of 36 per cent in the spring of 1946, the SPD increased its following to 68 per cent by December 1946; less than two in ten expressed a preference for the CDU; and very few people indicated that they had no party preference.

Reorientation. Although about 35 per cent of the population felt that the occupation was a humiliation, about 55 per cent did not think so. In the course of eleven surveys made between November 1945 and December 1946, an average of 47 per cent of the people thought that National Socialism was a good idea, badly carried out; 41 per cent said that it was a bad idea; 12 per cent held no opinion. The percentage of persons indicating satisfaction with the denazification process decreased from 57 per cent in March 1946 to 34 per cent in December 1946. The proportion of the German population indicating a preference for neither communism nor National Socialism rose from 22 per cent to 66 per cent between November 1945 and November 1946. Those favoring communism decreased in number, those favoring National Socialism remained constant, and a considerable decrease was noted in the number of those holding no opinion. About seven in ten said that the Germans were not responsible for the war. Approximately one in three people indicated that they were troubled by rumors, with the most frequently heard rumor being that of an impending war with the Soviet Union. Only half the respondents said that they considered themselves sufficiently well informed about political events. A majority of AMZON residents felt that the best way to achieve the reconstruction of Germany was through "hard work." Between ten and 15 per cent hoped for a new strong Fuehrer and/or the rebirth of the old national spirit.

Report No. 61 (12 June 1947)

SOME ATTITUDES TOWARD THE SCHOOL SYSTEM IN WUERTTEMBERG-BADEN

Sample: 650 people representing a cross-section of adults in Wuerttemberg-Baden.
Interviewing dates: first three weeks of May 1947. (6 pp.)

A solid majority (62%) of the public in the *Land* of Wuerttemberg-Baden expressed satisfaction with the ability of the schools, under normal conditions, to fulfill the needs of German youth. Only a minority (30%), however, felt that school children could receive training equal to their abilities, 44 per cent felt such complete training depended on the financial and social position of the parents.

A large majority (71%) supported the idea of school boards elected in each *Kreis* (county). A large majority of those supporting such elections was firmly convinced that economic bias operated to deny some children the training that their talents would seem to demand. Leadership groups – the well-educated, men, residents of large towns and cities – were more dissatisfied with the school system than were the poorly educated, the women, or small town and village residents. Catholics were less informed and had less interest in public school matters, possibly because they relied more heavily upon private institutions.

Report No. 62 (14 June 1947)

GERMAN ATTITUDES TOWARD A PEACE TREATY AFTER THE CONCLUSION OF THE MOSCOW CONFERENCE

Sample: 600 people living in Hesse, Wuerttemberg-Baden, and West Berlin.
Interviewing dates: during the last week in April and the first week in May 1947. (8 pp.)

Most people knew that a conference had been held among the Allies and that it had broken up. Asked about the latest news they had heard concerning the conference, replies varied from the simple statement that it had ended (31 per cent in West Berlin; 28 per cent in Hesse; 24 per cent in Wuerttemberg-Baden) to more specific replies such as reference to Secretary of State Marshall's radio address upon his return home, or reports on the disunity of the Allies.

Not surprisingly, majority opinion held that the conference had accomplished nothing. A few took a more sanguine view, pointing out positive measures helpful to Germany or suggesting that at least Allied differences were finally out in the open. Those interviewed tended to blame the Soviet Union for the lack of results at the Moscow Conference (49 per cent in West Berlin; 31 per cent in Hesse; 41 per cent in Wuerttemberg-Baden). About half this number spoke of disunity among the Allies as the reason.

Although many people believed that a delay in signing a treaty would mean milder terms (58 per cent in West Berlin; 39 per cent in Hesse; 42 per cent in Wuerttemberg-Baden), majority opinion favored an immediate treaty (65 per cent in West Berlin; 57 per cent in Hesse; 52 per cent in Wuerttemberg-Baden). Only in West Berlin did a majority (57%) think that a treaty would be signed by the summer of 1948. In Hesse and Wuerttemberg-Baden majorities either thought that it would take more than two years to complete a treaty or had no idea how long it would take. Most Germans had a good idea of what they thought ought to be included in the treaty. Uppermost in their minds were economic reconstruction, boundaries—especially to the east—the return of prisoners of war, reparations, disarmament, form of government. Whatever the terms of the treaty, those interviewed were certain that the mere fact of settlement would lead to improved conditions in Germany (85 per cent in West Berlin; 74 per cent in Hesse; 79 per cent in Wuerttemberg-Baden).

A great number of Germans agreed that there were two major problems facing the Allies: Allied unity or disunity and the problem of food. Aside from the treaty, majorities in West Berlin (55%), Hesse (63%), and Wuerttemberg-Baden (68%) considered food to be the most important problem facing Germany itself. Economic reconstruction followed in second place.

Report No. 63 (8 August 1947)

GERMAN OPINION TOWARD THE PROSPECTIVE PEACE TREATY

Sample: 2,986 respondents in the American Zone and in the American and British Sectors of Berlin.
Interviewing dates: June 1947. (10 pp.)

A majority of the public, looking back at the Moscow Conference, condemned the Russians for obstructionism. A fourth of those questioned felt that the Conference definitively outlined the separate points of view held by the Allies or, at least, were conducted with good will on all sides.

A very large majority of AMZON Germans (82%) thought that a peace treaty would mean an improvement in Germany's situation. This feeling was so general throughout the population that there were no significant differences among any of the major population groups. Among those who credited the United States with giving aid to German reconstruction, however, an even larger majority (88%) looked forward to an improvement in their lot after a peace treaty. Those denying the existence of such aid were less apt (76%) to expect improvements.

About half (49%) the people did not expect that the Allies would complete a peace treaty by the summer of 1948, although a large minority (35%) did believe that Allied unity on the matter would be achieved by then. Those expecting agreement tended to be drawn from the broad masses of the population, whereas critics and skeptics were much more often upper class, well-educated men, or former NSDAP members.

The most important thing hoped for by all population groups was a revival of German trade and commerce. Higher socioeconomic status groups suggested, as the next in importance, provision for widened national boundaries, a unified democratic government, and relief from financial difficulties, including reparations payments. Lower socioeconomic status groups spoke in more simple terms, stressing the return of prisoners of war, relief from the burden imposed by the presence of evacuees, and an improvement of the food situation.

Report No. 64 (25 August 1947)

TRENDS IN ATTITUDES TOWARD THE FOOD SITUATION

Sample: a cross-section of the adult population in the American Zone and in the American and British Sectors of Berlin.
Interviewing dates: from several surveys made between February 1946 and June 1947. (7 pp.)

In the course of the year, the German public became increasingly skeptical about the amount of food that the United States sent to Germany. Whereas in July 1946, 73 per cent believed the American claim that they were providing a fifth of the total food supply, by June 1947 only 49 per cent believed this claim. Relatively more Bavarians were skeptical of the claim than residents of either Hesse or Wuerttemberg-Baden. Support for the claim tended to come more from among men, the better educated, the self-styled upper class, and former Nazi Party members.

In June 1947, regular newspaper readers were more likely (52%) than occasional readers and nonreaders (45 per cent each) to believe that America's imports amounted to a fifth of the Zone's food. Fewer nonreaders, however, than readers denied the claim. Proportionately as many urban as rural people reportedly believed the American claim although the number of denials increased with city size: 45 per cent of the residents of large cities in contrast to 33 per cent in small villages rejected the claim. Some of these opinions evidently resulted from the fact that urban residents had a harder time getting food than did rural residents. In fact, in June 1947, when 64 per cent of the people in rural areas said that they had enough food to get along, only 22 per cent of the urban dwellers could make this claim. And when the question was refined still further to whether or not they had enough food to do their work well, the figures for the two groups went down even further, to 50 per cent for rural residents and nine per cent for urban dwellers.

Despite dissatisfaction with the food supply, AMZON residents felt that they were the best fed in the four zones. In June 1947, 41 per cent of AMZON Germans thought that the rations were smallest in the Soviet Zone, 28 per cent mentioned the French Zone, 18 per cent said the British Zone. Interestingly enough, West Berliners placed the French Zone at the top of the list with 40 per cent and the Soviet Zone second with 31 per cent.

Report No. 65 (27 September 1947)

ATTITUDES OF BAVARIANS TOWARD LORITZ' DISMISSAL

Sample: 1,614 Bavarians.
Interviewing dates: between 14 July and 4 August 1947. (4 pp.)

This survey was made to test reactions to the dismissal of Alfred Loritz from his positions as Denazification Minister in Bavaria and leader of the WAV.

A solid majority (69%) had heard of the affair and most of these (63%) knew that both posts were involved in the ouster. Nearly four in ten (38%) felt that the post of Denazification Minister was of greater concern to the public and had an opinion on this move whereas only 24 per cent were ready to judge his removal from the party leadership.

Those best informed about Loritz' dismissal from these posts tended to come from among former NSDAP members, men, upper classes, and the well educated.

Very few respondents opposed the dismissals: Only five per cent thought that he ought to have remained as Denazification Minister, as opposed to 33 per cent who favored the dismissal; and four per cent favored his continuance as party leader, with 20 per cent against it and 32 per cent not interested.

Report No. 66 (27 September 1947)

GERMAN ATTITUDES TOWARD CORPORAL PUNISHMENT

Sample: 3,400 adults living in the American Zone and in the American and British Sectors of Berlin.
Interviewing dates: not specified. (5 pp.)

Most German adults living in the American Zone (78%) and in the American and British Sectors of Berlin (66%) were either uninformed or misinformed on whether corporal punishment was permitted in German schools. (Although there was no directive against such punishment, in practice it did not exist in AMZON schools.)

Large majorities (65%) in AMZON and a smaller majority of 51 per cent in West Berlin approved granting teachers the right to whip or beat "very disobedient and very unruly children." Significantly, however, those who opposed (30%) tended to hold their opinion more strongly than proponents: 54 per cent of the former group in AMZON said that their feeling was very strong whereas only 48 per cent of those favoring corporal punishment said that their opinion was very strong; comparable figures in West Berlin were 61 and 46 per cent, respectively.

Parents gave high approval to corporal punishment in the schools regardless of whether their children were in or out of school (between 62 and 69 per cent). Only three groups in the AMZON population failed to register majority approval of the proposal to permit corporal punishment: the highly educated, communist party affiliates, and those with no church affiliation. Among CDU/CSU followers, those with seven years or less of schooling, women, Catholics, those who were never affiliated with the NSDAP, and small town people there were more proponents of corporal punishment than among their counterpart groups.

Report No. 67 (10 October 1947)

GERMAN ATTITUDES TOWARD INTERNATIONAL LEADERSHIP

Sample: an unspecified number of adults in the American Zone.
Interviewing dates: August 1947. (2 pp.)

A large number of AMZON Germans (70%) thought that the United States would have the greatest influence on world events in the following ten years. The Soviet Union took a poor second place with 13 per cent. No other country received any significant mention. Comparison with results from the same question when it was asked one year earlier showed that in the interim more Germans had become convinced that the United States would exert a predominant influence.

Of those who thought that the United States would have a dominant role, 78 per cent thought that this influence would be for peace. Of those who had chosen the Soviet Union for the dominant position, 88 per cent felt it would result in war.

Report No. 68 (10 October 1947)

TRENDS IN ATTITUDES TOWARD NATIONAL SOCIALISM

Sample: unspecified number, representing a cross-section of the adults in the American Zone and the American and British Sectors of Berlin.
Interviewing dates: between November 1945 and August 1947. (5 pp.)

Despite fluctuations, the percentage of Germans describing National Socialism as a good idea badly carried out remained at a fairly high number – starting at 53 per cent in November 1945, dipping to a low of 42 per cent in July 1946, and rising again to 55 per cent by August 1947. Those regarding it as a bad idea rose from 41 per cent in November 1945 to 48 per cent in July 1946 but dropped once more to 35 per cent in August 1947. Another way of describing this trend is to say that, in the period from November 1945 to July 1946, the average number of people who thought National Socialism basically a good idea was 48 per cent; between December 1946 and August 1947 it was 52 per cent.

In July 1947, opinions on this issue were related to attitudes toward democracy, individual liberty as against economic security, and the responsibility of Hitler and his advisers for his acts. People who tended to excuse National Socialism were most ready to pick flaws in the working of democracy (42%), to choose security (70%) rather than liberty (22%), and to throw the blame for Hitler's acts on his advisers (32%) rather than on Hitler himself (25%), with another 37 per cent blaming both.

In August 1947, the population groups containing the largest proportion of persons describing National Socialism as a good idea badly carried out were persons with eight years of education (60%), those under 30 (68%), Protestants (64%), LDP/DVP party adherents (68%). More West Berliners (62%) held this view than Hessians (61%), residents of Wuerttemberg-

Baden (60%), and Bavarians (50%); Bavarians led the list of those who rejected Nazism as a bad idea (38%), followed by West Berliners and Hessians (33%), and residents of Wuerttemberg-Baden (31%).

Report No. 69 (16 October 1947)

GERMAN OPINIONS REGARDING THE ORGANIZATION OF EUROPE

Sample: 3,400 people living in the American Zone and the American and British Sectors of Berlin.
Interviewing dates: August 1947. (5 pp.)

This report deals with German reactions to two issues involved in the possible organization of Europe: a "United States of Europe," and the Marshall Plan.

On many issues of the day, the German people were apathetic, resigned, or persistently deluded. On some issues, however, such as turning to the west for economic and world leadership, their opinions were crystallized in positive directions. Regarding intra-European matters, their orientation was also largely western.

Asked to select from a checklist of 23 countries those which they thought should become part of a European nation, majorities of varying degrees voted to include each of the countries named except the Soviet Union, for which 38 per cent of the AMZON respondents voted.

In this climate of opinion the Marshall Plan could not fail to elicit high approval. In August 1947, however, knowledge of the plan was neither extensive nor definite. Only 47 per cent claimed to have heard of it, and the amount of information held by about half of this group was extremely shaky. Not unexpectedly, educational background had a great deal to do with the level of information. After a brief description of the plan, all those interviewed were asked whether they thought it would solve Europe's economic difficulties; a large majority in AMZON (78%) and even more West Berliners (88%) thought it would. Separate population groups did not differ significantly in their estimation of the possibilities of working out Secretary of State Marshall's proposal. There was nonetheless one telling factor that differentiated those expressing confidence in the plan from those who did not. Among the confident, 75 per cent were convinced that the United States would have the greatest influence on world affairs during the next decade and only 12 per cent thought that the Soviet Union would play this dominant role. Those expressing skepticism about the Marshall Plan were much more likely than the confident to believe that the Soviet role would be dominant (27%) and less often expected American leadership (58%).

Report No. 70 (17 October 1947)

GERMAN UNDERSTANDING OF THE REASONS FOR THE FOOD SHORTAGE

> *Sample:* 3,008 respondents from the American Zone in November 1946 and 3,007 in July 1947; 399 and 400, respectively, in West Berlin.
> *Interviewing dates:* November 1946; July 1947. (6 pp.)

In May 1946, immediately following the reduction in rations for the general public, 41 per cent of the AMZON Germans said that they thought food shortages in Germany and throughout the world had necessitated the cut; 27 per cent thought that poor crops and insufficient stocks were responsible.

By November 1946, 46 per cent of the respondents attributed the situation to overpopulation through the arrival of DPs, evacuees, and "foreigners." This percentage held through midsummer 1947. Two significant changes, however, did take place between November 1946 and July 1947. Whereas at the earlier date 22 per cent felt that the lost war was responsible for the bad food situation, only ten per cent gave this as the reason in July 1947. More, however, had come to blame the black market: Instead of eight per cent making this charge, as was the case in 1946, 26 per cent considered this reason pertinent in the summer of 1947.

Both of these changes were reflected in West Berlin thinking, too, but in addition the summer poll showed 37 per cent accusing the occupying powers (read "Russians") with taking away too much; only 18 per cent had made a similar charge a year earlier.

Report No. 71 (17 October 1947)

BERLIN: SYMBOL OF A NATIONAL STATE

Sample: 3,400 adults from the American Zone and the American and British Sectors of Berlin.
Interviewing dates: August 1947. (4 pp.)

This report summarizes German opinion on Berlin as the capital. Among West Berliners there was virtually unanimous agreement (93%) that Berlin ought to be the capital. In AMZON, however, opinion was rather differentiated. Hessians, with 70 per cent, were most in favor of Berlin as capital, the residents of Wuerttemberg-Baden followed with 58 per cent, and the Bavarians trailed behind with 52 per cent. In small towns and villages in AMZON the number of people withholding opinions was larger than in towns and cities, although Hessian villages tended to display more structured thinking than rural residents of Wuerttemberg-Baden and Bavaria. Thus in communities with less than 10,000 residents, 72 per cent of the Hessians favored Berlin as the capital city, 59 per cent of those in Wuerttemberg-Baden, and only 49 per cent of the Bavarians. In medium-sized towns, the largest amount of support for Berlin as capital city came from Hesse (63%). In both Bavaria and Wuerttemberg-Baden, residents of these medium-sized towns were more favorably disposed toward Berlin (59 and 61 per cent, respectively) than their large city counterparts (58 and 53 per cent, respectively).

In sum, the particularism of Bavarian villages had more influence than local civic pride among city dwellers in negating national feelings, whereas in Hesse national pride in the villages induced more centrist thinking than was evident in the cities. In Wuerttemberg-Baden, community pride in the large cities acted as a damper to national feelings when compared with centrist dispositions in the smaller towns.

About half (47%) of those not in favor of Berlin as capital said they would prefer Frankfurt; Munich was the next most popular choice (32%).

Report No. 72 (November 1947)

A REPORT ON GERMAN MORALE

Sample: a representative sample of about 3,000 people from the American Zone and about 400 persons from the American and British Sectors of Berlin.
Interviewing dates: first half of May 1947. (47 pp.)

The report deals chiefly with four broad attitudinal areas which were thought to be basic elements in German morale: (1) satisfaction or dissatisfaction with the aims and practices of the Nazi regime; (2) awareness of and interest in public affairs; (3) voluntary participation in political and community life; and (4) optimistic or pessimistic outlook regarding the future. Participation and awareness were most closely related but attitudes toward Nazism were found to be the variable showing the closest relation to all the others, suggesting that a good index to low morale is disposition toward the aims and practices of National Socialism.

Those dissatisfied with Nazism tended to be more liberal, more tolerant, and more optimistic, whereas those who were satisfied with it tended to show the opposite traits. People who were aware tended to have a coldly realistic but pessimistic outlook on life; the unaware displayed greater optimism. Those in the former group were in general the better educated, city dwellers, business and professional people, communists, former soldiers, and NSDAP members. The least aware were in general from the lower class, women, farmers, the least educated, and the elderly.

Very few Germans participated in community life to any appreciable extent; those that did had characteristics and attitudes similar to those of the "aware" group described above. Confidence in the future did not vary with any population dimensions except education: Those with the best education were the least confident. Those under thirty exhibited a pessimism that went far beyond that of any other population group. The upper social classes were better informed than the lower and tended also to be more pessimistic. There were indications that wealthy people were more afraid of communism than the lower class respondents and, therefore, if forced to choose, would tend to select National Socialism over communism.

Each political party showed a characteristic pattern of responses distinguishing it from the others. SPD affiliates appeared relatively optimistic and relatively satisfied with the way in which the occupation powers were working. CDU/CSU followers were found to be the least well informed, whereas LDP/DVP supporters were among the best informed. WAV voters showed the greatest sympathy with the aims of National Socialism.

The final section of the report is an appendix containing the questions asked together with the breakdown of responses by AMZON Germans.

Report No. 73 (28 October 1947)

A GUIDE TO SOME PROPAGANDA PROBLEMS

Sample: a representative sample of 500 adults in West Berlin.
Interviewing dates: unspecified. (11 pp.)

Four types of statements on 14 topics were used: One set was unfavorable to the United States, another was phrased favorably, the third presented alternative propositions in as fair and objective a manner as possible, and the fourth was unfavorable to the United States with the source of the charge given as the Soviet Union.

The average number giving favorable responses to the "objective" or "balanced" questions was 75 per cent. This figure moved up only three percentage points to 78 per cent in response to the statements with a pro-American bias but moved down ten percentage points to 65 per cent in response to anti-American propositions. When these anti-American propositions were identified as Russian-sponsored, the average moved up to 81 per cent.

The claim presented in one question that imperialistic aims underlay United States foreign policy had real plausibility to the Germans unless presented as a Soviet claim. Statements dealing with capitalistic domination of America were particularly disadvantageous to the United States; counterclaims to these did not relieve the effectiveness of such charges. At least one "favorable" overstatement, regarding the treatment of Negroes in the United States, elicited a more negative response (with 58 per cent of the sample responding in a pro-American fashion) than the comparable "unfavorable" (77%) and "balanced" (81%) statement.

Asked after the interview (which included 15 or more additional questions) to recall the one or two statements which first came to mind, people tended to recall unfavorable rather than complimentary statements about the United States. Generally best remembered were statements about the treatment of Negroes, followed by the charge that a third of America's population was ill-fed, ill-housed, and ill-clothed, allegations that the United States was determined to dominate the world, or that American society was composed of money-grabbing people.

Report No. 74 (27 October 1947)

ATTITUDES OF AMZON GERMANS TOWARD GOVERNMENT AND POLITICS

Sample: more than 3,400 Germans in the American Zone and in the American and British Sectors of Berlin.
Interviewing dates: August 1947. (17 pp.)

Although a majority of AMZON Germans (59 per cent as contrasted to 44 per cent in West Berlin) said that they did not know enough about what was happening politically, 78 per cent (73 per cent in West Berlin) did not want to know more and 64 per cent (45 per cent in West Berlin) never thought about politics, preferring to leave that to others. Most (61%) would not take any effective measures to protest an unpopular political measure and 96 per cent said that they had never written to an official about a political matter. Nonetheless, more were inclined to hold officials responsible for government than to put the responsibility on the electorate.

More people thought a democratic republic to be the most probable form of government for Germany (40%), preferred it (56%), and thought it best for the German economy (47%) than any other kind. Regardless of the form of government, however, six in ten AMZON residents and 89 per cent of the West Berliners preferred that that government have its headquarters in Berlin.

AMZON and West Berlin Germans not only claimed preference for a democratic republican form of government, but they were also unable, or unwilling, to criticize the idea of democracy to any important extent. In contrast, 71 per cent in AMZON and 57 per cent in West Berlin did not hesitate to say that communism was entirely bad. Small, well-informed groups, however, did specify faults in democracy and point out good aspects of communism.

Despite the claimed preference for democracy, when forced to choose between a government guaranteeing liberty and one providing economic security, 62 per cent selected the latter and 26 per cent the former. Moreover, less than half (44%) of the AMZON Germans and half (50%) of the West Berliners felt that the Germans were capable of running a democratic government at that time, with corruption and disunity cited as the primary reasons. Further, almost four in ten could not mention any way in which democracy could help their country.

Considering the avowed disinterest in political matters and the confusion attending their thinking about government, the Germans were fairly well informed about politics.

Report No. 75 (28 October 1947)

WHAT BERLINERS EXPECT FROM THE LONDON CONFERENCE

Sample: 254 people from the borough of Neukoelln in West Berlin.
Interviewing dates: between 12 and 21 October 1947. (7 pp.)

If the Berliners of Neukoelln had had their way, the Allies would have agreed on a peace treaty for Germany at the London Conference and they would have agreed to reconstitute Germany as a political and economic unit. As a second best solution, they hoped for free economic exchange between zones. Hopes and actual expectations, however, were quite different. Only 14 per cent believed that the Conference would result in a treaty, although 60 per cent thought there would be agreement at least on some points. One in four (24%) felt that there would be no agreement whatsoever, and about the same number (23%) thought that there would never be agreement among the Allies on a peace treaty. In fact, a plurality (32%) expected that the result of the Conference would be a Germany divided into two autonomous areas. At the same time, such a division was what they feared most as a possible outcome.

If a split came, 74 per cent predicted that the United States would remain in Berlin. If the Americans were to have left, however, 59 per cent said that they too would have wanted to go.

Of those familiar with the Marshall Plan (69%), a majority hoped to see it carried out. A plurality (41%) believed that the United States had political aims in suggesting the plan and quite a few (23%) thought it was primarily to secure profits for Americans. A sixth (16%) expected the United States to profit more from the Marshall Plan, nine per cent Europe, and 40 per cent expected both to profit equally.

Report No. 76 (29 October 1947)

GERMAN ATTITUDES TOWARD THE FOUR OCCUPYING POWERS

Sample: an unspecified number of respondents in the American Zone and in the American and British Sectors of Berlin.

Interviewing dates: spring and summer of 1947. (4 pp.)

AMZON Germans were not convinced that the Allies or the United States were doing all they could to rebuild Germany, although more of them were ready to acknowledge American than Allied help. Thus 44 per cent of the AMZON Germans (as contrasted to 74 per cent in West Berlin) said that the United

States had furthered the rebuilding of Germany, whereas only 31 per cent (47 per cent in West Berlin) admitted such help from the Allies. Equally noteworthy is the fact that 33 per cent (16 per cent in West Berlin) claimed that the United States had hindered reconstruction; 43 per cent (45 per cent in West Berlin) made the same charge against the Allies.

AMZON Germans were strongly convinced (70%) that the United States would wield the most influence in world affairs during the next ten years, and 55 per cent of the total population felt that this influence would be directed toward peace. Of the 13 per cent who thought such world influence would be wielded by the Soviet Union, most (11%) thought it would lead to war.

Of the four Allies, the Germans most trusted the United States to treat Germany fairly (63%); 45 per cent placed much trust in the British, only four per cent in the French, and none in the Russians. An overwhelming number of AMZON Germans (84%) would have picked the United States as an occupying power if history could have been turned back. AMZON Germans were also firm in their opinion that they were better off than people in any of the other three zones.

Report No. 77 (5 November 1947)

OPINIONS ON THE PRESS IN THE AMERICAN ZONE OF GERMANY

Sample: approximately 3,400 people living in the American Zone and in the American and British Sectors of Berlin.
Interviewing dates: July 1947. (13 pp.)

Almost half (47%) of the AMZON respondents felt that there was a free press in AMZON; in West Berlin the figure was as high as 66 per cent. Over two-thirds (68%) of those who read the *Neue Zeitung*, which was published by the American authorities, considered this paper to be free.

Six out of ten (60%) of those interviewed did not think that German editors were permitted to print everything they·considered to be correct and two-thirds (64%) felt that they ought to be allowed to do so.

About one in ten (6 per cent in AMZON; 12 per cent in West Berlin) preferred a party press to an independent press although a large number of people (27 and 42 per cent, respectively) were willing to have political parties publish newspapers if independent papers continued to be published as well. Much of the sentiment against the party press reflected the negative attitudes toward political parties generally. At the same time there was a great deal of misinformation about the party press; over half of those living in AMZON did not know that existing papers were independently edited. Among the informed respondents, there was more sentiment in favor of an independent press than among the uninformed.

Report No. 78 (6 November 1947)

BAVARIAN ATTITUDES TOWARD NEWSPAPERS

Sample: 1,613 adults representing a cross-section of the population in Bavaria.
Interviewing dates: August 1947. (4 pp.)

Half the people in Bavaria (53%) claimed to be regular newspaper readers, as compared with 55 per cent who had made the same claim one month earlier in AMZON. Not unexpectedly, regular readers tended to be the well-educated, from the upper social classes, men, and former NSDAP members. Among former NSDAP members, 76 per cent claimed regular readership, in contrast to 50 per cent of the nonaffiliates.

About three-fifths of the Bavarians questioned felt that the newspapers carried enough Bavarian as well as community news items. Almost a fifth, however, wished there were more of both. Regular readers were more likely than occasional readers to say that the papers they were reading were good, although 48 per cent of them thought that they were only fair.

Report No. 79 (22 November 1947)

ATTITUDES TOWARD AMERICAN CAPITALISM

Sample: about 2,250 residents of Wuerttemberg-Baden and Bavaria, and an unspecified number of respondents in West Berlin.
Interviewing dates: between 15 September and 15 October 1947. (7 pp.)

The heart of the questionnaire was comprised of fourteen questions, each one of which had been cast into four different forms for presentation to four separate but comparable cross-sections of the people. One set was phrased unfavorably to America; a second preceded each of these statements with an identification of the source of the charge as Russian; a third presented alternative propositions on the fourteen topics; and the fourth presented favorably phrased propositions in as fair and objective a sense as possible.

The average of the favorable responses to all 56 questions was 59 per cent in the two southern *Laender* and 75 per cent in West Berlin. The average percentage of favorable responses varied with the wording of the question – from unfavorable statements with the source identified (64 per cent in Bavaria and Wuerttemberg-Baden), to statements favorable to the United States (63%), to objective or balanced statements (59%), to statements unfavorable to the United States (49%).

In addition to a simple reply to the questions asked, respondents were requested to indicate the strength of their feelings on the various topics. No fewer than seven in ten persons were favorably disposed toward the United States on the issue of national capitalism. Scarcely more than one in ten held the opposite view. Both groups, however, held their opinions with a high degree of intensity. The most significant characteristic of the people who were firmly and favorably disposed toward the United States and the Americans was their high educational level. In addition, the majority of the group were men of rather high socioeconomic status. There were relatively few regular churchgoing Catholics, 95 per cent of them read newspapers, and about six in ten sometimes listened to the radio. The people on the other side of the fence — those who were firmly and unfavorably disposed toward the United States and to Americans — were markedly average in their educational background; they were mainly women; 52 per cent of them might be classified as upper lower socioeconomic status; and they tended to be nonchurchgoing Protestants. The in-between group — those open to persuasion by one or the other point of view — comprised primarily people with only seven years or less of schooling, more than six in ten were women, nearly half attended Catholic services regularly, more than seven in ten came from the lowest socioeconomic group, and nearly half lived in villages with fewer than 2,000 population.

Report No. 80 (26 November 1947)

OPINIONS ON DENAZIFICATION

Sample: a random selection of 300 names from the *Meldebogen* files of former NSDAP members as well as 3,000 people representing a cross-section of the American Zone population.
Interviewing dates: September 1947. (9 pp.)

This report on the impact of the denazification program deals with three groups: former party members (PGs) whose *Meldebogen* were still on active file, those who during the interview admitted former affiliation with the NSDAP, and those who claimed no connection with the Nazi party and were not affected by the Law of National Liberation.

Among the *Meldebogen* group and the claimed PGs, about four in ten had not yet been cleared. The members of the two groups differed from each other to a certain extent, but, as compared with the population as a whole, they were more alike than different. Each group contained more well-educated people, more upper middle-class people, more former soldiers, and more men than did the nonaffected public; they also contained more apolitical people.

Although many more former PGs than other Germans lost their jobs temporarily after 1945, only about eight per cent were still unemployed in September 1947. Almost all of the former PGs who had new jobs thought they were worse than their former ones.

There was no clear-cut division on whether the purpose of denazification was to remove National Socialist influence from public life or to restore followers to their old jobs. Large majorities in both groups, as compared with only 56 per cent of the general public, knew that the denazification procedures were conducted by Germans under Allied supervision. Those not affected by the procedures gave majority approval to denazification in principle, but majority disapproval to its methods.

A majority of former PGs felt that denazification had had a greater impact on the economic life than on the political life of Germany; those not affected who had opinions on the matter tended to divide evenly on the two aspects.

The most frequently mentioned result of denazification was the lack of capable officials and businessmen.

Report No. 81 (3 December 1947)

GERMAN REACTIONS TO EXPELLEES AND DP'S

Sample: a cross-section of native residents and expellees in the American Zone.
Interviewing dates: March 1946, November 1946, June 1947, and September 1947. (9 pp.)

Expellees and native Germans were almost unanimous in the belief that the expulsions were unjustified. Dissatisfaction among both groups increased, with seven per cent of the expellees saying in March 1946 that they were not satisifed with the way they had been treated and 45 per cent expressing this view by September 1947; among native residents, in March 1946 a fourth (25%) predicted that the expellees would not get along with the native population and in September 1947 almost half (46%) made this prediction. Six out of ten native Germans (59%) considered the expellees to be German citizens; they were also the respondents most likely to think that the expellees would adjust to their new surroundings.

A vast majority of the expellees (85%) would go back to the place of their birth if they had a chance; nine out of ten native residents (91%) also felt that the expellees would go home if they could.

Two-thirds (66%) of AMZON residents predicted that the displaced persons would not be able to get along with the native population, and as few as three per cent of those interviewed considered the DPs to be German citizens. About one in seven

(25%) thought that Germany should be responsible for the support of the DPs, with one-third (32%) placing this responsibility at the door of the DPs' native country.

Report No. 82 (8 December 1947)

GERMAN SENTIMENT FOR PEACE AND ECONOMIC SECURITY

Sample: in the course of three surveys, 1,470, 3,005, and 3,004 interviews were conducted in the American Zone. *Interviewing dates:* 26 April 1946, 10 December 1946, and 4 August 1947. (5 pp.)

Large and solid majorities of the public consistently rejected many of the propositions, presented to them in the interviews, expressing a basic inclination toward the values of militarism or war. At the same time, more than half the public did not deny the idea of racial superiority with its implication of a right to rule. The three statements with which respondents most frequently agreed were: "The human spirit is not glorified by war alone" (96%); "War does not pay" (94%); and "A civilian is not less worthy than a soldier" (90%). (Complete wordings and results appear in an appendix in the report.)

Reaction to the propositions suggests that the German public saw only a partial or indirect relationship between the actions of their government and themselves. Probably still more basic to this problem is the German outlook on individual rights. Asked to choose between a government that provides economic security and one which guarantees civil liberties, the majority (62%) preferred the former and many fewer (26%) chose the latter. Asked which was the most important of the basic freedoms, 31 per cent mentioned commercial freedom, 22 per cent chose religious freedom, 19 per cent free elections, and only 14 per cent free speech.

Report No. 83 (9 December 1947)

NEWSPAPER READERSHIP AND NEWSCAST LISTENING

Sample: more than 1,500 Bavarian adults and over 600 adults from Wuerttemberg-Baden, as well as 500 West Berliners.
Interviewing dates: latter part of September 1947. (10 pp.)

More than half of the people interviewed in Bavaria (53%) and Wuerttemberg-Baden (58%) considered themselves to be regular newspaper readers; in West Berlin nearly three-fourths (73%) made this claim. The most widely read paper in West Berlin was the British licensed *Telegraf*, followed by the American licensed *Tagesspiegel*.

A fourth (25%) of the people in Bavaria and Wuerttemberg-Baden (and 31 per cent in West Berlin) said that they listened to radio newscasts regularly. In both areas 90 per cent or more of the respondents listened to the local station. In West Berlin, Radio Berlin had 47 per cent of this audience, followed by RIAS with 38 per cent.

Those who considered themselves regular newspaper readers or radio listeners were generally inclined to think that the news they were getting was more reliable than what had been available during the war. Nonetheless, more than a quarter apparently felt that there had been little change.

Regular readers and listeners were also more inclined than others to assert an interest in political matters. Neither newspaper reading nor radio listening, however, appeared to influence opinions on the intention of the Allies regarding Germany; only about two in ten of all groups felt that the Allies would unite Germany.

Not unexpectedly, the more educated, men, urban residents, and those of higher socioeconomic status were more likely than their counterparts to read newspapers and listen to radio newscasts. In September 1947, only seven per cent of the Bavarian respondents and 13 per cent of the people in Wuerttemberg-Baden said that they read newspapers from other zones. More than eight in ten of those out-of-zone newspaper readers claimed preference for AMZON papers. The readers themselves possessed, for the most part, those characteristics usually associated with the most alert, best informed population groups.

Report No. 84 (17 December 1947)

WHO ARE THE EXPELLEES AND WHAT DO THEY THINK?

Sample: 466 expellees and 2,373 native Germans in the American Zone.
Interviewing dates: September 1947. (10 pp.)

According to the October 1946 German census – one year before this survey was made – 16.2 per cent of the AMZON population came from former German territories; 8.3 per cent from Czechoslovakia, 4.3 per cent from territories east of the Oder-Neisse, 1.8 per cent from southeastern Europe, and 1.8 per cent from other foreign countries. This report compares the socioeconomic characteristics and attitudes of these expellees with those of the native residents of the regions to which they had moved.

The expellees were rather similar to the native population, both in their socioeconomic characteristics and in their attitudes. Six out of ten expellees (60%) were living in small towns of under 2,000 population and as few as five per cent lived in cities of over 100,000; for native AMZON residents the figures were 49 and 22 per cent, respectively. The age distribution of both groups was about the same, as was their education.

The economic situation of the expellees, however, was considerably worse than that of the native residents. A third (34%) of the expellees received less than 70 *Reichsmarks* a month as compared to 19 per cent of the native population. Conversely, as few as 15 per cent of the new arrivals had monthly incomes above RM 200, whereas 34 per cent of the native Germans received this sum every month. The work status of expellees followed about the same pattern as that of the native Germans, except that few expellees were tradesmen and farmers and twice as many were working as unskilled laborers. Only 18 per cent of them were unemployed, and of these only three per cent were employable.

About three-fourths (72%) of the new arrivals were Catholics, whereas only 52 per cent of the native population was Catholic. Twenty-six per cent of the expellees and 45 per cent of the native Germans were Protestants. Native Germans tended to go to church more regularly than the newcomers.

Over half of the expellees (54%) as compared to 41 per cent of the native Germans said either that they favored none of the existing parties or that they had not yet decided which one they preferred. Among those who did express a party preference, about the same number of expellees (28%) and native Germans (27%) chose the SPD.

Whereas 66 per cent of the native population claimed that they did not get enough to eat, 80 per cent of the expellees made this claim. Their greatest worry, however, was simply the fact of being an evacuee coupled with the desire to return to their homes.

Close to 80 per cent of both expellees and native Germans lacked confidence in Allied reconstruction efforts. And the same number of new arrivals and native residents (41%) felt that local officials were working primarily for their own benefit. In addition, four out of ten expellees and long-time residents did not consider it worthwhile to hold political meetings. If forced to choose between communism or National Socialism, as few as two per cent of the expellees and four per cent of the native Germans chose communism. Almost the same number (37 and 38 per cent, respectively) felt that National Socialism was a bad idea; whereas 52 per cent of the native population thought it was a good idea badly carried out, 46 per cent of the expellees held this viewpoint.

Report No. 85 (17 December 1947)

SUMMARY OF TRENDS OF GERMAN PUBLIC OPINION

Sample: not specified.
Interviewing dates: between November 1945 and late 1947. (6 pp.)

Food. In November 1945, 20 per cent of the population mentioned food as their chief source of concern. This figure held, on the average, until March 1946 when it rose to 30 per cent — following a cut in food rations — and then to 40 per cent where it remained until February 1947; by the end of 1947 it had risen still higher, to 50 per cent. In Berlin the situation was consistently worse, with the figures rising from 52 per cent in March 1946 to a high of 74 per cent in July 1947, just before the harvest, and then back down to 57 per cent at the end of the year, following the harvest.

Fuel. Concern about fuel closely followed seasonal needs, dropping almost to nothing in the summer, rising sharply in September, and with the peak in February. In AMZON, however, this peak was 14 per cent whereas in Berlin during the same winter the figure was 41 per cent.

Other Worries. Mentions of clothing and shoe shortages rose, with eight per cent citing this in 1945 but 35 per cent concerned about it by 1947. The percentage concerned about prisoners of war decreased. Financial worries increased slightly.

Politics. In the fall of 1945, 69 per cent of the population held political meetings to be desirable but, by August 1947, the number responding in this way had dropped to 45 per cent. Local government officials did not maintain the confidence of the people: Whereas in August 1946, 42 per cent thought they were doing their jobs well, only half as many

(22%) gave them the same credit in October 1947. In 1945, 62 per cent said that they felt these officials were working for the good of the community, but by late 1947 only 45 per cent felt that this was the case. The number feeling that the jobs were being done for selfish reasons rose from 12 to 42 per cent.

Loss of confidence in the Americans also occurred. In August 1947, 44 per cent of the people said that they thought the United States was helping in the reconstruction of Germany; in November 1945, however, this positive attitude had been expressed by 70 per cent of the people. Confidence in Allied cooperation deteriorated radically as well: In January 1946, 15 per cent were pessimistic on this count; by the fall of 1947 the figure had risen to 70 per cent.

Confidence in news sources also declined, from a high of 75 per cent reporting daily in January 1946 that they read a newspaper to 55 per cent saying they did so in the fall of 1947.

Concomitant with the loss of confidence in the Allies was a consistent reduction in the number of persons who would choose communism over National Socialism if forced to pick one: In the fall of 1945, 35 per cent of the people said that they would take communism; in late 1947 only four per cent made this choice. Those saying "neither" tripled during this time from 22 to 66 per cent.

One figure that remained constant was the number of people (62%) who said they preferred economic security to guarantees of certain civil liberties.

Report No. 86 (17 December 1947)

SUMMARY OF REACTIONS TO END OF LONDON CONFERENCE

Sample: 188 West Berliners.
Interviewing dates: 16 December 1947. (3 pp.)

The interviews were conducted covertly on the streets of West Berlin following the conclusion of the London Conference. Two out of three (65%) had already heard about the end of the Conference. Many more (40%) blamed the Soviet Union for the breakup of the Conference than blamed the United States (1%). A plurality, however, spoke in terms of allotting some responsibility to both sides (42%), although even these people put primary blame on the Soviets for the outcome.

A large majority expected greater difficulties for Germany following the Conference. One in three persons (32%) believed that Germany would eventually be divided into two parts. Another one in four (26%) felt that there would be no change in the current state of affairs. About 15 per cent thought the situation would deteriorate, possibly into war. About the same number (14%) suggested that a new conference might be called.

Of those who felt that Germany would be split, 63 per cent expected no change in Berlin's status, 16 per cent thought that the Western Allies would leave and that the Soviets would take over the entire city, and 13 per cent thought that the city would also be split.

The morale of the general public did not seem noticeably affected by the results of the Conference although there were indications that the people felt that events were taking place over which they had no control. The report ends with the suggestion that the Germans might be induced to see that it was the Russian refusal to accept principles rather than Allied disagreement that caused adjournment.

Report No. 87 (9 January 1948)

THE TREND OF GERMAN ATTITUDES TOWARD ALLIED COOPERATION

Sample: an unspecified number comprising a representative sample of Germans in the American Zone and West Berlin. *Interviewing dates:* 25 July 1946, 5 June 1947, 25 August 1947, and 15 September 1947. (3 pp.)

The failure of the Foreign Ministers' Conference in London was widely interpreted as responsible for the gloomy outlook of the German people toward Allied cooperation. The data from the present study indicated, however, that the pessimism could not be attributed solely or even chiefly to the failure of that conference, since the attitude had been apparent six months before it took place.

In July 1946, a solid majority reportedly believed that the Allies would work together toward the unification of Germany. One year later, in the summer of 1947, a solid majority denied that the Allies would work together toward this end. Only in West Berlin were there more – but only a very few more — optimists in September (27%) than there had been in August 1947 (21%). Within the *Laender*, fewer Hessians tended to expect cooperation than did residents of Wuerttemberg-Baden or Bavaria; in fact, Bavarians were almost as optimistic as West Berliners.

Throughout the period under consideration, there was a marked difference in response between educational groups. Consistently, the best educated people were more dubious about Allied cooperation. The pessimists tended to be those who claimed to think about political affairs and claimed to be newspaper readers. Significantly, more of the optimists appeared ready to accept broad German responsibility for the war.

Report No. 88 (20 January 1948)

GERMAN OPINION ON THE PEOPLE'S PART IN POLITICAL AFFAIRS

Sample: a cross-section of over 3,400 Germans living in the American Zone and West Berlin.
Interviewing dates: October 1947. (9 pp.)

Opinion was divided on the issue of whether or not an increased interest in politics would help in the reconstruction of Germany: 41 per cent said it would help and 46 per cent felt it would not. Significantly, former members of the Nazi Party (48%) and people with 12 years or more schooling (51%) were more likely than others to deny the usefulness of an interest in politics. Of those who said that political activity would be of no help, 11 per cent said that they had lost confidence in politics and ten per cent said that working directly on the problems of reconstruction would be worth far more.

Seven in ten AMZON Germans (70%) would reportedly turn down a reasonable political office if they were offered one. In contrast to this, 82 per cent expressed a willingness to work an hour longer every day for the reconstruction of their country.

According to a third (34%) of the AMZON population and almost a half of the West Berliners (46%), the individual could not influence the activities of the political parties. About two-thirds of the AMZON respondents (63%) and 78 per cent of the West Berliners, however, felt that in the future the people ought to have more influence on political activities.

Report No. 89 (22 January 1948)

RECEPTION OF THE PAMPHLET "OFFEN GESAGT"

Sample: 140 persons in the American Sector of Berlin.
Interviewing dates: not specified. (8 pp.)

Several pamphlets were published and sold to the German public in fairly large numbers as an overt orientation operation of Military Government. This is the first study made of such a pamphlet and concerns *Offen Gesagt (Speaking Frankly)* by former Secretary of State James Byrnes. The respondents were chosen to represent three specific groups: age groupings, social status groupings, and men and women.

Slightly more than half (56%) of the people tested read the pamphlet from beginning to end. The pamphlet appealed most strongly to people in middle status positions: those with nine to eleven years of education (63%), those between 30 and 45 years of age (59%), and those from the lower-middle class (55%) as well as the upper and upper-middle class (57%); also, many more men (59%) than women (39%) found it very interesting.

Although young people and women were not as keenly interested as the middle-aged and men, both the young and the women claimed as frequently as their counterpart groups that they had learned something from the booklet. Among those who claimed to have learned something, 21 per cent mentioned details about the Yalta Conference, 19 per cent mentioned Allied disagreements with a negative emphasis upon the Soviet Union, and 16 per cent cited the Berlin-Moscow pact indicating that Hitler's meeting with Molotov showed the latter's unreasonable attitude.

Practically all respondents (93%) said that the translation was good and half (49%) of the respondents felt that stylistically it was clear and understandable. Two in three (66%) said that they would have bought the pamphlet on the newsstand if they had seen it there.

Report No. 90 (23 January 1948)

GERMAN OPINIONS ON SOCIALIZATION OF INDUSTRY

Sample: unspecified number of respondents in the American Zone and West Berlin.
Interviewing dates: November 1947. (8 pp.)

The survey attempted to get at attitudes toward the socialization or nationalization (*Verstaatlichung*) of industry.

Four in ten AMZON respondents (41%) and 50 per cent of the West Berliners felt that the workers would not be better off if industry were socialized; only 30 per cent in AMZON and 36 per cent in West Berlin said that they would be better off. There was more support for the socialization of heavy industry (49 per cent in AMZON and 57 per cent in West Berlin).

When asked whether the responsibility of German industrialists for World War II was very great, great, or slight, 51 per cent of the people in AMZON said that it was very great or great. Two-thirds of those people who thought workers would be better off under socialization as well as two-thirds of those who favored socialization in part or in total also placed heavy blame on the industrialists.

No population or geographical groups favored total socialization of industry in significant numbers. Tending to approve the socialization of heavy industry only were adherents of the SPD, independent businessmen, officials, skilled laborers, and the middle classes. Opponents of any socialization at all were found in largest numbers among LDP/DVP sympathizers, people from upper socioeconomic levels, and the highly educated.

Comparison of opinions on socialization of industry with those on the workers' lot under such a regime showed some interesting results. Not surprisingly, people opposed to any or all socialization were almost completely agreed (89%) that it would not be a good thing for the worker. Similarly, advocates of complete socialization rallied in equal numbers (87%) to the claim that it would be a good thing for the worker. In contrast, the group favoring partial socialization (30 per cent in AMZON) did not fall clearly into either extreme. As many of them claimed the workers would be badly off under socialization (45%) as claimed they would gain from it (41%).

Report No. 91 (24 January 1948)

GERMAN CONCEPTIONS OF AMERICAN BARTERING AND BLACK MARKETEERING

Sample: not specified, in the American Zone and West Berlin.
Interviewing dates: not specified (5 pp.)

Three out of ten AMZON Germans (30%) thought that there were Americans in Germany who were enriching themselves through barter activities; in West Berlin the figure was 48 per cent. A similar proportion in AMZON (29%) felt that the United States occupation troops were using German food supplies; but in West Berlin only five per cent thought this to be true. A somewhat larger number (36 per cent in AMZON and 30 per cent in West Berlin) reported hearing that Americans wasted or destroyed food.

A close relationship was found between attitudes on black marketeering and alleged American barter and food practices. In AMZON, 71 per cent of the population said that black marketeering was being practiced in their communities and 73 per cent felt that the German officials were not doing all they could to stop it. Of those who thought that there was a great deal of black marketeering going on in their community, 49 per cent said that Americans were enriching themselves in Germany by bartering; of those who said that there was no black market, only 15 per cent said that the Americans were gaining from barter.

A large number of persons who knew Americans (42%) said that the Americans were enriching themselves, but only 26 per cent of those who did not know any Americans felt this to be true.

Better-educated groups and upper-class groups tended more frequently than their counterparts to think that Americans gained from barter. Otherwise there were no marked differences among the various population groups in attitudes on these matters.

Report No. 92 (9 February 1948)

READERS OF "MEIN KAMPF"

Sample: 3,000 residents of the American Zone and West Berlin.
Interviewing dates: November 1947. (4 pp.)

Two in ten AMZON Germans (19%) admitted having read all or part of *Mein Kampf*. People who had read it in the greatest numbers were those considered to be among the book reading public, the well educated, professional and businessmen, and those in the upper and upper-middle socioeconomic levels. More men than women had read it, as well as more men who had been in military service than those who had not. About the same number of people in all age groups had read the book.

Among former NSDAP members, 72 per cent of those who had read *Mein Kampf* but only 50 per cent of the nonreaders said that every person has certain inalienable rights; among those who had not belonged to the party, 64 per cent of those who had read it and 43 per cent of those who had not felt that there were such rights.

Report No. 93 (11 February 1948)

"THE CREAM OF THE CROP" TWO YEARS LATER

Sample: 78 former prisoners of war who had attended a course on democracy at Fort Getty and who filled out a mailed questionnaire.

Interviewing dates: spring 1947. (15 pp.)

At the end of the war, a group of specially selected German prisoners of war in the United States was sent to a school at Fort Getty to learn about democracy and the principles for which the United States stands. They were later released in Germany with no special provision having been made for their future. Some maintained contact with each other and with their former teachers. Not surprisingly, the proportion of professional people and white collar workers among the group was very high (73%) and their political attitudes differed considerably from the picture presented by the population as a whole.

The Fort Getty respondents said that, on their return to Germany, they were more impressed by the chaotic state in the mental attitudes of the people than by the physical and material conditions. Nearly half of them mentioned widespread corruption, low levels of both morals and morale.

Four in ten said that the length of the occupation would depend on what happened in the international arena; one in ten felt it would last until there was a functioning democracy in Germany. Four in ten thought it should last until democracy was established in the country. On the future of Germany, less than a fifth thought the country would recover regardless of outside help and an equal number were completely pessimistic.

Seven out of ten considered the general economic, political, and social conditions to be the greatest obstacle to the democratization of Germany. Half of all respondents accused the Germans of political apathy, intolerance, and lack of a genuine concept of freedom. Three out of ten were severely critical of the denazification process and many felt that this hindered the education of the German population to democratic ways.

Nearly a fourth of the respondents (23%) were members of one of the political parties, whereas only about five per cent of the general public claimed membership. Over a third (35%) preferred the SPD, one in seven belonged to the LDP/DVP, and one in ten to the CDU/CSU. The third of the respondents who had disclaimed preference for any party said that the parties pursued self-centered policies, inspired little confidence, were old-fashioned, and many blamed them for Hitler's rise to power.

Quite a large number refused to make predictions concerning their own futures but half of all respondents were rather confident and considered their prospects good. One point worth noting was the concern expressed by many over whether or not to take an active part in politics. Siding with any political party was considered dangerous, but a strict neutrality was also thought to be disadvantageous.

Three-fourths of the group had already thought about emigrating. Four in ten had decided not to leave, an equal number said that they did hope to emigrate, and another two in ten said they would consider it if the economic or political situation in Germany turned out to be hopeless.

Less than half claimed to be sufficiently well-informed on current events. One-fourth mentioned the lack of newspapers, radio sets, and preoccupation with burdens of daily life.

Significantly, 64 per cent of the group was employed at the time of the questionnaire in some sort of government work. The Fort Getty certificate proved to be helpful to four out of ten in obtaining such work. A fifth had never made use of the certificate. Nine per cent were white-collar workers and professionals, and five per cent worked in private business.

Report No. 94 (24 February 1948)

CONTACTS BETWEEN GERMANS AND AMERICANS

Sample: a representative sample of people in the American Zone and West Berlin.
Interviewing dates: November 1947. (16 pp.)

About a quarter of AMZON Germans (27%) and West Berliners (25%) said that they had become acquainted with Americans after the war. Most of these contacts were made by chance or through professional and work channels, and most of the acquaintanceships remained extremely casual. Germans who knew Americans tended to be predominantly from the upper socioeconomic and educational strata; more men and younger people than women and older people had American acquaintances. Very few people (12%) had received gift packages from Americans; recipients were more likely to be residents of medium-size cities than those of large cities or rural areas.

Although knowing Americans appeared to have little influence on general attitudes and opinions, it did affect opinions relating to Americans in Germany. Of those who knew Americans, 63 per cent said that German employees were well treated by the Americans, whereas among those who did not know Americans only 52 per cent felt this to be true. On certain issues, such as American wastefulness and negligence regarding property, people who knew Americans were more critical than those who did not.

More significantly, personal relationships with Americans did not affect views on certain basic issues. Among those under 40 years of age with nine or more years of education, National Socialism was a good idea badly carried out for a sizable majority of both those who knew Americans (68%) and those who did not (70%). In both groups, just over 40 per cent felt that the Germans were responsible for Hitler's rise to power and about a fourth said they were to blame for his staying in power.

A third of the AMZON Germans thought that the United States occupation troops were more popular then than they had been a year earlier, another third said the popularity level was the same, and 22 per cent felt it had diminished. Those who said that they were more popular also held generally more favorable attitudes towards Americans. Those who said that the Americans had become less popular than formerly were also more prone to attitudes consistent with Nazism; 53 per cent felt that some races are more fit to rule than others.

More West Berliners than AMZON Germans thought that the Americans had gained in popularity. The same was true of men, people with eight years of education, and older people, whereas the young and those with nine to eleven years of education tended toward the belief that the Americans were less popular.

Report No. 95 (25 February 1948)

APPRAISAL OF THE CONTENT OF EDUCATION AND EDUCATIONAL FACILITIES

Sample: 451 adults in West Berlin and 223 in Stuttgart, all 18 years of age and over.
Interviewing dates: January 1948. (8 pp.)

The outlook toward educational problems in themselves did not differ markedly between the two cities. More people in West Berlin (55%) than in Stuttgart (18%) expressed concern about the lack of clothing and shoes for the children. Shortage of buildings, however, concerned the respondents in Stuttgart (43%) more than it did those in West Berlin (16%).

Nearly everyone in both communities (90%) supported the teaching of religion in the schools and large majorities (60%) felt that such instruction should be compulsory. In Stuttgart, however, 63 per cent felt it ought to be handled by clerics whereas in West Berlin only 37 per cent favored clerics as contrasted with 47 per cent who felt school teachers should give religious instruction.

Only minorities supported beating of students as a basic right of teachers (under 30 per cent). Large majorities in West Berlin (86%) and Stuttgart (85%) favored the formation of a school board in every city. Few West Berliners (24%) and Stuttgart residents (14%) thought that the dismissal of teachers who were former NSDAP members had had favorable effects upon the educational system.

In both cities, residents gave as the chief aim of general education "a comprehensive general education" (37 per cent in West Berlin and 52 per cent in Stuttgart); for West Berliners the second most important goal was discipline (28%) whereas in Stuttgart it was training for a future job (20%). The educational philosophy of various groupings showed a primary emphasis upon order and conduct, with a fairly heavy vote for vocational training among the old, the lower class, and those with eight years or less education. The youth of Germany, however, those with nine or more years of education, and the upper and middle-class members overwhelmingly selected the other two objectives – a rounded education and the development of independent thinking.

About half (49 per cent in West Berlin and 51 per cent in Stuttgart) the public said that the failure to teach history would have very serious effects. Teaching of history was considered least important by those who regarded vocational training as the prime aim of education (57%) and most important by those who considered critical thinking the main objective (55%). Asked why history was not being taught at the time of the survey, the bulk of those who had opinions pointed to a general confusion in the political situation, a revision in the conception of history, or the fact that the Allies and the "experts" disagreed on matters of interpretation (48 per cent in West Berlin; 31 per cent in Stuttgart). About a fifth of the total sample (22 and 21 per cent, respectively) responded that nothing more dared be said about militarism or Nazism. Only eight and four per cent, respectively, thought it necessary or a good idea to remove the influence of militaristic and Nazi ideas. Ten per cent in West Berlin and 26 per cent in Stuttgart had no opinion on this question.

Report No. 96 (3 March 1948)

GERMAN YOUTH VERSUS ADULTS ON QUESTIONS OF DEMOCRACY

Sample: 1,000 adults and 2,000 young people from the American Zone and samples from both groups in West Berlin.
Interviewing dates: December 1947. (5 pp.)

German youth and adults gave an edge to democratic principles when they were asked to choose between a democratic and an authoritarian way of forming a new club. Of the AMZON young people between 13 and 25 years old, 57 per cent thought that the leader should be chosen by majority vote, as compared to 40 per cent who would have the leader appointed. About the same number of adults (54%) were in the same democratic camp. Young people between the ages of 13 and 25 who lived in cities were the most democratic, and boys and men over 16 voted for majority rule considerably more often than girls and women. Youngsters belonging to youth clubs that elected their leaders supported democratic principles (71%) to a greater extent than members of clubs that appointed their leaders (49%). Youngsters and adults who might be considered politically informed were more likely to choose the democratic alternative than were those who were uninformed. Although in general those who kept up with current events were also most likely to favor electing their leader, mass media did not seem to affect the opinion of those between ten and 17 as much as the older groups.

Report No. 97 (3 March 1948)

BERLIN REACTIONS TO NAGY'S PAMPHLET "MACHTRAUB IN UNGARN"

Sample: 149 people from the American Sector of Berlin (controlled for age, social status, and sex only).
Interviewing dates: not specified. (7 pp.)

Machtraub in Ungarn (*Power Grab in Hungary*) by Ferenc Nagy, like Secretary of State James Byrnes' volume, *Offen Gesagt* (*Speaking Frankly*), was published and sold to the German public as an overt orientation operation of the Military Government (cf. Report No. 89).

Unlike *Offen Gesagt*, whose appeal was concentrated in middle status, middle-aged, and slightly above average educational groups, Nagy's booklet evoked interest among all groups. The least interested seemed to be those under 30 (39%), the well educated (54%), and women (49%). Lower interest among the more sophisticated seemed to be attributable to the sensational character of the pamphlet.

About 75 per cent of those given the booklet actually read it through from cover to cover. Within the individual groups, those who had finished it were predominantly in the age group from 46 to 60 (80%), those with a high school education (78%), men (84%), and people of lower middle-class status (78%). Only 59 per cent of the respondents reported recommending it to someone else; for the Byrnes book the figure had been 71 per cent.

While 70 per cent of the respondents claimed to have learned something from *Offen Gesagt*, only 48 per cent made the same claim for *Machtraub*. Many more women (57%) than men (39%) felt they had come upon some new fact. More persons under 30 (53%) admitted having learned something than the middle-aged (44%) or the old (49%). Pressed to indicate what it was they had learned, most (54%) of these people referred to the "crass brutality" of the Russians.

A very large majority (84%) of those who read the pamphlet thought it good rather than fair (11%) or poor (2%). Only three per cent expressed no opinion.

Practically everyone (87%) thought the presentation of the facts to be fair rather than one-sided. Poorly educated people and those under 30 were slightly more likely to criticize the factual presentation than was any other group.

Technically, there were almost no objections to the booklet. Nearly all approved the style of writing and the translation. To some, the cover seemed to smack of sensationalism, but relatively few sharply rejected the cover on this ground. Almost no one (5%) said that the price was beyond their means.

Report No. 98 (6 March 1948)

GOVERNMENT BY POLITICIANS, EXPERTS, OR THE PEOPLE?

Sample: a cross-section of residents in the American Zone. *Interviewing dates:* November 1947. (4 pp.)

An overwhelming majority was in favor of the popular determination of policy as opposed to its determination either by politicians or experts.

Those most strongly opposed to both politicians and experts were members of political parties; they appeared most consistently in favor of determination of policy by the people. Educated people appeared to differentiate sharply between the two choices: When they could choose between politicians and the people, they rejected the former emphatically (13%) in favor of the people (85%), but when the choice was between the people and the experts, the vote for the former dropped below the average for the entire population; almost three out of ten (29%) educated people preferred experts rather than the people.

When asked whether they thought some human rights to be inalienable, or whether the state had a right to suspend any rights when necessary, those who had voted for rule by the people tended also to vote for the inviolability of human rights (52%), while the others tended to vote for their suspension when necessary (46%). Similarly, when questioned about racial theory, those who thought that the experts should determine policy also tended to think that some races were more fit to rule than others (48%).

Report No. 99 (5 March 1948)

A REPORT ON GERMAN YOUTH

Sample: 1,996 respondents between ages of 10 and 25 from the American Zone and 341 from West Berlin; and 1,171 over the age of 26 from the American Zone and West Berlin.
Interviewing dates: late December 1947. (17 pp.)

The purpose of the study was to analyze three aspects of German youth: the membership, organization, and activities of youth clubs; club members contrasted with nonmembers as to interests, activities, attitudes, and group activities; young Germans contrasted with older Germans regarding interests and activities.

In AMZON, 15 per cent of the younger sample claimed membership in youth groups; in West Berlin the figure was 11 per cent. City youth were more likely to belong than were rural youth. Most members (78%) went to the club at least once a week. In most areas, the majority of clubs had either a special room or club house. Over half the members said that their clubs had no financial support and only a third in AMZON (37 per cent in West Berlin) reported paying dues.

Positions of leadership were limited among AMZON club members as a whole. Only seven per cent held any office. In West Berlin 17 per cent held some office. Older members tended to hold office more often than younger members. Office-holders tended to be male (68%), from the middle class (68%). A majority, both in AMZON (51%) and West Berlin (53%), said that their leaders were appointed by outsiders.

Few AMZON club members (11%) but as many as 32 per cent in West Berlin complained about the lack of good leadership and discipline and the fact that groups of different ages were in the same room.

Of those club members who had also belonged to the Hitler Youth, 63 per cent contrasted the militarism of the earlier group with the freedom and democracy of the new. The most popular activities in the Hitler Youth had been social activities (36%) followed by sports and games (32%). The most disliked aspect was the militarism of the organization (43%).

Club members, although more likely than nonmembers to read youth magazines and other publications and to listen to the radio, were not better informed on such matters as world leaders or the name of their local mayor. Attitudes toward democratic and ethical values did not differ greatly between members and nonmembers. Both groups selected similar figures as the greatest German: Goethe and Schiller ranked first, nonpolitical figures came second, nationalist or military figures third; almost half gave no reply. Club members appeared to come from a relatively higher socioeconomic level than non-members and were more often regular churchgoers. Members and nonmembers did not differ with respect to the occupation of the head of the family.

Among all age groups, the most read sections of the newspapers were the local news and the advertisements. A majority of radio listeners preferred musical programs. Older people liked news and commentaries more than did the younger. Large majorities of all age groups did not like to attend lectures. Leisure-time activities were fairly similar in all age groups, with handicrafts and studying, writing, and reading mentioned most frequently.

Report No. 100 (March 1948)

TRENDS IN GERMAN PUBLIC OPINION

Sample: the number of respondents varied from 365 in the first survey to 4,000 interviewed in January 1948; the total number of persons interviewed was over 16 million in the American Zone and West Berlin.
Interviewing dates: from 26 October 1945 to 5 January 1948 during which time more than fifty full-scale surveys were conducted. (43 pp.)

This report summarizes in graphic form major trends of German opinion in the American occupied areas, and covers seven major issues: reorientation, politics, media, the occupation, economic affairs, food, and expellees.

Reorientation. In 1947 surveys an average of 52 per cent accepted National Socialism as a good idea badly carried out; this was a rise of five percentage points over the previous year but only two points higher than it had been in 1945. If forced to choose between communism and National Socialism, a plurality preferred the former in 1945, most people rejected both in 1946, and by 1947, although the "neither" category remained large, more chose National Socialism, and almost no one picked communism. Two years after the war's end, the number of Germans willing to assume responsibility for their country's part in bringing on the war continued a downward trend. About four in ten AMZON Germans felt that some races are more fit to rule than others.

Whereas before January 1948 over half the public had accepted the right of communists to speak on the radio, after this date only a little more than a third did so. From the outset, large majorities of AMZON Germans said that, if they had to choose, they would prefer a government guaranteeing jobs rather than one that promoted personal liberty.

Politics. The number of Germans who claimed to be informed about politics continued to drop after 1947 and the number of people who did not wish to see their sons enter politics remained at over 75 per cent. In all surveys, about a third of the people said that they thought about politics, with the rest leaving this task to "the others." In early 1947 a high of 72 per cent said that they thought political meetings were of value, but by the end of that year the figure had dropped to 45 per cent; in early 1948 it had again risen, but only to 58 per cent. Confidence in the motives of local German officials showed a definite downward trend; disenchantment with the performance of these officials was also growing.

Throughout AMZON, the CDU/CSU lost half the popular support it had enjoyed in the fall of 1945. Meanwhile the LDP/DVP gained, particularly in Wuerttemberg-Baden. At the same time, the number of people liking none of the parties tripled.

Media. Regular newspaper readership declined between early 1946 and the spring of 1947, leveling off at about half the AMZON population; in West Berlin about three-quarters claimed to be regular readers. In January 1948, 56 per cent of the AMZON population were regular or occasional radio listeners; more than four in ten consistently claimed to be nonlisteners. In January 1948 only 47 per cent felt that they were getting more accurate news coverage than during the war; the "no opinion" replies rose sharply from 22 per cent in January 1947 to 49 per cent in January 1948. In early 1946, 50 per cent of the AMZON public felt that newspaper coverage was more complete than that given on the radio; by January 1948 the two were given equal ratings.

The Occupation. Confidence in Allied efforts to rebuild Germany dropped from 43 per cent in September 1946 to only three in ten by January 1948. Confidence in American efforts to rebuild Germany, which had dropped from 70 to 44 per cent between 1945 and 1947, rose to 55 per cent in January 1948, possibly because of the Marshall Plan. No more than a third ever felt that the four powers would cooperate in rebuilding Germany; in early 1948, in fact, less than one in ten held this view.

Between January 1946 and January 1948, there was a sharp increase in pessimism regarding a united Germany as an end product of the occupation, from 71 per cent saying that the Allies would cooperate to 80 per cent saying that they would not.

Ever increasing numbers of Germans said that the United States would be the most influential country in the world throughout the next ten years and that this influence would be toward peace. Almost all who named the Soviet Union saw war as a result. Majority opinion continued to hold that the Americans ought to reconstruct Germany as soon as possible in order to prevent its falling prey to communism.

Economic Affairs. In January 1946, 67 per cent of the AMZON population said that their family incomes were sufficient to meet necessary expenses; two years later, however, only 57 per cent did so. Large majorities in West Berlin claimed that they could not meet living costs. There was no discernible trend on opinions concerning the direction which prices would take. Fluctuations also marked the trend in opinions on the future conditions in AMZON. On the whole, between January 1946 and June 1947 about as many people thought that the *Reichsmark* would not maintain its value as thought it would.

Increasingly large numbers of AMZON residents had come to the conclusion that a local black market existed and was serious. In February 1946, 51 per cent thought that there was no black market but by January 1948, 71 per cent recognized there was; similarly, at the earlier date only 15 per cent felt that it was serious, but by the later date 47 per cent thought so. At the same time, confidence in official efforts to stop the black market decreased sharply, although in early 1948 the trend seemed to be on the upswing once again.

Food. Increasing numbers of people cited food as their chief source of concern, having risen from only 17 per cent in AMZON in 1945 to 53 per cent in 1948. Clothing and shoes followed in importance and the percentage mentioning them had also increased. Majority opinion in AMZON continued to hold that the ration card system was being handled fairly, although the number thinking so had decreased sharply from 93 per cent in late 1945 to 64 per cent in January 1948. Majorities, often large ones, maintained that they did not get enough food to do their jobs well; in West Berlin the figure was as high as eight in ten.

Expellees. By January 1948, as many as 93 per cent of the Germans held the opinion that the expulsions had been unjustified. Both expellees and native residents were almost unanimous in feeling that the expellees would like to return to their homelands. As in the previous year, about half of the AMZON population said that the expellees would get along well with the local residents and about four in ten said that they would not; Hessians were most optimistic on this score, the residents of Wuerttemberg-Baden the most pessimistic. The expellees themselves were less satisfied in January 1948 with their reception in Germany than they had been in the fall of 1946.

Report No. 101 (24 March 1948)

GERMAN YOUTH AND ADULTS VIEW
INDIVIDUAL RESPONSIBILITY

Sample: 1,000 adults and 2,000 young people in the American Zone and West Berlin.
Interviewing dates: late December 1947 and early January 1948. (7 pp.)

Few German youngsters between 10 and 12 considered an individual member of a club responsible for the actions of other club members. When asked if a boy should help pay for a window broken by other members of his club while he was not present, about a fourth (23%) of the children between 10 and 12 thought he should help pay, while over half of those between 13 and 25 and 38 per cent of those 26 years old and over supported such group responsibility. In Bavaria, Hesse, and Wuerttemberg-Baden, youth and adults tended to have about the same idea on this question. The size of town that children between 10 and 12 lived in seemed to have little or no effect on their attitudes although those between 13 and 25 who lived in large cities were considerably more conscious of the group spirit than the same age group living in small towns. Of the children who had belonged to one of the Hitler youth groups, 48 per cent thought the boy ought to help pay for the window.

In considering what a young boy should do whose club friends have decided to steal a lamp, respondents between the ages of 18 and 25 as well as adults — especially West Berliners — were most likely to recommend that the boy take some positive steps registering his disapproval. Those who advocated such action were from the middle socioeconomic groups, former members of the Hitler youth groups, the more highly educated, and those who kept up with current events. Children of ten and eleven were least likely to say that, if they were the young boy in question, they would go as far as to leave the club, try to prevent others from stealing, or tell someone about the plan.

The next and final sketch continued the previous one, with the young boy accompanying his friends in the theft of the lamp and the entire group being caught. Since he had opposed the action, was the young boy to blame or not? In AMZON, 80 per cent of the children between 10 and 17, 85 per cent of those between 18 and 25, and 79 per cent of the adults considered him guilty. In West Berlin, young people between the ages of 18 and 25 almost unanimously (97%) gave the verdict guilty, while 81 per cent of those between 10 and 17 and 87 per cent of the adults gave the same verdict.

Report No. 102 (24 March 1948)

PATRONAGE OF U.S. INFORMATION CENTERS

Sample: an unspecified number of adults in the American Zone, West Berlin, and Bremen.
Interviewing dates: March 1948. (3 pp.)

One out of every 100 adult Germans in the American Zone said he had visited an *Amerika Haus* (United States Information Center). In West Berlin the figure was slightly higher with two out of every 100, and in Bremen it was as high as three out of 100.

Knowledge of what the centers had to offer was not very extensive, either. More than nine out of ten in AMZON claimed to know nothing about them, in West Berlin 89 per cent disclaimed any such knowledge, and in Bremen the figure was 78 per cent.

People living in cities were both more likely to have heard about the information centers and to have visited one. Even in the largest cities (250,000 and over), however, knowledge of them was only at the eight per cent level and a mere one per cent had visited one.

When people were asked about the *Amerika Haus* nearest them it turned out that the best known were those in Heidelberg (14%), Wuerzburg (11%), Darmstadt (8%), Bamberg (8%), and Regensburg (7%).

Although very few AMZON residents frequented information centers, those who did represented the leadership groups, those with higher levels of education, men, and readers of foreign periodicals.

Report No. 103 (24 March 1948)

READERSHIP OF POLITICAL BOOKS AND PAMPHLETS

Sample: 3,000 residents of the American Zone.
Interviewing dates: February 1948. (3 pp.)

The purpose of the report was to ascertain the readership of five political books or pamphlets: *Der SS-Staat* by Eugen Kogon (read by 2.4 per cent of the sample), *Offen Gesagt* by James Byrnes (2.0%), *Hinter dem eisernen Vorhang* (2.9%), *Machtraub in Ungarn* by Ferenc Nagy (0.5%), and *Marshall stellt klar* (0.7%). Readership was extremely limited, with more men having read them than women. And compared with the population as a whole, the readers tended to be better educated, city dwellers from the upper socioeconomic levels.

Report No. 104 (24 March 1948)

THE MARSHALL PLAN IN PROSPECT

Sample: 3,003 adults in the American Zone.
Interviewing dates: March 1948. (5 pp.)

In August 1947 nearly half (47%) of a representative cross-section of adults in the American Zone said that they had heard of the Marshall Plan. By March 1948, six months later, 69 per cent claimed to know about it. Among those who had heard of it, 75 per cent were in favor of it and 85 per cent thought that it would have a favorable effect upon living conditions. About twice as many people thought that the chances for success were poor (13%) or nonexistent (1%) as believed the chances were very high (6%); most people thought they were only high (36%) or just fair (32%).

Many people in AMZON (53%) felt that American aid would not be sufficient; in West Berlin the figure was even higher, at 59 per cent. Women (27%) were less confident of the sufficiency of American aid than men (35%), the young less so than the old. People whose education or status was low tended, also, to be slightly more pessimistic than those with more education or higher status.

Among those who had heard of the Marshall Plan, 80 per cent felt it had been set up to help keep western Europe from turning communist; the second most frequently chosen reason (44%) was America's sincere desire to help Europe; 29 per cent thought it was to ensure allies in case of war with the Soviet Union; and about the same number (25%) said it was a way for the United States to dump goods resulting from overproduction. The percentages of young people who accepted American intentions as sincere (37%) was smaller than it was among the middle-aged (45%) or among those over 50 (51%). Attitudes of confidence that the plan would be carried out were strongly related to the belief in the sincerity of American motives.

Report No. 105 (27 March 1948)

INTERNATIONALISM IN GERMANY

Sample: 3,750 people 18 years of age or older in the American Zone, West Berlin, and Bremen.
Interviewing dates: first three weeks of March 1948. (7 pp.)

Half (49%) of the people interviewed had heard of plans to create a Western European Union; those with more than twelve years of education were much more likely to have heard of it (94%) as was true of those with upper- and upper-middle-class status (85%).

Almost no one opposed the idea of such a union and confidence in its realization was fairly high. Nonetheless, obstacles were known to exist. Only one in 20 (5%) saw no obstacles, while about 35 per cent gave no response. Of those who thought the chances for realization of such a union were very high, 48 per cent cited the Soviet Union and communism as possible difficulties, another 16 per cent mentioned nationalism. Of those who thought the chances were poor or even nil, 35 per cent mentioned the Soviet Union and communism, 41 per cent cited nationalism, and 14 per cent could give no reason.

While a solid majority (59%) of the general public and even more West Berliners (66%) believed that there would be another world war within a generation, a large number of people (45%) thought that a Western European Union would decrease the possibilities of such a war. Only 13 per cent felt the union would increase the possibilities for war. Significantly, of the small percentage of persons (3%) who opposed the idea of a Western European Union, two-thirds (65%) thought that it would either increase or not affect the chances for a third world war.

Practically the same people who knew about the Western European Union also knew about the United Nations. But confidence that the UN could secure peace was markedly lower than was confidence in the possibility of realizing a Western European Union. Only about a third (35%) of the people who had ever heard of the UN granted that it had a fair or better than fair chance of ensuring peace. In contrast, 45 per cent of all the people believed that a Western European Union would decrease the chances of war, if not prevent one.

Report No. 106 (27 March 1948)

THE RADIO AUDIENCE IN AMZON, BERLIN, AND BREMEN

Sample: 3,700 respondents in the American Zone, West Berlin, and Bremen.
Interviewing dates: the last three weeks of February 1948.
(9 pp.)

More than half (52%) of AMZON adults listened to newscasts regularly or occasionally. This audience comprised 67 per cent of the sample in West Berlin and 76 per cent in Bremen. The metropolitan station in each *Land* virtually monopolized the audience in its area. Radio Stuttgart had more listeners outside the borders of the *Land* than any of the other *Laender* stations and Radio Leipzig had the largest audience of any station outside the American Zone. Whereas Radio Berlin was the most popular station (47%) in West Berlin in September 1947 and RIAS was a close second (37%), by February 1948 the situation had reversed itself: RIAS had 57 per cent of the audience and Radio Berlin had only 31 per cent. Only in West Berlin was there an important fraction that had tuned out because a broadcast was considered untrue (36%) while 26 per cent had done so when they thought that a program was bad.

More listeners (31%) than nonlisteners (18%) favored a government whose aim was to protect freedom of elections, speech, and press, although both listeners (62%) as well as nonlisteners (69%) favored a government whose aim was peace and order.

Exactly half of those who listened to news on the radio (50%) felt that the news they were getting was more accurate than what they had heard during the war. The main source of political information for newscast listeners was the radio (66%), while for nonlisteners it was newspapers (61%).

Newscast listeners tended to be of higher socioeconomic status (72%) than nonlisteners (28%), and to have more education (66%) than nonlisteners (34%). Men (59%) were more likely to listen than women (47%), city people more than rural people, and the younger more than the older.

About a fourth of the AMZON radio audience had listened to the Military Government's Thursday evening broadcasts, although only ten per cent of the entire AMZON population had done so. People who had listened and were also able to describe the programs accurately gave strong majority approval (68%).

Three-fourths of the AMZON radio audience listened to the "Voice of America" broadcasts. Regular VOA listeners differed from radio listeners in general, and even more so from nonlisteners, in their attitudes toward various issues: 64 per cent of them thought the news was more accurate at the time than it had been during the war, 39 per cent would hope for a government guaranteeing civil liberties as against one whose chief concern was peace and order, and 61 per cent felt that the exercise of the right to criticize the government would not endanger the peace and order of the state. Regular VOA listeners were also the ones who made a point of turning on that station, as compared with listeners to other stations who claimed indifference as to whether or not they turned on any particular station.

Report No. 107 (29 March 1948)

PUBLIC RECEPTION OF THE BIZONAL ADMINISTRATION

Sample: 3,000 in the American Zone, 500 in West Berlin, and in the third part of the study 316 people in Bremen. *Interviewing dates:* 6 October 1947; 5 January 1948; and the first weeks of March 1948. (5 pp.)

The report presents a summary analysis of attitudes toward the Bizonal administration. In October 1947 only about a third (31%) of the AMZON public had heard of the Bizonal Council, which by that time had been in operation for some months. By

January 1948, an additional ten per cent claimed to know of the new organization. And two months later the number had risen sharply to six in ten.

Between October 1947 and January 1948 confidence that Bizonia would improve living conditions dropped from 73 per cent to 53 per cent. In March 1948, 44 per cent said that conditions had been unfavorably affected, while only 36 per cent said that they were better. Indeed, at this time, only 20 per cent were satisfied with the work of the Bizonal Economic Council, whereas 64 per cent expressed dissatisfaction. Half of the dissatisfied commented that nothing was getting done.

Not unexpectedly, the more alert, the better educated, and the more sophisticated members of society were those most likely to be informed about the existence of a Bizonal administration. Almost all (96%) of the college educated adults but less than half (47%) of those with only seven years of schooling could claim in March to have heard of Bizonia. Again, more men (78%) than women (46%) said they were informed. The well educated also tended to be somewhat more dissatisfied (70%) than the poorly educated (60%).

In March 1948, when asked whether they thought Bizonia would aid or impede the unification of all four zones, a plurality (39%) in AMZON and still more in West Berlin (47%) and Bremen (46%) felt that Bizonia increased the possibility of four-zone unity. Among those who knew of Bizonia, 43 per cent thought that it would help and 28 per cent felt that it would impede unification; a third (33%) of those who had not previously heard of Bizonia responded, when informed of the plan, that it would help, and half that many (16%) thought it would impede reunification.

Report No. 108 (29 March 1948)

MAGAZINE READERS

Sample: more than 3,700 adults in the American Zone, West Berlin, and Bremen.
Interviewing dates: during the last three weeks of February 1948. (5 pp.)

About a quarter (24%) of the AMZON Germans 18 years of age and over claimed to be magazine readers. This represented an increase since December 1946 when the figure had been 18 per cent. The three overt American publications, *Heute, Neue Auslese,* and *Amerikanische Rundschau,* were mentioned more frequently by AMZON readers than any other single magazine. In West Berlin, which had a greater ratio of magazine readers in the first place (42%), the publication *Sie* was more popular (13%) than *Heute* (8%), and the Berlin *Illustrierte* had the same number of readers (8%) as *Heute.*

Very few Germans (nine per cent in AMZON; seven per cent in West Berlin; 12 per cent in Bremen) appeared to read foreign magazines. Those who did read primarily American and British periodicals.

As is usually the case, magazine readers, although they constituted only a minority of the sample, tended to be people of superior socioeconomic status and educational attainment. They were more likely than nonreaders to choose civil liberties over the maintenance of law and order, if a choice was required: 35 per cent of the readers chose a government whose aim is to preserve freedom of elections, speech and press, while only 21 per cent of the nonreaders made this choice; a government whose main aim is to maintain peace and order was the choice of 56 per cent of the readers and 69 per cent of the nonreaders.

Of those who were magazine readers, 84 per cent were regular newspaper readers, 72 per cent listened to newscasts on the radio regularly or occasionally, 16 per cent had recently read political books or pamphlets (in contrast to six per cent of the total public), and 12 per cent had visited United States information centers one or more times (whereas only five per cent of the general public had done so).

Report No. 109 (5 April 1948)

THE EFFECT OF FOREIGN TRAVEL ON KNOWLEDGE AND ATTITUDES

Sample: not specified (595 respondents on the linguistic question).
Interviewing dates: March 1948. (4 pp.)

A fifth (20%) of the AMZON public claimed to know at least one foreign language, with English and French as the most frequently mentioned. Knowledge of a foreign language was almost entirely a matter of schooling.

Two-fifths (40%) of the adult population in AMZON had been in a foreign country. Not unexpectedly, many more men (65%) than women (20%) had had this experience. Those who had been outside Germany tended to be better informed than those who had not, and they also differed somewhat in their attitudes, but not greatly. Of the men who had been in a foreign country, 76 per cent had heard of the United Nations, whereas among those who had never left Germany only 63 per cent had heard of it. Among the women who had been outside of Germany 50 per cent had heard of the UN; among those women who had not travelled abroad the figure dropped to 28 per cent. On the question of the formation of a Western European Union, 80 per cent of the men who had travelled abroad and 72 per cent of those who had not were in favor; 61 per cent of the women who had been outside of Germany and 42 per cent of those who had not were for the idea.

Report No. 110 (15 April 1948)

BREMEN ATTITUDES COMPARED WITH BERLIN AND AMZON

Sample: not specified.
Interviewing dates: not specified. (16 pp.)

Following January 1948, the city of Bremen was included in all surveys. This report details results found in Bremen on a number of trend questions previously described in Report No. 100. Munich, Frankfurt, and Stuttgart are the "major AMZON cities" mentioned in the report.

Bremen residents expressed somewhat more confidence in future economic conditions in AMZON (49%) than did AMZON residents themselves (42 per cent in the major cities) but less than West Berliners (64%). More people in Bremen (45%) than in other places thought that prices would go up.

Bremen residents evidenced greater awareness (69%) of the Bizonal Council in Frankfurt and far greater approval of it (85%) than others in Germany. They were also more inclined to expect local advantages from Bizonia.

Residents of Bremen mentioned anxieties over food, particularly, but also over clothing and housing more frequently than other Germans. And although 86 per cent said they were not getting enough food to work efficiently, a strong majority (75%) approved the handling of the ration card system.

As in other German cities, nine out of ten people in Bremen said there was a large or very large black market operating in the city and 84 per cent felt that the local German authorities were not doing enough to stop it.

The people of Bremen showed about the same level of interest in politics as West Berliners, but very few were in favor of a political career for their sons. Bremen opinion was divided on whether local officials were more concerned with the welfare of the people (48%) than with their own interests (51%) whereas the residents of West Berlin, Munich, and Nuremberg inclined more toward the less favorable view of local officials.

Like West Berliners — and unlike AMZON residents — people in Bremen gave majority preference (59%) to a strong central government with headquarters in West Berlin.

Almost three-fourths of the Bremen residents (72%) said that they thought National Socialism was a good idea badly carried out. This was a higher degree of favor than was found in West Berlin (62%) and markedly higher than in AMZON (54%). When asked what they would do if they had to choose between communism and National Socialism, almost two-thirds of the Bremen respondents said they would take neither; the same held true in AMZON.

Only half of the Bremen residents considered the Germans capable of democratic self-government, with the main reason given being that the people would not accept majority rule.

As in AMZON and West Berlin, a large majority of Bremen residents said that the news in Germany was more truthful than it had been during the war. Three-fourths of Bremen adults claimed to be regular newspaper readers, as was true in West Berlin and AMZON cities.

Bremen respondents, like others throughout Germany, thought in overwhelming numbers that the four occupation powers were not working together successfully to reconstruct Germany or to unify it. In fact, more people felt that the Allies had hindered reconstruction than felt they had furthered it. More Bremen than AMZON respondents, but fewer than West Berliners, nonetheless asserted that the United States had furthered German reconstruction. And three-fourths of the Bremen residents, as compared to half the West Berliners and AMZON population, felt that the behavior of the American occupation troops had improved since the end of the war.

Report No. 111 (9 April 1948)

ATTITUDES TOWARD THE BAVARIAN PARTY

Sample: a cross-section of more than 1,600 adult Bavarians.
Interviewing dates: March 1948. (3 pp.)

Half a year before this survey was made, the *Bayernpartei* (Bavarian Party) entered the political arena in Bavaria expressing separatist, anti-Prussian sentiments and calling for a rise in the Bavarian standard of living as well as the ouster of non-Bavarians from the *Land.*

In the survey almost half (47%) had some judgment – favorable or unfavorable – to make about the party; even more people (53%), however, withheld judgment, either because they did not know anything about it or because they had not yet made up their minds. Those who did have something to say were a majority of those with nine or more years of education, men, people who did not attend church regularly, those in the middle and upper social levels, city people, businessmen, and officials.

Among those who had an opinion about the party, 34 per cent spoke favorably of it, 66 per cent made derogatory remarks. Emphasis was put on the fact that it called for Bavarian autonomy and that it defended Bavarian particularism. Some said that they were attracted by the call to oust expellees and DPs from Bavaria.

About two-fifths of small town and rural people were likely to be for the *Bayernpartei* as against somewhat more than one-fifth from towns with more than 5,000 population. Five out of ten regular Catholic churchgoers, three out of ten irregular Catholic churchgoers, and one out of ten Protestants saw good points in the party. Practically none of the expellees or refugees had anything good to say about it, while four out of ten of the native Bavarians did. Among occupational groups, only the farmers – with six out of ten – showed a majority in favor. While less than two out of ten of those who preferred either the SPD, KPD, or LDP and a like number of those without party preferences saw good points in the *Bayernpartei*, four out of ten CSU sympathizers (44%) did so. Few people (15%) with eight years or more schooling considered the party favorably, but a slight majority (53%) of those with only seven years or less schooling spoke well of it. Since Catholics, people with little education, farmers, rural people, and CSU followers were the groups that predominated in Bavaria, it seemed safe to conclude that the *Bayernpartei* was best received among "typical" Bavarians.

Report No. 112 (12 April 1948)

REACTIONS TO A FOREIGN POLICY PAMPHLET

Sample: 155 persons in the American Zone and 156 persons in West Berlin.
Interviewing dates: not specified. (6 pp.)

The study follows the same pattern described in two previous reports, Nos. 89 and 97, concerning the pamphlets *Offen Gesagt* (*Speaking Frankly*) by Byrnes and *Machtraub in Ungarn* (*Power Grab in Hungary*) by Nagy. The pamphlet under discussion here was *Aspekte der Gegenwaertigen Aussenpolitik* (*Aspects of Present American Foreign Policy*), published by the United States Department of State.

The pamphlet *Aspekte* had relatively less appeal than either *Machtraub* or *Offen Gesagt*. In West Berlin only 41 per cent had read it through completely as compared with 75 and 56 per cent for the other two. And, again in West Berlin, only 26 per cent found it very interesting while 57 and 49 per cent had described the previous two pamphlets in this way.

More than half the readers (58 per cent in Berlin and 55 per cent in AMZON) claimed not to have learned anything from the pamphlet. On the question of whether *Aspekte* presented a one-sided or fair picture of American policy, the majority (72 per cent in West Berlin and 55 per cent in AMZON) thought that it stated the American case fairly, while 22 per cent in West Berlin and 35 per cent in AMZON felt that it was one-sided. Almost everyone (95 per cent in West Berlin and 91 per cent in AMZON) thought the translation good. The presentation also won majority approval, although quite a few people found it boring. Most people found the cover good and most of those who did not like it said that it was too American.

Report No. 113 (15 April 1948)

AMZON ATTITUDES AND INFORMATION ABOUT RUSSIA

Sample: a representative sample of Germans living in the American Zone.
Interviewing dates: February 1948. (6 pp.)

Very few people in AMZON (2%) and only 11 per cent in West Berlin reported thinking that Soviet policy was determined to a large extent by the will of the people; about the same small number (2 and 4 per cent, respectively) believed that all the people got along well in the Soviet Union. The groups most frequently mentioned as able to get along were the party leaders (50 per cent in AMZON), government officials (29%), party members (21%), industrialists and managers (14%), and the upper classes (12%). Very few (9 per cent in AMZON; 14 per cent in West Berlin) mentioned the workers.

Although the AMZON Germans had very strong opinions about the Soviet Union and its people, their factual information about the country was in general at a fairly low level. In AMZON, 78 per cent said that Russians may not own automobiles, 85 per cent said the same about factories, 75 per cent about apartment houses, and 57 per cent about radios. On the question of literacy, 31 per cent said that less than half the Russians could read and write, 36 per cent placed the figure at about half, and only 22 per cent said most or all could do so. Group breakdowns of score groups ranging from the least informed to most informed revealed that those who were well informed about the Soviet Union were in general also those who were well informed about anything else.

There was no clear relation between information about the Soviet Union and the belief that the government was oriented by and for the people. People who had been in the Soviet Union within the past few years seemed almost unanimously to give a negative picture of the country.

Report No. 114 (23 April 1948)

GERMANS ASSAY THEIR FREEDOMS

Sample: a cross-section of over 3,500 Germans living in the American Zone and West Berlin.
Interviewing dates: March 1948. (9 pp.)

When asked if they felt they had five rights and freedoms — protection from the police, the right to express their opinions, to choose a job, to vote in an election, and to own a business — over half of the AMZON (51%) and West Berlin (54%) respondents answered that they had all five rights to a satisfactory degree. Of the 40 per cent who said they did not have all these rights, the largest number mentioned the right to choose a job as the one they did not have to a satisfactory degree. In AMZON, the next most frequent concern was about free speech. In West Berlin, 15 per cent mentioned the right to vote in free elections.

A majority (69%) of those with 12 years or more of education as compared with 36 per cent of those with eight years or less schooling said that they did not have certain rights to a satisfactory degree. Those who felt their rights to be restricted were asked if they expected greater freedom in ten years: Of this group a good majority in AMZON and even more West Berliners were optimistic about the future with regard to freedoms.

Asked which two of the listed freedoms they considered most important, people mentioned free speech (55 per cent in AMZON; 68 per cent in West Berlin) and free elections (51 and 60 per cent, respectively) more often than the right to choose their own jobs (41 and 43 per cent, respectively), to own a business (25 and 12 per cent, respectively), or to be protected from the police (8 and 13 per cent, respectively).

Three-fourths (75%) of the AMZON Germans and 79 per cent of the West Berliners said that the Russians were not free to express their opinions without fear of punishment, and over half (56 and 57 per cent, respectively) felt that this was also true of the Czechs. Seven out of ten (68 and 69 per cent, respectively) said that Russians were not able to vote in fair and free elections, and as many (69 and 74 per cent, respectively) said that Russians could not own a private business.

Well-educated people in AMZON were almost unanimous (97%) in saying that free speech did not exist to a satisfactory degree in some countries as compared to 78 per cent of those with eight years or less schooling. Seven out of eight (86%) of the well-educated, but only half (51%) of those with little education, said that the people in Czechoslovakia could not express their opinions freely.

Report No. 114A (11 May 1948)

GERMANS ASSAY THEIR FREEDOMS

Sample: over 300 people in Bremen.
Interviewing dates: March 1948. (3 pp.)

The report compares attitudes of Bremen residents with those of people living in West Berlin and AMZON, as described in Report No. 114.

Asked if they felt they had five rights and freedoms – protection from the police, the right to express their opinions, to choose a job, to vote in an election, and to own a business – 69 per cent of the residents of Bremen said they did not have all these rights to a satisfactory degree. This was considerably more dissatisfaction than was found in either AMZON or West Berlin. Over half of those living in Bremen (58%) thought they did not have the right to work at any job they chose, an attitude which was twice as prevalent in Bremen as in AMZON.

When asked which of the five listed freedoms they considered most important, more Bremen residents (58%) emphasized the right to work at any job they chose than did the West Berliners (43%) or AMZON residents (41%).

Bremen residents were slightly more often skeptical of the degree of freedom found in the Soviet Union than were West Berliners or AMZON residents; 86 per cent said that the Russians could not express their opinions without fear of punishment, while 78 per cent said that they could not vote in a fair and free election.

Report No. 115 (26 April 1948)

THE "ADVERTISING PILLAR" AS AN INFORMATION MEDIUM

Sample: a cross-section of 240 West Berliners.
Interviewing dates: 19 April 1948. (3 pp.)

About a quarter of the population could be considered regular and attentive readers of the notices on the pillars *(Litfass-saeulen)*. Forty per cent said they never looked at or read them while 60 per cent said they did. Of the latter group, 40 per cent had not looked at one during the previous week, ten per cent said they only glanced at them, and 26 per cent had looked at one or more pillars during the week as well as spent some time reading them. In the last mentioned group there were more men than women, more people under 40 than over, and more upper- and middle-class people than lower-class people.

Eight in ten said they read notices about theaters, concerts, and the like; two in ten read the lost and found ads, notices of robberies, rewards for apprehension of criminals, etc.; and smaller proportions of respondents read notices about sports events, official notices, ads for missing persons, etc.

For half of the people who read the notices, some action resulted, such as going to the theater or attending a sports event.

Report No. 116 (28 April 1948)

THE MOVING PICTURE AUDIENCE IN AMZON

Sample: a cross-section of more than 3,700 adults in the American Zone, West Berlin, and Bremen.
Interviewing dates: February 1948. (4 pp.)

In AMZON, 28 per cent of the people 18 years and over attended a movie once a month or more often; this regular moviegoing audience was larger in Bremen (40%) and larger still in West Berlin (54%).

More people living in medium-size cities than in very large cities or in small towns were regular moviegoers. The regular movie audience was drawn largely from higher socioeconomic groups (38 per cent in AMZON), the well educated (45%), the young (56%), unmarried people (44%), and from among white-collar workers (51%).

Most moviegoers (88 per cent in AMZON) said they had seen the newsreel *Welt im Film.* Of these, 65 per cent expressed satisfaction with it, 25 per cent were dissatisfied with it, and nine per cent withheld judgment. Criticism centered around the view that the newsreel tended to be superficial or frivolous, ignoring the serious aspects of life in Germany at that time.

Report No. 117 (27 April 1948)

BERLINERS VIEW THE CZECHOSLOVAKIAN SITUATION

Sample: a cross-section of 260 West Berliners.
Interviewing dates: 12 to 21 April 1948. (5 pp.)

Concerning the communist coup in Czechoslovakia, 80 per cent of the respondents said they had heard that a new government had taken over in that country. The 20 per cent who had not heard about it consisted almost entirely of poorly educated women from the lower socioeconomic levels. A large majority (80%) of the informed were of the opinion that the change was the result of foreign pressure. Three-fourths (75%) of the informed believed that the consequences of the coup were not favorable to the Czechoslovakian people. People who thought that the Czechs had benefited from the change were more inclined (65%) than those who took the contrary view (41%) to think that the same thing was possible in Berlin.

A small majority held that the events in Prague could not be repeated in Berlin, although 44 per cent of those who knew what had happened thought a similar coup was possible. More than half of those who thought it possible, however, believed it would not actually occur.

Among newspaper readers, more occasional readers (22%) than regular readers (11%) thought that the change in government in Prague had been carried out democratically and that the Czech people had gained from the change, although in both groups majorities held the opposite view. A majority of the occasional newspaper readers (58%) held that a similar coup was possible in Berlin; 56 per cent of the regular readers said it was not possible.

A similar study made in April 1948 in the Austrian cities of Linz and Salzburg revealed more extensive knowledge concerning the change in Czechoslovakian government, with 96 per cent of the people in Linz and 85 per cent of those in Salzburg knowing of the coup. In Linz 77 per cent of the people and in Salzburg 67 per cent felt that the change resulted from foreign pressure. More Linz residents (69%) than Salzburgers (57%) or Berliners (60%) felt the change not to be to the advantage of the Czech people. About one in ten, both in Linz and Salzburg, thought that a similar coup was possible in Austria, although 67 per cent in Linz and 51 per cent in Salzburg thought it not possible. About half of those who believed it to be possible, however, did not personally expect such a coup.

Report No. 118 (3 May 1948)

NEWSPAPER READERSHIP

Sample: a cross-section of over 3,000 residents in the American Zone, 513 West Berliners, and 235 residents of Bremen.
Interviewing dates: February 1948. (5 pp.)

In AMZON, 64 per cent reported reading newspapers regularly; over three-fourths of the West Berlin and Bremen residents (76 per cent and 79 per cent, respectively) made the same claim.

Throughout AMZON, as well as in Bremen, people said that they read their local paper or papers most frequently. The

American-licensed *Neue Zeitung* had a readership of over one-fourth of the AMZON population as well as of 17 per cent of the people in Bremen. Relatively large proportions of the *Neue Zeitung* readers preferred it to their local paper, such as in Wuerttemberg-Baden where 27 per cent read it and 24 per cent preferred it. More people in the higher socioeconomic groups, more professional and business men, more of the better educated, and more evacuees were counted among *Neue Zeitung* readers than people in other groups.

In West Berlin, the British-licensed *Telegraf* was the most widely read and best-liked paper, with more than six out of ten (64%) saying they read it and four out of ten saying they liked it best. The next most popular paper was the American-licensed *Tagesspiegel* with 38 per cent saying they read it and 17 per cent saying they preferred it. Six out of ten West Berliners (60%) read only western-licensed newspapers, and fewer than one in ten (7%) read only Soviet-licensed papers; the remainder (33%) read both western- and Soviet-licensed newspapers. Almost all of the well-educated people (89%) and 71 per cent of those in the higher socioeconomic group said they read only western-licensed papers. Fully a third of the people on the lowest rungs of the economic ladder — 33 per cent of those of "lower lower" socioeconomic status and 37 per cent of the "upper lower" group — said that they read Soviet-licensed papers exclusively.

Report No. 119 (10 May 1948)

CUMULATIVE IMPACT OF THE MASS MEDIA

Sample: about 3,000 persons residing in 225 communities in the American Zone.
Interviewing dates: February 1948. (7 pp.)

This report presents the overall picture growing out of a large-scale study on mass media (cf. Reports #102, 103, 106, 113, 116, 118). The interrelationships of three composite sets of scaled questions were examined, measuring (1) participation or nonparticipation in the audience of at least six major media of mass communication, (2) attitudes toward the United States, Americans, and aspects of American policy toward government and economics, and (3) information about the Soviet Union.

One in eight people (12%) seemed to have no source of topical information at all, except perhaps conversations. Another one in six (17%) indicated that no source of information reached him with any regularity. The number of audiences within which AMZON Germans participated was strikingly related to attitudes toward the American way of life. Regardless of social class, the more sources of information which an AMZON German had, the more likely he was to be favorably disposed toward American policies in government or economics, ways of life, and activities. Similarly, regardless of social class, the better informed Germans consistently were more often favorably disposed toward the United States than were the poorly informed. Regardless of the information level, however, people with most sources of information proved better disposed toward American policies than those who participated in few or no audiences.

A consistent relationship was also found between levels of information about the Soviet Union and attitudes toward American capitalistic life. Again, regardless of social class, those who could give the most correct answers to a set of factual questions about the Soviet Union more frequently displayed favorable attitudes toward American capitalism. Those with relatively little factual knowledge about Russia, by way of contrast, appeared more often less favorable toward the American system.

Report No. 120 (20 May 1948)

GERMAN OPINIONS ON DAYLIGHT SAVING TIME

Sample: an unspecified number of respondents in the American Zone, West Berlin, and Bremen.
Interviewing dates: April 1948. (3 pp.)

The German people were generally in favor of daylight saving time (54 per cent in AMZON; 75 per cent in West Berlin; 63 per cent in Bremen). The two groups most opposed to the idea were the farmers and residents of towns with less than 1,000 residents. Of the farmers, 40 per cent were against daylight saving time, 31 per cent were for it, and 29 per cent expressed no opinion. Among people living in small towns, 29 per cent were opposed, 37 per cent were in favor, and 35 per cent had no opinion on the matter.

People who did not like the idea of putting their clocks ahead gave a variety of reasons, the most frequently mentioned of which was that they would be deprived of much needed sleep. Others said it was bad because people did not have enough food to carry them through such a long day.

Men tended to be more favorable (57%) than women (51%). Trade union members were also more favorable than the general public (59%). Other differences were not great except, as the West Berlin and Bremen attitudes indicated, large city dwellers tended to be most favorable to daylight saving time. Among occupational groups, those who worked indoors – office workers, professional and business men – gave more frequent approval than others.

These findings compared with those of a Gallup poll made in the United States in April 1948. There, too, a majority agreed to daylight saving time; farmers were the only people who were largely opposed to it. Indeed, more American farmers were opposed, and also more positive in their opposition, than were German farmers. City dwellers in the United States, as in Germany, were most favorable to the change.

Report No. 121 (19 May 1948)

UNIFORMITY OF RELIGIOUS PREFERENCES IN AMZON COMMUNITIES

Sample: data from October 1946 census of the German population. (4 pp.)

The report gives an analysis of some of the data gathered in the October 1946 census to ascertain the percentage of Catholics in each community or city. A basic table at the end of the report shows the number of towns of under 5,000 population within each administrative district containing a certain percentage of persons who claimed adherence to the Catholic church.

Practically all the towns (97%) within the American Zone contained less than 5,000 residents. This figure was consistently high for each administrative district but was lowest in Baden (92%) and highest in Schwaben and Unterfranken (99%). The percentage of the total population represented in this set of communities was, however, much more variable. Throughout the entire Zone a majority of the population (56%) lived in towns under 5,000. But in Baden less than half the people (42%) lived in these smaller communities, while in Unterfranken a large majority (78%) was found in towns of this size.

It is particularly striking that a great number of towns (71%) fall at the extremes; they were either very largely Catholic or very largely non-Catholic. Of 10,355 towns with under 5,000 residents, 2,299 (22%) had zero to 20 per cent Catholic population, while 5,008 (49%) had 81 to 100 per cent Catholic population.

Heavily Protestant towns were concentrated in Wuerttemberg (59 per cent of which had Catholic populations of less than a fifth and 80 per cent of which had Catholic populations of less than a half), Kassell (51 and 82 per cent, respectively), Darmstadt (30 and 88 per cent respectively), Wiesbaden (36 and 78 per cent, respectively) and Mittelfranken (21 and 73 per cent, respectively). Heavily Catholic towns were in Oberbayern (94 per cent of which had Catholic populations of more than four-fifths and 100 per cent of which had Catholic populations of more than a half), Niederbayern (93 and 100 per cent, respectively), Schwaben (88 and 94 per cent, respectively), Oberpfalz (87 and 95 per cent, respectively), and Unterfranken (75 and 81 per cent, respectively). Of Oberfranken's small towns, 31 per cent were predominantly Protestant and 33 per cent were predominantly Catholic. In Baden, 14 per cent of the small towns were predominantly Protestant and 44 per cent predominantly Catholic.

Report No. 122 (22 May 1948)

PREJUDICE AND ANTI-SEMITISM

Sample: a cross-section of persons 15 years of age and older in the American Zone.
Interviewing dates: April 1948. (11 pp.)

This study was a repeat of a survey made in December 1946 (cf. Report No. 49). Its purpose was to ascertain whether there existed a general anti-Semitism among the German people and, if so, to measure both the spread and its incidence within certain groups of the population. One historical note should be borne in mind: Whereas in 1933 there were about 503,000 Jews in Germany (0.8 per cent of the total population), in 1948 there were less than 20,000.

A comparison of the two detailed studies on anti-Semitism made in December 1946 and April 1948 revealed that overt anti-Semitism had not increased during the year. Indeed, it had decreased slightly, from 21 per cent to 19 per cent for anti-Semites and 18 per cent to 14 per cent for intense anti-Semites.

However, at the same time, racist attitudes – the basis of anti-Semitism – had increased sharply, from 22 per cent to 26 per cent.

An objective estimate of population divisions (overcoming possible objections to the wording of the questions) showed that about two in ten persons were clearly anti-Semitic, about three in ten were indifferent or unconcerned, and just over half could be termed "not anti-Semitic." Group differences paralleled those found in the earlier report: women, the poorly educated, and rural persons were more likely to be anti-Semitic than men, the well-educated, or city dwellers. More detailed analysis, however, revealed that locale was even more important than education in shaping outlooks on this issue. Examination of the *Regierungsbezirke* (administrative districts) showed that in Wuerttemberg, for instance, there was more prejudice (gradient score of 129 per cent on a scale ranging from 0 per cent equalling the total absence of prejudice to 100 per cent equalling absolute anti-Semitism) than in Baden (gradient score of 103 per cent).

Knowledge reduces prejudice. However, parents of German youth were more frequently carriers of prejudice than childless couples. Germans between the ages of 15 and 19 showed more anti-Semitism than other age groups. Trade union members were less often anti-Semitic than nonmembers. Expellees from the East did not differ from natives of an area in their degrees of prejudice.

Report No. 123 (25 May 1948)

REACTIONS TO THE VOLKSKONGRESS PETITION IN BERLIN AND DARMSTADT

Sample: representative cross-sections of over 450 adults in West Berlin and almost 200 in Darmstadt.
Interviewing dates: May 1948. (5 pp.)

As had been expected, almost everyone (96%) in both West Berlin and Darmstadt hoped that Germany would again be united. However, people did not want this unity at any price. Most people (78 per cent in West Berlin and 87 per cent in Darmstadt) said that they would not sign a petition if they knew it came from a communist organization. Likewise, most people (78 per cent in West Berlin and 85 per cent in Darmstadt) said that they would not favor uniting Germany if union could only be achieved under Soviet influence. And in Darmstadt, almost eight in ten (78%) favored the establishment of a provisional government for western Germany, although in West Berlin only 49 per cent did.

A petition for German unity under the auspices of the *Volkskongress* had some appeal, especially in Darmstadt where fewer people than in West Berlin had heard or read anything about the council. People who had heard of the *Volkskongress* (80 per cent in West Berlin and 51 per cent in Darmstadt) were much less inclined to sign its petition (32 per cent in West Berlin and 53 per cent in Darmstadt) than those who had not heard of it (44 per cent in West Berlin and 62 per cent in Darmstadt). By the same token, regular newspaper readers were more skeptical of the *Volkskongress'* efforts (30 per cent in West Berlin and 53 per cent in Darmstadt) than were nonreaders (53 per cent in West Berlin and 76 per cent in Darmstadt).

Both in West Berlin and in Darmstadt women, older people, those from the lower socioeconomic groups, nonreaders of newspapers, and people opposed to the creation of a provisional west German goverment were more likely than their counterpart groups to say that they would sign a petition sponsored by the *Volkskongress*. Interestingly enough, however, many of those who said they would sign such a petition also favored a provisional government (29 per cent in West Berlin and 62 per cent in Darmstadt); evidently they wanted unification but were ready to accept separation.

Men, those from the middle class, regular newspaper readers, those who would not sign a petition circulated under communist auspices, and those who opposed unification if it meant Soviet leadership were more favorable toward a provisional government in the west than were their opposite numbers. Those most strongly opposed were the KPD/SED sympathizers, those who would sign a communist-sponsored petition, and those willing to see a united Germany under Soviet leadership.

Report No. 124 (1 June 1948)

SOCIAL CHARACTERISTICS OF THE GERMAN PEOPLE IN THE AMERICAN ZONE AND IN BERLIN (BRITISH AND AMERICAN SECTORS)

Sample: 14,973 respondents in the American Zone, and 1,999 in West Berlin, comprising the combined total of respondents in several surveys.
Interviewing dates: 15 February to 8 July 1947. (41 pp.)

The report comprises 34 tables cross-tabulating the AMZON and West Berlin population according to education, social status, age, religion, occupation, monthly income, former NSDAP membership, current party membership, political party preference, and size of community. An appendix compares the sample data with data from the census of 29 October 1946; another appendix shows religious affiliation and church attendance broken down by the sex, education, and social status of the respondents.

Report No. 125 (22 June 1948)

BERLIN RADIO LISTENERS APPRAISE "AMERICAN VOICES"

Sample: a cross-section of West Berlin residents.
Interviewing dates: during the last two weeks of May 1948.
(3 pp.)

In this study an attempt was made to gather evidence about the desirability of using as radio announcers persons with clearly marked American accents or those with no accent at all.

Assuming that the speaker made himself understood, there was no strong sentiment favoring the use of an American accent. In fact, among all listeners – those who had heard an American on radio as well as those who had not – almost as many favored a voice without an accent (35%) as said they favored German spoken with an American accent (37%); the remainder (28%) indicated no preference between the two.

A surprisingly large percentage (62%) said they had heard an American speaking on the radio while about 15 per cent said they had never heard one. Half of those who preferred an accented voice said that this was one way of knowing that the speaker really was an American; most of the others expressing this preference said it sounded nicer.

Report No. 126 (29 June 1948)

RELIGIOUS INSTRUCTION IN THE SCHOOLS

Sample: 3,007 people 15 years and older in the American Zone, 511 in West Berlin, and 315 in Bremen.
Interviewing dates: April 1948. (6 pp.)

Almost everyone (96 per cent in AMZON; 92 per cent in West Berlin; 93 per cent in Bremen) favored religious instruction in the elementary schools (*Volksschulen*). In AMZON, 71 per cent felt that it ought to be obligatory. Even in West Berlin, 51 per cent of the population wanted compulsory instruction in religion. Only in Bremen was a majority (54%) in favor of such instruction on a voluntary basis.

Opinions differed along regional lines on who should give religious instruction. In Bavaria, 87 per cent voted for the clergy, as did 75 per cent in Wuerttemberg-Baden. In Hesse, however, almost as many (38%) favored classroom teachers as favored the clergy (43%). In West Berlin, 49 per cent voted for teachers, while in Bremen a majority of 62 per cent favored teachers.

Only a minority, however, supported the idea of confessional schools (28 per cent in AMZON; 26 per cent in West Berlin; 30 per cent in Bremen). Of those in the American Zone who did favor confessional schools, equal numbers (13%) were opposed and in favor of having common schools as well.

There were mixed reactions to the question of financial aid to schools whose curricula were determined by the church. Bavaria split evenly on the question. A small majority in Wuerttemberg-Baden (53%) and a larger one in Hesse (59%) were opposed to such aid from the state. In West Berlin and Bremen the opposition was even greater (73 per cent and 70 per cent, respectively).

Report No. 127 (8 July 1948)

SOME OPINIONS ON THE UNIVERSITY OF BERLIN

Sample: 200 people living in the Neukoelln district of West Berlin.

Interviewing dates: first two weeks of May 1948. (4 pp.)

In late April 1948 three students who had played an active part in University affairs were dismissed from the University of Berlin for allegedly defaming the Institute and its head. This survey was made in order to measure Berlin reactions to the underlying issues of the matter, as well as to related problems.

Slightly more than half of the respondents (53%) knew that the University was located in the Soviet Sector of Berlin. Only four out of ten claimed to have heard of the expulsions, and of these only 14 per cent said that the students had been engaged in anticommunist or anti-Soviet activities; 63 per cent had a general idea of why they had been expelled; and 16 per cent could give no reason at all. Those who did give a reason were overwhelmingly (85%) opposed to the dismissals. Whether or not the respondents knew anything about the case of the three students, however, most of them were of the opinion that students should have the right to criticize University affairs. Those opposed to the right to criticize based their belief on three arguments: that students ought to confine themselves to studying, that public criticism only harms the University's reputation, and that students are too immature to offer criticism.

Seven in ten people thought it would be a good idea to establish another university in West Berlin. Two-thirds of those in favor of this idea said that there was no freedom of opinion or security at the University in the Soviet Sector. Six out of ten of the minority opposing the idea argued that setting up another institution would simply widen the East-West split.

Concerning the question of selecting university students, the largest number (67%) chose as a criterion the ability to think independently. The possession of knowledge was the second most frequently cited value (46%), political background was mentioned by only six per cent, and the traditional German test of university admission – social status – was accorded fourth place with four per cent.

Report No. 128 (8 July 1948)

A PILOT STUDY OF ATTITUDES TOWARD THE JOINT EXPORT-IMPORT AGENCY

Sample: 187 adults living in West Berlin.
Interviewing dates: not specified. (3 pp.)

Only 36 per cent of the West Berliners questioned claimed to have heard or read anything about the Joint Export-Import Agency (JEIA) and half of these were either unable to describe its functions or described them vaguely or incorrectly. Few who had heard or read of the Agency felt able to pass judgment on its work. By the same token, only 22 per cent of the total number of those interviewed could suggest any specific improvements.

Almost half of the "informed" group (15 per cent of the total) agreed that an exchange of goods with foreign countries was a good thing, but an equal number withheld judgment on the matter. The main reason given for advocating exports was that Germany would receive food and raw materials in return.

A plurality (45%) favored German control of the Agency, although a large minority (26%) felt that the trade program would be worse off if run by German experts. The latter based their statements primarily on German disunity.

Report No. 129 (19 July 1948)

REACTIONS OF A PANEL OF READERS TO THE PAMPHLET "MIT VEREINTEN KRAEFTEN"

Sample: 155 people in American Zone cities and 88 in West Berlin.
Interviewing dates: not specified. (6 pp.)

Mit Vereinten Kraeften (With United Force) was one of a series of pamphlets issued by the Military Government. The purpose of the study was not to predict general readership, but rather to explore the reactions of various kinds of people who had been exposed to the pamphlet.

Mit Vereinten Kraeften appeared to be less popular than the three previously published pamphlets. As few as 35 per cent in AMZON said that they had read it in its entirety, whereas as many as 77 per cent had read all of *Machtraub in Ungarn (Power Grab in Hungary)*; about two-thirds claimed to have read *Offen Gesagt (Speaking Frankly)*, and almost half had read *Aspekte der Gegenwaertigen Amerikanischen Aussenpolitik (Aspects of Present American Policy)*. As was true in the case of the other pamphlets, men, those in the upper socioeconomic group, and the better-educated were more likely to read *Mit Vereinten Kraeften* than were their counterpart groups.

Of those who had read the pamphlet, 57 per cent in AMZON thought the whole thing was interesting, 51 per cent thought that in general it was good, 41 per cent had recommended it to friends or relatives, and 54 per cent said they would be willing to pay 50 *Pfennig* for it if they saw it on the newsstand.

Less than two-thirds of those interviewed in AMZON (63%) thought that *Mit Vereinten Kraeften* gave a clear picture of the facts, and over half (54%) said they had not learned anything new from it.

Technical appraisal of the pamphlet was generally favorable. Nine out of ten said it was well translated, most liked the style in which it was written, and considered the cover attractive.

Report No. 130 (23 July 1948)

BERLIN REACTIONS TO THE AIR LIFT AND THE WESTERN POWERS

Sample: 300 people in West Berlin.
Interviewing dates: 19, 20, and 21 July 1948, one month after suspension of land traffic to the city. (8 pp.)

Almost unanimously (98%), West Berliners said that the Western Powers were doing the right thing by staying in Berlin. In fact, 100 per cent of those with nine or more years of education said the West should remain.

Confidence that the Americans would in fact stay had risen in the course of the previous nine months. In October 1947, 74 per cent thought that they would stay; by July 1948, the figure had risen to 89 per cent.

Five out of six West Berliners (84%) expressed confidence that the air lift could supply enough food to maintain current rations. Almost half (48%) said, however, that they personally had not been making out as well with food during the previous few weeks. Of these, 28 per cent blamed their worsening food situation on the blockade and 11 per cent blamed the currency reform. Opinion was divided on whether or not the air lift could keep the city going through the winter. Those with nine or more years of education were more skeptical of the possibilities of maintaining life in West Berlin (61 per cent said no, 38 per cent yes) than those with less education (47 per cent no, 49 per cent yes). Most of those interviewed (86%) predicted that the blockade would not last through the winter.

Three-fourths (77%) said that the Western Powers were doing their utmost to relieve the distressed condition of West Berlin. Of those who felt that the Western Powers could do more (22%), 14 per cent suggested the use of more planes, five per cent said that the blockade should be lifted by force; men and those with more education advocated force more often than women and those with less education.

Of those interviewed, 82 per cent thought that the Western Powers had gone up in the estimation of the German people; the same number thought the Soviets had lost popularity.

A plurality of those interviewed (43%) thought that the Americans were more interested in strengthening their power than in the welfare of West Berliners.

In August 1947, 42 per cent of the West Berliners predicted war within a decade; in April 1948, 66 per cent felt this way; and by July 1948 the figure had risen to 82 per cent. Almost three-fourths (73%) thought the Berlin situation serious enough that it in itself could cause a war in the near future. Again, those with more education tended to be more pessimistic.

Report No. 131 (4 August 1948)

GERMANS VIEW THE SIX POWER CONFERENCE PROPOSALS

Sample: 500 people in the American Zone, 100 in Bremen, and 100 in West Berlin.
Interviewing dates: early July 1948. (6 pp.)

The study showed widespread ignorance of the Six Power Conference held in London and a lack of enthusiasm for the proposals among those who claimed to be informed about them.

Although Berlin had not been included in the plan, a majority of "informed" people, even in West Berlin itself (65%), thought that it had been; and vast majorities in AMZON (84%) and Bremen (90%) and half the respondents in West Berlin, regardless of whether or not they knew about the specific London proposal, felt that the city ought to be included.

There was general agreement among respondents on the practicability of setting up a western German government although there was still strong sentiment in favor of a single united Germany governed from Berlin. If, however, people were asked to choose between a western German government and a united communist Germany, then the overwhelming majority opted for the former.

Relatively few people knew that any proposals regarding the Ruhr had been made at London. Of those who knew about the proposal for international control of this region, three in ten favored it and two-thirds were opposed.

Large majorities (72 per cent in AMZON and 79 per cent in Berlin) regarded the addition of the French Zone to the Bizonal organization as a step toward the unification of Germany.

Report No. 132 (10 August 1948)

SOME ASPECTS OF MORALE IN BERLIN

Sample: 284 adults in West Berlin.
Interviewing dates: 22, 23, and 24 July 1948. (7 pp.)

A large majority of West Berliners (63%) expressed confidence in their own ability to withstand further rigors imposed by the blockade. Men and women did not differ markedly in their expressed capacity to endure. Persons with nine or more years of education, however, had greater confidence than those with less.

Opinions were more divided on the question of how long the population could withstand the imposed restrictions. Men and the better educated were more inclined to be optimistic than their counterpart groups, should the blockade last for a long time or even indefinitely.

Almost unanimously (92%), West Berliners said that even though the Russians had announced their willingness to take over the food supply of the city, the Americans would have to continue the airlift; 40 per cent said they had no confidence in the Russians, that they did not keep their word. An almost equal number (38%) said it would be physically impossible for the Soviets to feed all of Berlin, and ten per cent linked the Soviet food plan with political ambitions.

Most respondents had negative reasons to explain the Soviet offer of food: 42 per cent thought it was propaganda, 25 per cent thought that the USSR wanted to draw West Berlin to their side, and 14 per cent felt it was in order to get rid of the Americans.

Seven out of eight West Berliners (86%) thought that their own lives would be affected if the Americans were to leave West Berlin. About half expressed a basic fear of the Russians; one in six (17%) mentioned political consequences.

Report No. 133 (10 August 1948)

REACTIONS TOWARD CURRENCY REFORM IN THE U.S. ZONE OF GERMANY

Sample: 500 people in the American Zone and 100 in Bremen.
Interviewing dates: 21 to 25 July 1948. (11 pp.)

One month after the currency reform, the per capita cash on hand reported by respondents was DM 22.41 in AMZON and DM 21.39 in Bremen. One-half of the AMZON respondents asserted that their food supply had increased during the previous weeks and almost eight in ten made this claim in Bremen.

Almost everyone (90 per cent in AMZON and 96 per cent in Bremen) thought that the currency reform had been necessary and 53 per cent even felt it should have come sooner. In AMZON only a third of the respondents were satisfied with all the regulations implementing it, with the most frequent criticism concerning the effect of the ten to one conversion rate on small savings accounts.

Three in ten (31%) in AMZON reported expecting another currency reform and half of these expected it to come within one or two years. Slightly more than half thought that the new Mark would retain its value during the coming year. Well over half (58%) of the AMZON residents as well as 66 per cent of Bremen residents expected to be better off during this time period. Men and women shared similar expectations regarding the future effects of the currency reform, but the better educated and upper socioeconomic groups were more inclined than their counterparts to take an optimistic view. Seven in ten AMZON residents expected to buy more of certain goods than before, with clothing and shoes heading the list. Four in ten in AMZON (38%) and a fourth in Bremen (23%) said, however, that they planned to cut down on purchases of certain items.

A fairly large majority (71 per cent in AMZON and 73 per cent in Bremen) felt that the currency reform would cut down the extent of the black market. Moreover, the proportion thinking a local black market existed dropped sharply from 48 per cent who said it was a serious problem in June to 16 per cent in July.

Huge majorities felt that the currency reform would increase unemployment, as was indeed the case. Equally large majorities were willing to work more to earn more, but large fractions felt that there would be little chance to do so.

Attitudes toward the currency reform were closely related to the adequacy of the food supplies at the time. People who said that their rations had improved tended also to think that the reform had been necessary, it should have come earlier, the new Mark would retain its value, they would be better off during the coming year because of the reform, it would reduce the black market, and they would increase their purchases of certain items.

Report No. 134 (2 September 1948)

SOME TRENDS IN BERLIN MORALE WITH SIDELIGHTS ON RECREATION

Sample: a representative sample of 300 people living in West Berlin.

Interviewing dates: 19 August 1948, two months after suspension of land traffic to West Berlin. (5 pp.)

The second month of the Berlin blockade saw an outstanding increase in long term confidence in the air lift. Whereas in late July a majority of Berliners (52%) believed that the Western Powers could not maintain life in the city through the winter by air lift alone, by August almost eight out of ten Berliners (77%) thought it would be possible to do so. The greatest rise in confidence was among the more educated Berliners – the opinion leaders. In July, only a minority of 38 per cent of the better educated felt that the air lift could cope with the winter; in August a very large majority (82%) felt this way.

By August 69 per cent of the West Berliners believed that the Western Powers were doing their utmost to relieve distressed conditions in the city (as opposed to 77 per cent in July). But, at the same time, slightly more Berliners in August (29%) than in July (22%) also felt that more could be done.

A majority of West Berliners (58%) felt that the blockade had not appreciably reduced their opportunities for recreation. A majority (60%), however, thought it would be a good idea if, in the circumstances, the Military Government helped increase recreational possibilities. One in five (21%) nonetheless felt such assistance would be a bad idea since there were more serious matters to attend to.

Report No. 135 (13 September 1948)

RADIO LISTENING IN BERLIN SINCE THE BLOCKADE

Sample: an unspecified number; a representative cross-section of adults in West Berlin.
Interviewing dates: August 1948. (5 pp.)

RIAS (Radio in the American Sector) had by far the largest share (80%) of the West Berlin radio audience and was also the most popular (80%), thus continuing the gains noted in February 1948 (Report No. 106). The proportion of radio listeners to the total Berlin population decreased slightly since February, no doubt as a result of the cuts in electricity: 61 per cent of the population claimed to listen to the radio in August as compared with 67 per cent in February.

The three most popular listening periods were from 9:00 a.m. to noon (26%), in the afternoon (31%), and evening until midnight (38%).

Three-fifths (59%) of the radio audience listened regularly or occasionally to the RIAS program *"Varady funkt dazwischen,"* which satirized the current Berlin political scene with special reference to the East. Eight in ten (80%) of the people who listened to the *Varady* broadcasts found them very good or good. Their realism as well as their humorous irony were the two most frequently mentioned characteristics.

Seven in ten of the radio audience − or 45 per cent of the total adult population − claimed to hear "Voice of America" broadcasts and six per cent of all listeners volunteered the information that these were their favorite broadcasts.

Men and women differed somewhat on the kinds of radio programs they preferred, although in general their tastes were similar. Women liked musical and variety programs best of all (73%), followed by newscasts (54%), discussions and talks (27%), and news commentaries (17%). With men, newscasts were the top favorite (65%), musical programs followed as a close second (60%), and discussions and commentaries were equally popular (about 30%).

Report No. 136 (21 September 1948)

ATTITUDES TOWARD A GOVERNMENT
FOR WESTERN GERMANY

Sample: 3,000 residents of the American Zone, 511 in West Berlin, and 329 in Bremen.
Interviewing dates: August 1948. (7 pp.)

In AMZON 70 per cent of the residents favored setting up a provisional government for western Germany while only about one in eight (12%) was against the proposal. In West Berlin, 74 per cent were in favor, while 23 per cent – almost twice as many as in any other area – were opposed and very few (3%) were undecided. In Bremen, 79 per cent favored and 13 per cent opposed the idea.

More than half of those supporting the new government (39 per cent in AMZON, 35 per cent in West Berlin, 56 per cent in Bremen) did so because they thought Germany needed a government of her own. Significantly, more West Berliners (13%) than residents of AMZON or Bremen regarded the new government as a move toward unification.

Most (6 per cent in AMZON, 12 per cent in West Berlin) of those opposing the formation of a West German government did so because they considered a united government essential for Germany.

Asked whether they thought that a provisional West German government should control foreign trade or whether the Western Powers ought to continue in this field, 51 per cent of AMZON residents, 69 per cent of those living in Bremen, and 52 per cent of the West Berliners responded that they considered foreign trade within the domain of the German government. Those with higher education and socioeconomic status were more likely to hold this opinion than were those with less education and of lower socioeconomic status.

Although a majority believed that the new government should control foreign trade, 65 per cent in AMZON, 72 per cent in Bremen, and 85 per cent in West Berlin felt that the

Western Powers would keep Germany's interests in mind were they to retain control over foreign policy.

About half of the respondents (47 per cent in AMZON, 51 per cent in West Berlin, 53 per cent in Bremen) thought that a new western German government would widen the East-West split of Germany, with the percentage thinking that it would have little influence varying from a third (33%) in AMZON to 38 per cent in Bremen, to almost half (46%) in West Berlin. Those who felt it would widen the split were more likely to be men, the well educated, and those of higher socioeconomic status.

Report No. 137 (21 September 1948)

THE MUNICH MOVIE AUDIENCE

Sample: a representative cross-section of 302 residents of Munich, 15 years of age and over.
Interviewing dates: 29 and 30 July 1948. (4 pp.)

Two-fifths of the residents of Munich were regular moviegoers by their own estimate. The same proportion said they went less than once a month and 21 per cent claimed never to attend a film.

The Munich movie audience was drawn largely from the 15-24 age group: Two-thirds (65%) of this age group were regular moviegoers, the other third went irregularly. Educational differences appeared to be as important a factor as age in marking the moviegoer: Although only a third (33%) of the poorly educated were regular moviegoers, two-thirds (61%) of the well educated were. Socioeconomic status was also related to movie going: Half (51%) of those of higher socioeconomic status went to the cinema as compared with one-third (34%) of those of relatively lower status.

Every third moviegoer (36%) voted for musicals as the preferred type of full-length film; historical films were second with 22 per cent, and no one said that he preferred war films. When asked what hypothetical film title they found most attractive, 33 per cent chose *"Bauernhochzeit"* (The Farmer's Wedding); this was followed by *"Abenteuer im Dschungel"* (Jungle Adventure) with 16 per cent.

The ten most popular films of that period included six of American origin, with *Gaslight* heading the list (15 votes). Of the total list of movies named, the number of German titles mentioned as favorites exceeded that of any other country, although the largest number of votes indicating favorite films went to those made in the United States. Despite this popularity of American films, over two-thirds (69%) of the respondents expressed a general preference for German over American films; nearly a quarter (23%) gave qualified answers, five per cent had no preference, and only three per cent indicated a preference for American over German films.

Report No. 138 (17 September 1948)

NEWSPAPER READING IN BERLIN SINCE CURRENCY REFORM AND THE BLOCKADE

Sample: a representative cross-section of 300 residents of West Berlin.
Interviewing dates: latter part of August 1948. (4 pp.)

In West Berlin, 72 per cent claimed to read a newspaper regularly and 14 per cent said they read one occasionally; this represented a slight drop since March 1948 when the question had also been posed. In August, 83 per cent of the men and only 66 per cent of the women were regular readers.

The British-licensed *Telegraf* continued to be the most widely read and popular newspaper in West Berlin with almost six in ten (57%) of the total public reading it and over a third (36%) preferring it. The American-licensed *Tagesspiegel* remained in second place both in readership (32%) and preference

(22%). Neither newspaper, however, gained in popularity or readership since the spring; the same was true for the Soviet- and French-licensed papers.

People who read one or more newspapers published in West Berlin were asked whether they paid for their papers in West or East Marks. Six in ten (62%) replied West Marks, 21 per cent said East Marks, and ten per cent said that they sometimes paid with one currency and sometimes with the other.

Of the 37 per cent of those who cut down on their purchases of newspapers after the currency reform, 14 per cent had stopped reading the *Telegraf,* nine per cent the *Tages-spiegel.* The main reason given for cutting down on newspaper purchases was the lack of money, specifically a lack of West Marks.

Newspapers seemed to have an adequate "pass along" rate, with an average of 2.38 people reading each copy of a paper, and with most (80%) of the exchanges going on between members of a family.

Report No. 139 (22 September 1948)

CHIEF CARES AND WORRIES SINCE THE CURRENCY REFORM

Sample: not specified.
Interviewing dates: nine surveys taken between February and August 1948. (5 pp.)

During the spring of 1948, the cares and worries of the German people were much the same as they had been the first time this question was asked in the first survey. In June 1948, however, when the Western Powers introduced the currency reform, a change occurred in the German situation and consequently in the cares and worries expressed by the public.

Before the currency reform, the most frequently reported chief worry had always been food. Indeed, during the winter and spring of 1948, over half the people in AMZON, two-thirds in Berlin, and three-fourths in Bremen mentioned food among their chief cares and worries. After the currency reform, however, the picture changed markedly in AMZON and Bremen, while in West Berlin, where the blockade was instituted along with the currency reform, the food situation remained serious and 47 per cent of the population was still seriously concerned with it.

During the winter and spring of 1948 clothing and shoes ranked second as an expressed worry, with about four in ten AMZON adults mentioning it. But after the currency reform this figure dropped and by August only eight per cent thought it important enough to mention. In Berlin, however, the drop was only from 32 per cent to 14 per cent.

Fuel was a less pervasive worry but one which showed the same tendency as food and clothing. In Berlin, after dropping to its usual summer low of one or two per cent in late spring, it rose again to one in ten during August.

Although worries over basic necessities tended to decrease after the currency reform to nearly manageable proportions, anxiety over the means of obtaining them skyrocketed. By midsummer, half the AMZON population (48%) said that they had no means of livelihood and by August this figure had risen to 59 per cent.

In all the surveys, a small group of people in AMZON (less than 5%) mentioned concern about the future in general. In West Berlin, however, it rose from about five per cent to 13 per cent in mid-April, dropped again in May and then rose again, remaining relatively high (10% to 14%) during June, July, and August.

Most of the other kinds of cares and worries remained fairly constant: anxiety about prisoners of war and missing persons (6-9%), loss of housing (8-14%), Nazi Party membership (0-2%), health (3-6%), evacuee difficulties (8-9%). The number claiming to have no worry varied from one to five per cent of the AMZON sample.

Report No. 140 (24 September 1948)

OPINIONS ON THE PROPOSED WITHDRAWAL OF THE FOUR OCCUPYING POWERS

Sample: an unspecified number; a representative sample of residents of the American Zone, West Berlin, and Bremen. *Interviewing dates:* August 1948. (4 pp.)

The proposal by the Soviet Union calling for the withdrawal from Germany of all four occupying powers was greeted with mixed feelings by many Germans. On the one hand, they favored the idea of the withdrawal but, on the other hand, they were dubious of the proposal since it emanated from the Russians. In AMZON 39 per cent said they would like to see the proposal carried out while 49 per cent were distrustful of it. The lack of enthusiasm for the proposal was most marked in Bavaria, where over half (54%) rejected it.

Throughout AMZON, those with more education and higher economic status were less ready to accept the suggestion. In West Berlin and Bremen, however, people tended to be more favorably disposed toward the proposal than in AMZON. In both cities, half the people (51 and 52 per cent, respectively) hoped it would be carried out.

In AMZON, respondents who perceived that the Americans had hindered the reconstruction of Germany were more likely to favor (58%) than to oppose (35%) the Soviet proposal; those for and against the formation of a West German government (54 and 53 per cent respectively) were almost equally against the Soviet idea; and persons who thought that the formation of a West German government would have no influence on the East-West split were more likely to oppose the idea (58%) than were those who thought that the establishment of such a government would widen this split (51%).

Report No. 141 (4 October 1948)

BERLIN ATTITUDES ON THE AIR LIFT:
FURTHER TRENDS

Sample: 300 people in West Berlin.
Interviewing dates: 16 and 17 September 1948, three months after suspension of land traffic to Berlin. (3 pp.)

While in July only 45 per cent of the Berlin population thought the Western Powers would be able to bring in enough supplies by air to maintain life in the city, by September this figure had risen to 85 per cent. At the same time, indications were that the accomplishments of the air lift had brought some West Berliners to the belief that Western capabilities were limitless. In July, 77 per cent had felt the West was doing its utmost and only 22 per cent thought they could do more; by September, 66 per cent thought they were doing their utmost and 32 per cent felt they could do more.

Confidence in the fact that the Americans would stay in Berlin as long as they stayed in Germany remained high and constant between July and September (87-89%); a year earlier, however, the figure had been appreciably lower (74%).

Despite the restrictions and hardships caused by the blockade, West Berliners were almost unanimous (88%) in saying that they preferred things as they were rather than a united city under the control of the communist-dominated Socialist Unity Party (4%).

Report No. 142 (5 October 1948)

ATTITUDES TOWARD JEIA

Sample: a representative sample of residents of the American Zone, West Berlin, and Bremen.
Interviewing dates: latter part of July 1948. (3 pp.)

Only 30 per cent of AMZON residents claimed to have heard or read something about the Joint Export-Import Agency (JEIA). In Bremen the figure was twice as high (59%), while less than a fourth (24%) of the West Berliners said they had heard of it.

Of those who had heard of JEIA, half knew that it regulated both German exports and imports. Only half of the informed respondents in AMZON and Bremen and a third of the informed West Berliners could evaluate its work. Most of those with opinions thought that it functioned well or fairly well.

Report No. 143 (14 October 1948)

GOVERNMENT OR ADMINISTRATION FOR WESTERN GERMANY?

Sample: 1,500 people in the American Zone, 250 in West Berlin, and 162 in Bremen.
Interviewing dates: August 1948. (6 pp.)

To the majority of AMZON respondents (58%) it made no difference whether the proposed provisional western German organization was called a "government" or an "administration." Of those who did express a preference, more people favored, especially in Bavaria (27%), the label "government" as proposed by the Western Powers. Only in Berlin was a majority (56%) even concerned about drawing this distinction, and then the respondents split evenly in their support of the two terms.

More men than women felt it was important to decide between the rival conceptions; the same was true of those with higher educational and socioeconomic levels.

Of those favoring the notion of "government" rather than "administration," the majority in AMZON (66%), Berlin (73%), and Bremen (63%) referred to what they considered to be desirable implications of greater power, responsibility and prestige. For the smaller group of people who favored the term "administration," the reasons were more diversified although the greatest number (40%) explained that, as long as Germany was controlled by the Western Powers, one could not speak of a government.

In addition to the usual questions, this survey contained a series of 12 questions designed to yield a scale of confidence in the Western Powers and support for the term "government." Those with the least confidence in the West most favored the "administration" label.

Report No. 144 (26 October 1948)

U.S. ZONE GERMANS VIEW THE AIR LIFT

Sample: 500 American Zone residents in July and 3,000 in August; 300 West Berliners in July and 511 in August; 107 people from Bremen in July and 320 in August.
Interviewing dates: July and August 1948. (5 pp.)

The number of AMZON residents who expected the Americans to stay in Berlin increased from 59 per cent in July to 71 per cent in August. In West Berlin itself, the vast majority of respondents thought they would stay although the figures did decrease from 89 per cent in July to 87 per cent in August. In all three areas, in AMZON, Bremen, and Berlin, respondents were almost unanimous in saying that the Western Powers were doing the right thing by staying in Berlin; this opinion did not vary significantly in the July and August surveys. Although most people agreed that the Western Powers should remain in Berlin, they had different reasons for feeling this way: Almost half (45%) of the AMZON residents and over half (56%) of those living in Bremen felt that if the West withdrew at that time it would mean a victory for communism. In West Berlin, by way of contrast, 58 per cent mentioned drastic personal implications for the Berliners.

Almost nine out of ten AMZON Germans (88%) as compared to 75 per cent in West Berlin thought that the West was putting all of its might into the air lift. Nonetheless, although 84 per cent of the Berliners said that the air lift would in the future supply West Berlin with enough food to maintain rations at their then-current level, only 56 per cent of the AMZON Germans expressed such confidence.

Most Germans, especially West Berliners (82%), felt that the prestige of the Western Powers had gone up as a result of the air lift, and conversely that Soviet prestige had gone down.

In August 1947, 44 per cent of the AMZON residents predicted war within the next decade. By April 1948 an even 50 per cent held this expectation. And in the summer of 1948, 67 per cent said they expected war; in West Berlin the figure was as high as 82 per cent. In fact, 73 per cent of West Berlin respondents felt that the situation at that time was serious enough to cause a war within the near future; in AMZON only 59 per cent thought this to be true.

Report No. 145 (1 November 1948)

THE "AMERIKA HAUS" IN FIVE GERMAN CITIES

Sample: a random sample of 300 adults from each of five cities: West Berlin, Bremen, Frankfurt, Nuremberg, and Stuttgart, as well as Munich as presented in an appendix. *Interviewing dates:* last two weeks of September 1948. (19 pp.)

The report consists of three parts: a general discussion of the five cities, the summary of a similar study done in Munich in late July 1948, and a series of 20 tables giving detailed statistics from each of the five cities.

Majorities ranging from 52 per cent in West Berlin to 74 per cent in Nuremberg knew that there was an *Amerika Haus* in their city, and four in ten of the total adult population in each of the five cities could mention specific things offered there.

Asked how they had found out about the *Amerika Haus*, most people mentioned newspapers, although the radio and conversations with others were also frequently mentioned. A comparison with a survey made in March 1948 showed that knowledge of *Amerika Haus* offerings had increased approximately fourfold.

In each of the cities, the most frequent visitors to *Amerika Haus* programs were the better-educated groups, particularly community and opinion leaders. And in all cities except West Berlin and Nuremberg, about twice as many men as women said they had visited one.

In Munich, 26 per cent of the respondents could name offerings of their city's *Amerika Haus*, a smaller proportion than in any of the other cities studied. The most frequently listed facilities of the center were the libraries and books (65%). Only four per cent said that they had actually been in the *Amerika Haus* there.

As in the other cities, majority opinion (56%) viewed the purpose of the *Amerika Haus* to be giving visitors the opportunity to take part in various activities and to read books from the United States and other countries.

Report No. 146 (13 November 1948)

THE PROBLEM OF CLEANLINESS IN PRESENT-DAY GERMANY

Sample: a representative sample of 1,500 people in the American Zone, 242 in West Berlin, and 160 in Bremen. *Interviewing dates:* August 1948. (11 pp.)

In their own eyes the Germans ranked first in prewar standards of cleanliness as compared with the peoples of the four occupying powers. Asked about Germany's international ranking in cleanliness under current conditions, 23 per cent of AMZON residents and 26 per cent in Bremen still placed German standards first.

West Berliners (and it should be remembered that the study was made during the blockade) were least satisfied with the level of cleanliness which they were able to achieve (69%); men and people from the upper and upper-middle classes were also less satisfied than their counterpart groups.

When asked whether the inability to keep sufficiently clean had any effect on their character, 83 per cent of the West Berliners and 80 per cent of the Bremen residents replied in the affirmative. The most frequently mentioned effect (67%) was a feeling of inferiority and irritability. Questioned specifically about soap supplies, 76 per cent of the West Berliners, 74 per cent of the Bremen residents, and 50 per cent of the AMZON residents said that they managed poorly with the amount of soap at their disposal. This was true despite the fact that large proportions in both West Berlin (79%) and Bremen (77%) said that they supplemented their soap ration through outside sources. In fact, the largest proportion of West Berlin and Bremen respondents felt that three times as much soap as they currently were getting was needed as a minimum supply.

In West Berlin, 39 per cent of the respondents said that they were never able to take a bath or shower, but a further 23 per cent said that they did so once a week. In AMZON, without the handicaps of the blockade, fully three out of ten still maintained that they could never take a bath and 43 per cent said they did so once a week.

The problem of soap aside, the most irritating difficulty on the score of cleanliness reported in AMZON and in Bremen was the lack of sufficient clothing. In West Berlin it was the lack of fuel.

Report No. 147 (17 November 1948)

HOW BERLINERS EXPECT AND WANT THE CRISIS SETTLED: WITH THEIR RECOMMENDATIONS

Sample: a representative sample of 400 people living in West Berlin.
Interviewing dates: middle of October 1948. (8 pp.)

Four months after the suspension of land traffic to West Berlin, residents of the city expressed little hope that the crisis would be settled in a desirable way. Most (46%) expected only further disagreement and quite a few (27%) thought that the city would be divided into East and West Berlin. What they hoped for was that the Four Powers would agree peacefully and return to Four Power administration of the city (39%); a quarter hoped that the Soviets would leave Berlin with only the West remaining; and 24 per cent said that they would like all four occupying countries to leave.

If the West Berliners had been in a position to decide how the Western Powers should settle the Berlin problem, 58 per cent would have used more force against the Soviet Union than the West was doing. The intensity of this feeling was shown by the fact that 46 per cent of the respondents wanted the West to take active steps even if it meant war; 50 per cent said a war should be avoided even if it meant that the blockade would continue. Larger numbers of men, young people, the well educated, and those in the upper and middle economic levels than their counterpart groups considered breaking the blockade more important than avoiding war. Those whose morale was low enough to want to leave Berlin were more likely to say that the West should break the blockade (55%) than were those with higher morale who wanted to stay in the city (43%).

A large majority of Berliners (83%) considered the Americans to be in a superior military position and felt that the United States would win in case war did come.

Almost unanimously (95 per cent; in July the figure had been 98 per cent) West Berliners thought that the West was doing the right thing by staying in Berlin and about nine in ten thought that they would continue to stay. The large majority of West Berliners (65%) thought that the Western powers were doing their utmost to relieve distressed conditions in the city. A growing minority, however, (from 22 per cent in July to 34 per cent in October) felt that the West could do more. Asked what they could use more of, 14 per cent mentioned food and, with the approach of winter, 12 per cent said coal and solid fuel.

Report No. 148 (30 November 1948)

RADIO BREMEN EVALUATED BY BREMEN LISTENERS

Sample: 167 persons randomly selected from a listing of radio owners in Bremen as contained in the Deutsche Post file.
Interviewing dates: early September 1948. (5 pp.)

Nine out of ten radio-owners (89%) said that they were regular listeners. On an average, three people listened to each set. A vast majority (96%) reported listening to the radio in the evening. Every single person interviewed claimed to listen to Radio Bremen, with the Nord-West Deutscher Rundfunk being the second most popular station (63%).

Most people (87%) preferred news broadcasts with light music a close second (69%). Although the great majority of Bremen radio-owners (80%) were satisfied with Radio Bremen programs, about two in ten said that they would like some programs cut down or eliminated altogether so that others could be lengthened.

Over half (54%) of the respondents felt that the radio stations ought to be independently owned; only 22 per cent preferred state ownership. Those wanting independent ownership were most inclined to think that state ownership precluded really free expression of opinion (34%), private initiative produced better programs (17%), or only independent radio could be unpolitical (3%). Proponents of state ownership most frequently cited the need either for financial assistance (11%) or for governmental supervision (8%).

Report No. 149 (10 December 1948)

TRENDS AND PRESENT ATTITUDES
ON THE MARSHALL PLAN

Sample: approximately 3,000 cases in the American Zone, 500 in West Berlin, and 300 in Bremen.
Interviewing dates: 17 September 1948, with reference to four other surveys between 4 August 1947 and 2 August 1948. (11 pp.)

For a previous report on reactions to the Marshall Plan, see Report No. 104, 24 March 1948.

By September 1948 awareness of the Marshall Plan had spread to the point where fully nine out of ten in Berlin (90%) and Bremen (91%) said they had heard or read something about the European Recovery Program and as many as three out of four in AMZON (76%). Ignorance of the Marshall Plan in AMZON was most concentrated among the lowest socioeconomic level where 44 per cent were still unaware of the European Aid Program.

From the outset the majority reaction to the plan was one of approval (74 per cent in favor, 3 per cent against). In AMZON, this approval was greatest among residents of Wuerttemberg-Baden (87%), men (82%), the higher educated (82%), older (79%), and economically better situated (87%), and those living in larger cities. Increasing numbers of Germans viewed the American motives in promulgating the Marshall Plan in a favorable light, as a sincere desire to help Europe get back on its feet (51 per cent in September 1948). Prevention of communism, however, was the most frequently cited motive in all five surveys (74%). The upper socioeconomic levels saw more materialistic motivations in American support of the Marshall Plan than did the lower levels, but it was also the former group that was most favorably disposed to the Plan. Youth was less sold on it and more suspicious of American motives than their elders.

Although extremely few Germans (3%) thought that the United States would withdraw its support completely, there was a certain degree of pessimism concerning the continuing adequacy of American aid to Europe. AMZON and Bremen respondents seemed to be less confident of the continued sufficiency of American aid specifically to Germany than they were of the sufficiency of such aid to Europe in general. In Berlin, however, where the air lift was in progress, there was more widespread confidence in America's willingness to continue aiding Germany.

Report No. 150 (15 December 1948)

ATTITUDES AND RESOURCES OF BERLINERS AS THEY LOOK FORWARD TO A BLOCKADED WINTER

Sample: representative sample of 400 persons living in West Berlin.
Interviewing dates: mid-October 1948. (12 pp.)

In October, 71 per cent of the Berlin population thought that the blockade would last through the winter, while in July only ten per cent had thought so.

Similarly, opinions reversed on the potentialities of the air lift. In July, 52 per cent felt that the Western Powers would not be able to maintain life in Berlin through the winter and 45 per cent thought they could; by August, 19 per cent felt they could not do so and 77 per cent thought they could; and in October, ten per cent responded negatively while 89 per cent felt it could be done.

Along with the belief that the blockade would last through the winter, most Berliners expected little help with their heating problem. A majority (55%) thought they would get enough heating material to survive, 12 per cent thought they would get enough to be fairly comfortable, and 33 per cent expected to get none. Over half (54%) had no heating material in the house at the time of the interview and about one-third (32%) had no candles or lamps to light their homes during those times when the electricity would be turned off. Among those lacking both heat and light – as compared with the group having both – there were more old people, women, those with little education, and those in the lower socioeconomic group. Over half (54%) of this deprived group felt that the West could do more to help the distressed conditions in Berlin. Surprisingly, however, their outlook on the general situation in the city was somewhat more optimistic in that fewer expected war, and more thought the big four would come to an agreement about the Berlin situation.

The financial status of almost all Berliners was grave. Although, on the average, families had about as many East Marks as they needed, they lacked 85 West Marks in order to make ends meet. In addition, over half (55%) of the families with no way of heating or lighting their homes also reported having no West Marks whatever in their previous month's income.

About two-thirds (61%) of the Berliners reported that their mood was the same at the time of the interview as it had been before the blockade; one-quarter (25%) said it was worse, eight per cent said much worse, and, interestingly enough, six per cent said their morale had improved. Less than a third (30%) said they would want to leave Berlin if given the opportunity, as compared with 43 per cent who felt this way in July.

Report No. 151 (18 December 1948)

SECURITY VERSUS FREEDOM IN BLOCKADED BERLIN

Sample: unspecified.

Interviewing dates: summary of seven surveys made between February 1947 and November 1948. (4 pp.)

Until June 1948 there had been a slight trend toward an increased vote for "freedom" and a decreased vote for "economic security" in response to a question designed to measure their relative importance. In general, however, a clear majority of about six out of ten preferred "freedom." In November 1948 a definite change in the majority point of view took place: Over half (54%) told Military Government interviewers that they preferred a government which assured "freedom" to one which provides "economic security." These findings were all the more significant in view of the fact that they occurred at a time when the economic security of the Berliners had, if anything, been decreasing.

Report No. 152 (24 January 1949)

AMZON VIEWS ITS CIVIL SERVICE

I. Religion and Party Membership as a Factor in Government Employment

Sample: approximately 1,500 cases in the American Zone. *Interviewing dates:* December 1948. (7 pp.)

More than half (55%) of the Germans in AMZON said that members of SPD and CDU/CSU were equally well-qualified to hold government jobs; an even greater majority (75%) felt this was true of Catholics and Protestants. Of the few who did claim there was a difference, relatively more felt that SPD members were better qualified (15%) than members of the CDU/CSU (8%); and in Bavaria more people considered Catholics better equipped (14%) than Protestants (6%). Pluralities in all three *Laender* felt that members of both leading parties enjoyed an equal chance for government work, although in Bavaria 23 per cent felt that CDU/CSU members had a better chance. Majorities said that government jobs were also equally available to members of the two faiths. Again, however, Bavarians noted that they felt it was easier for the dominant faith there, the Catholics, to obtain such positions.

Although considerably more people believed that non-members of political parties were better qualified for government jobs (35 per cent, as opposed to 7 per cent who said that party members were better qualified, and 43 per cent who said that it made no difference), it was felt that party members could in fact obtain them more easily.

Opinion was evenly divided on whether or not government workers should be allowed to work actively for a political party (36 per cent in favor, 38 per cent against) but there was also a fairly large fraction of people (22%) with "no opinion" on the subject.

Report No. 153 (26 January 1949)

BOOK READING IN THE U. S. ZONE, BERLIN, AND BREMEN

Sample: 3,000 adults in the American Zone, 500 in West Berlin, and 300 in Bremen.
Interviewing dates: October 1948. (9 pp.)

In AMZON half (50%) the adult population claimed to be book readers; in Bremen and Berlin almost two-thirds (64%) made this claim. Residents of cities were more likely than small town and rural people to read books. Men, white-collar workers, and younger people were more likely to be book readers.

Entertaining literature and novels were far more popular than classics or nonfiction. The books most frequently mentioned were the Bible (71%) and the *Prayer Book* (27%), followed by the works of Goethe (19 per cent mentioning his *Faust* and 26 per cent listing other titles).

Half (45%) of the readers read fewer books then than before the war.

The currency reform did not greatly affect the overall availability of books since, on the one hand, it increased the number of books published although, on the other hand, it decreased the amount of money available to buy or rent them.

Report No. 154 (3 February 1949)

OPINIONS ON THE "NEUE ZEITUNG"

Sample: 1,500 adults in the American Zone, 250 in West Berlin, and 150 in Bremen.
Interviewing dates: December 1948. (10 pp.)

Claimed readership of the *Neue Zeitung* was largest in Berlin where 20 per cent said they read it regularly, smallest in Bremen where only four per cent claimed regular readership; in AMZON ten per cent were regular readers, with proportionately more readers in Wuerttemberg-Baden than in the other *Laender*. Sizable fractions had either stopped reading the paper or read it less frequently than before. Although the most frequently cited reason for no longer seeing the paper was lack of money, the absence of local news was probably as important a reason.

Large majorities of present and former readers (63%) said they liked the paper "well," and another large fraction (27%) said "moderately well"; very few of these respondents (3%) claimed not to like it at all. Few people recognized any change in the paper. Wide news coverage, the political news, and the literary and art features were most frequently cited as praiseworthy. But over one in ten (11%) criticized the literary and art features for being expressionist and too modern. Only bare majorities (51%) in AMZON called the paper "impartial" in its political reporting, as opposed to 22 per cent who thought the paper "one-sided."

Report No. 155 (3 February 1949)

THE TOWN HALL MEETING IN REILINGEN

Sample: 400 Reilingen residents between the ages of 15 and 50, selected from current ration card lists.
Interviewing dates: 25 September 1948. (9 pp.)

The survey is based on the first town hall meeting held in Reilingen, a typical small town in Wuerttemberg-Baden, on 15 September 1948. The town had at that time a population of 3,500, with most residents being small farmers, many of whom worked in nearby factories.

Ten days after the meeting, 19 per cent said they had attended, 68 per cent said they had heard of it but not attended, and only 13 per cent had neither attended nor heard of it. A large majority (78%) of the informed respondents felt that public forums of this kind were useful. Almost all of the Reilingen population approved the idea of future town hall meetings. Of those who had attended or heard about the first one, 95 per cent expressed such approval; of those who had not heard about it, 82 per cent thought it would be a good idea. If another meeting were held, more than three times as many people (63%) said they would attend than had been at the first one. Only a minuscule one per cent claimed they had no intention of going a second time.

Almost all (97%) of the respondents who took part in the Reilingen meeting felt that participation by Americans was desirable.

Just over half (52%) of the audience either had no criticisms to make of the meeting or could not or did not wish to articulate adverse comments. The criticisms that were made were directed primarily at the Military Government officials.

Four out of ten of those actually present at the Reilingen meeting claimed they had learned something new and interesting. Of even greater significance is the fact that just as many of those who knew of but had not attended the meeting also claimed to have learned something from it. Finally, although only one of three people interviewed before the meeting could name the *Landrat*, three out of four could identify him after the meeting.

Report No. 156 (9 February 1949)

AMZON VIEWS ITS CIVIL SERVICE

II. Men versus Women in Public Employ

Sample: 1,500 respondents in the American Zone.
Interviewing dates: December 1948. (5 pp.)

Both a majority of men (61%) and a majority of women (56%) felt that men were basically better qualified for government jobs. Only a third (34%) felt there was no difference. About two-thirds (64%) of men and women in AMZON agreed that it was easier at the time of the interview for men to obtain positions with the government than for women. More than a third (37%) felt that a woman did not have the same opportunity for government work even when she had the same abilities. Significantly enough, however, fully two-thirds (67%) of the group holding this last opinion approved of such a state of affairs.

Report No. 157 (3 February 1949)

OPINIONS ON THE WORK STOPPAGE IN BAVARIA

Sample: 1,600 residents of Bavaria.
Interviewing dates: late November and early December 1948. (5 pp.)

The report concerns the work stoppage in Bavaria on 12 November 1948. One-tenth (9%) of the respondents said that they themselves had participated in the demonstration while 12 per cent said that a member of their immediate family had done likewise. Support for the strikes came chiefly from men, those under thirty, and from urban dwellers. Only two per cent claimed that the stoppage affected their daily routine.

Asked whether such work stoppages were right or wrong, nearly two-thirds (64%) disapproved of them, 16 per cent approved, seven per cent had mixed feelings, and 13 per cent withheld judgment. Of those approving, most argued that it was an effective way to protest the high cost of living. The most frequently heard argument against the stoppages was that they were useless, did not accomplish anything.

Report No. 158 (4 February 1949)

BREMEN VIEWS THE PICTURAMA "AMERICA TODAY"

Sample: 188 write-in questionnaires.
Interviewing dates: 24 January 1948. (12 pp.)

Bremen audience reaction to the picturama *America Today* was overwhelmingly (96%) favorable, and 97 per cent would recommend it to friends. A third (34%) of the audience reported that their opinions of the United States became more favorable as a result of the program, while a majority (60%) maintained that their attitudes remained the same. Two-thirds (65%) thought the pictures and commentary equally interesting; a third (32%) preferred the pictures. Pluralities among university-educated people felt that the presentation of certain topics, such as American foreign relations and black Americans, was neither very impressive nor very realistic. Many respondents wrote on the questionnaire additional comments, the most frequent of which was that the program was crammed too full.

Report No. 159 (11 February 1949)

BAVARIAN REACTIONS TO TOWN HALL MEETINGS AND PUBLIC FORUMS

Sample: cross-section of Bavarian population with 1,608 respondents in 108 communities and towns, as well as mayors and deputy mayors in each community selected.
Interviewing dates: late October 1948. (10 pp.)

About one in four (27%) of the people in Bavaria (excluding Munich and Nuremberg) claimed to have heard of public forums, town hall meetings, or similar assemblies. Only six per cent said they had taken part in such a meeting, with four times as many men as women making this claim.

Over three-quarters (78%) of those who knew about the meetings approved them; approval was higher among those who had attended one than among those who had only heard of them.

Mayors' views on the meetings were divided. Among those from towns where no assemblies had been held, on the one hand, twice as many expressed negative views as positive opinions on their value. On the other hand, five times as many mayors of towns where meetings had been held made favorable rather than unfavorable comments.

Meetings without Military Government sponsorship had taken place in about 15 per cent of the localities included in the sample. It appeared that the Military Government sponsored meetings in larger towns and cities more frequently than in smaller villages.

Report No. 160 (23 February 1949)

GERMANS CONSIDER THE WITHDRAWAL
OF THE OCCUPYING POWERS

Sample: a representative sample of 1,500 adults in the American Zone, 250 in West Berlin, and 150 in Bremen. *Interviewing dates:* August and November 1948. (6 pp.)

The report stems from the Soviet proposal that all occupying powers withdraw from Germany. In November almost six in ten AMZON residents (57%) as compared with 49 per cent in August rejected this proposal. A third (34%) still saw virtue in the idea but the trend appeared to be toward rejection. A breakdown of replies of different groups in the population shows that people with university training or of higher socioeconomic status disapproved with greater frequency than others.

The inference that acceptance of the proposal arose in part from a failure to note some of its implications received strong support from replies to a further question concerning its effects on German security. Of the 65 per cent of respondents in AMZON who felt that Germany would not be in a politically secure position if the occupying powers withdrew, most feared civil war and chaos; they also mentioned the fear of Soviet aggression.

When questioned as to Soviet motives in making the proposal, only one per cent in AMZON had something nice to say about the Russians. By far the most common (65%) reason given was that it was a Soviet scheme to get control of Germany. Asked then whether any of the occupying powers would misuse this plan to gain greater influence in Germany, 65 per cent in AMZON mentioned the Russians and four per cent pointed to the Western Powers.

Report No. 161 (24 February 1949)

SOME GERMAN OPINIONS ON OCCUPATION COSTS

Sample: 1,500 adults in the American Zone, 250 in West Berlin, and 150 in Bremen.
Interviewing dates: December 1948. (6 pp.)

There was widespread ignorance of the German share of American occupation costs. Less than a quarter (22%) in Bremen, 39 per cent in Berlin, and 43 per cent in AMZON were unable even to hazard a guess as to the German share. Of the Germans who did give estimates, almost four out of ten (38%) in AMZON, and in Bremen a full majority of 61 per cent thought that the Germans were paying substantially all of these costs; in Berlin the proportion was not so large, but still an appreciable 29 per cent.

Breakdowns of the major population groups show first that those people who usually had fewer opinions on other subjects likewise had fewer opinions on the subject of occupation costs. The breakdowns also reveal that the groups who were usually best informed – men, the well-educated, those with higher socioeconomic status, and city-dwellers – definitely tended more often than did their counterparts to make the larger estimates.

Only one AMZON respondent in ten suggested that occupation costs were a major cause of the difficulties which the *Laender* had in balancing their budgets. This suggests that there was little support for the view of the German officials who pointed to occupation costs as the major problem regarding *Laender* finances.

Report No. 162 (4 March 1949)

CHARACTERISTICS OF NATIVES AND REFUGEES IN AMZON IN 1948

Sample: varies from as low as 1,500 to a maximum of 6,000.
Interviewing dates: during summer and fall of 1948. (6 pp.)

The report consists of seven tables showing differences between refugees and nonrefugees in AMZON. In general, the middle-aged population groups were overrepresented among the refugees; they were more inclined to support the SPD than were natives; their occupational and educational status was lower, as was their income; they had a higher rate of unemployment, were more Catholic, and lived in smaller towns than the natives.

Report No. 163 (7 March 1949)

SOCIAL CHARACTERISTICS OF THE GERMAN PEOPLE IN BAVARIA, HESSE, AND WUERTTEMBERG-BADEN

Sample: 8,056 in Bavaria, 3,643 in Hesse, and 3,274 in Wuerttemberg-Baden.
Interviewing Dates: between 15 February 1947 and 8 July 1947. (45 pp.)

The report consists of 34 tables cross-tabulating demographic variables of the populations in Bavaria, Hesse, and Wuerttemberg-Baden. The variables included are: sex, age, education, occupation, size of community, monthly income, social status, religion, former NSDAP membership, present party membership, and political party preference. A detailed explanation of sampling procedures as well as a definition of the various terms used throughout the report precedes the presentation of the data.

Report No. 164 (2 April 1949)

AMZON VIEWS ITS CIVIL SERVICE

III. Prestige Value of Government Work

Sample: approximately 1,500 cases in the American Zone.
Interviewing dates: December 1948. (7 pp.)

Fifteen per cent of AMZON adults claim that they were at that time or had at one time been employed by the government. Of the remaining 85 per cent, very few had ever considered doing so.

The prestige value of working for the government was not particularly high in AMZON. It was generally lowest among the better-educated and among the young; highest among those with less education and those over 50 years of age. Given a choice between a position with the government and an equivalent one in private industry, 31 per cent preferred government work, 16 per cent did not care which, and 48 per cent opted clearly for private industry. The chief argument in favor of private industry was freedom from bureaucracy, that for government work was security and pensions. Finally, more people (47%) preferred to see their sons work for the government than wanted to do so themselves.

Nearly four out of ten (37%) felt that some government offices were overstaffed. Those most frequently mentioned were the ration board, housing, and employment offices. These were also the offices mentioned most often by the 25 per cent of the population who felt that some offices could be eliminated entirely. On both questions, the young, the better-educated, and former government employees were more inclined to say that some offices could be reduced or abolished.

Report No. 165 (22 April 1949)

OPINION ON FUSION IN WUERTTEMBERG AND BADEN

Sample: about 600 respondents in Wuerttemberg-Baden. *Interviewing dates:* autumn 1948. (7 pp.)

A plurality of people (46%) in both Wuerttemberg and Baden hoped for unification of the three *Laender* of Wuerttemberg-Baden, Wuerttemberg-Hohenzollern, and Suedbaden. About a quarter (27%) felt that the entire territory should be divided into two *Laender*: Wuerttemberg and Baden, a return to prewar political boundaries. Only six per cent preferred the existing situation. The two groups most favorably disposed to unification were the better-educated (69%) and former members of the NSDAP (73%).

Almost all respondents who favored change also felt that the change ought to be made immediately. However, about one-half of the original number withdrew their support for change when it was suggested that this might mean a rise in taxes. Those who did not withdraw their support were primarily the higher-educated, men, and older people.

Although most people were unable to name any specific hindrance to unification, three such hindrances cited most frequently were: traditional differences, disunity among *Laender* governments, and differences among the occupying powers.

Report No. 166 (25 April 1949)

PUBLIC ATTITUDES TOWARD POSTWAR GERMAN POLICE

I. General Appraisals

> *Sample:* a cross-section of 1,900 residents of the American Zone, West Berlin, and Bremen.
> *Interviewing dates:* December 1948. (9 pp.)

Nearly two-thirds (64%) of the people in AMZON seemed reasonably well-satisfied with the German police force with regard to its primary function of maintaining order and security; the figures were higher in Berlin (71%) and Bremen (70%), and somewhat lower in Bavaria (61%). A plurality (47%) of AMZON respondents also thought that the police force provided as much security and order as in former times, although a large minority (37%) expressed the opposite view. Among those who thought the police force better in a prior era, the Nazi period was the one most frequently cited in this connection.

In AMZON 45 per cent thought the police should not have more authority. When the 31 per cent who would like the police to have more power in certain areas were asked to be specific, they most frequently mentioned the black market and control over displaced persons. Only four per cent in AMZON named areas in which they felt the police had too much power at that time.

Six in ten AMZON respondents (59%) did not want members of the police force to take an active part in political life. More than half (55%) felt that policemen should not run for public office.

Only a relatively small proportion (17%) of the respondents in AMZON thought that the members of the police force came primarily from certain groups in the population. A strong majority also felt that the police force should draw its members evenly from all parts of the population.

When asked whether they thought the local police should be under the mayor of the town or under the Ministry of the Interior, Bavaria and Wuerttemberg-Baden residents (38 and 40 per cent, respectively) favored decentralized control at the town level; in Bremen and Hesse, a plurality (22 and 21 per cent, respectively) favored control at the *Land* level. High "no opinion" figures show that the issue is not particularly salient for the respondents.

Report No. 167 (25 April 1949)

PUBLIC ATTITUDES TOWARD POSTWAR GERMAN POLICE

II. Awareness of Civil Rights versus Police Powers

Sample: a cross-section of 1,900 residents in the American Zone, Berlin, and Bremen.
Interviewing dates: December 1948. (10 pp.)

Only one person in twenty (5%) in AMZON and Bremen (one in 12 in Berlin) was aware of the fact that the new postwar constitution of their *Laender* or cities provided certain protections for the individual against the arbitrary use of power by the police. Still fewer could name a specific measure designed to protect civil rights. Large majorities nonetheless had a sensible proposal as to what they would do if they felt that the police had violated their rights.

About six people in ten in AMZON (62 per cent, as contrasted with 69 and 72 per cent in Berlin and Bremen respectively) were aware that an off-duty policeman is "just another citizen" with no particular authority.

Over three-quarters (77%) of the AMZON respondents thought that the police had a right to search a private dwelling without a warrant, merely on suspicion that a suspect might be there. When asked about a hypothetical case in which a policeman levied an on-the-spot fine, only 44 per cent in AMZON knew he had exceeded his authority. Over half (54%) the AMZON respondents, however, were aware of a suspect's right to be brought before a judge within a reasonable amount of time after his arrest. Even more people (55%) were aware that a police chief has no right to break up a peaceful public meeting on the grounds that he doesn't like the sentiments being expressed. Finally about six in ten (59%) were aware that a police chief has no authorization to precensor newspaper editorials of which he disapproves.

Report No. 168 (27 April 1949)

WEST BERLIN'S REACTION TO A SINGLE CURRENCY

Sample: a cross-section of 300 West Berliners.
Interviewing dates: 29-30 March 1949, ten days after the announcement that the East Mark would cease to be legal tender in the western sectors of Berlin. (7 pp.)

Eight in ten respondents (81%) felt that it was basically necessary to make the West Mark the only legal tender in West Berlin. Of those who thought it unnecessary, most cited the personal disadvantages they suffered.

Six in ten (62%) thought the conversion was carried out justly. Among those who felt it was unjustly carried out, 15 per cent thought the rate of exchange was too low.

Two-thirds (68%) of West Berlin's residents thought that they personally would be better off as a result of the currency change. More people could think of certain groups within the population that might be worse off as a result of the change than could think of groups that might profit from it. Those who had to cross into the Soviet Sector to work were considered by most to be the hardest hit.

The majority (59%) of respondents thought that the conversion would have little influence on the east-west split of Germany.

As another consequence of the change, 62 per cent felt that black market activities would decrease; 16 per cent felt they would stop altogether. Most West Berliners (84%) thought that they would continue to be able to use their East Marks. A majority (57%) also foresaw a currency change in East Berlin.

Report No. 169 (6 May 1949)

GERMAN APPRAISAL OF "LASTENAUSGLEICH"

Sample: about 1,500 residents of the American Zone, 250 West Berliners, and 150 people from Bremen.
Interviewing dates: November 1948. (12 pp.)

About three-quarters of the population in AMZON (73%) and Bremen (76%) knew the meaning of the term *Lastenausgleich*, a term used to refer to policies aimed at equalizing war losses among the people. In Berlin, however, only 30 per cent of the respondents could give a satisfactory definition of the term. In Berlin and Bremen an overwhelming majority (91 per cent and 89 per cent, respectively) was in favor of the programs; in AMZON the people were slightly less enthusiastic (74%).

More than half of the respondents felt that the program should be carried out immediately and more than eight in ten thought it would indeed be carried out eventually. A large minority in AMZON and Berlin (43 per cent and 41 per cent, respectively) and 50 per cent in Bremen, however, thought it could not possibly be carried out fairly.

Refugees and bombed-out persons were most frequently mentioned as the ones who ought to benefit from the program. Almost a fourth (24%) of the AMZON respondents expected to benefit themselves; almost a third (32%) expected that they would have to pay for a *Lastenausgleich*.

In AMZON only 40 per cent of the respondents knew that German authorities would develop the plans for the equalization program. Among those who knew about the program, 40 per cent wished that the Americans would carry it out as contrasted to only 26 per cent who wanted German authorities to implement the plan. Reasons given by the former group were almost without exception variants of the theme that the Military Government would be more just and more objective than German officials. This was particularly the case among those expecting to receive something from, rather than pay something to, the program.

Report No. 170 (16 May 1949)

GERMAN ATTITUDES TOWARD ECONOMIC AND POLITICAL STRIKES

> *Sample:* 1,500 residents of the American Zone, 250 West Berliners, and 150 people in Bremen.
> *Interviewing dates:* February 1949. (9 pp.)

The large majority of respondents in AMZON (68%), Bremen (81%), and Berlin (72%) disapproved of strikes for higher wages.

In AMZON, however, fewer people disapproved of political than of economic strikes, although more respondents expressed indecisiveness by giving "no opinion." The main reason advanced in support of strikes for political purposes was to call politicians' attention to the shortcomings of their decisions. The main counterargument was that such strikes are useless and accomplish nothing.

Respondents from the younger age group were more willing to express approval of both economic and political strikes, but even with them it was only a minority sentiment. As might be anticipated, people in the upper income and better-educated groups—where most employers are found—looked more askance at strikes for better wages or more food. Attitudes on political strikes could not be categorized so easily. Among political groups, SPD sympathizers registered widest support for strikes, although the extent of approval was still no greater than three out of ten. Even among union members, less than one out of three supported strikes as an economic or political weapon; moreover, present union members were less favorable toward the idea of strikes than were would-be members.

Group comparisons for the AMZON population add up to the clear suggestion that disapproval of strikes was not an attitude localized among particular groups, but was the dominating sentiment among all the major segments of German society.

Report No. 171 (23 May 1949)

CHARACTERISTICS AND ATTITUDES OF THE GERMAN MOVIE AUDIENCE

I. Impact of Currency Reform on Attendance

Sample: a representative sample of 3,000 American Zone residents, 500 West Berliners, and 300 people in Bremen. *Interviewing dates:* November 1948. (6 pp.)

The currency reform markedly reduced movie attendance, especially in West Berlin. About a fifth (21%) of the AMZON population went to a movie once a month or more frequently. Young people, the better-educated, and those of upper socio-economic status attended films more frequently than did others. Most moviegoers wished that they could see more movies; lack of money was the main reason given for not doing so.

As would be expected, theaters were least accessible to AMZON's rural population. They were most accessible to people living in towns between 5,000 and 10,000 population rather than in the largest AMZON cities. People living close to a theater saw considerably more movies than those at a distance.

Only a negligible number of Germans (4 per cent in AMZON) had seen an American movie in an American theater, thus being exposed to productions whose suitability for German consumption had not been controlled.

Report No. 172 (23 May 1949)

CHARACTERISTICS AND ATTITUDES OF THE GERMAN MOVIE AUDIENCE

II. Most Popular Type of Movie

Sample: 3,000 residents of the American Zone, over 500 West Berliners, and 300 people from Bremen. *Interviewing dates:* November 1948. (7 pp.)

Among those who went to movies, a large majority (67 per cent in AMZON) selected a film rather than going to any film that happened to be showing when they had time. Selection was based primarily on advice from friends and the film title, as well as advertising. Newspaper commentaries were also instrumental.

Most people who went to movies hoped to find entertainment and diversion rather than serious problems, although a sizable minority (21 per cent in AMZON) expressed an interest in problem films. Movies accenting a love theme appeared to be the most popular kind of film; in AMZON, movies featuring classical or operatic music vied with revues for second place.

Of the 26 films people listed as their favorites, 13 were produced in the United States, eight were German, four British, and one was from France. In West Berlin, foreign films were more popular: Of the fifteen favorite films listed by respondents, only four were made in Germany.

Report No. 173 (18 May 1949)

CHARACTERISTICS AND ATTITUDES OF THE GERMAN MOVIE AUDIENCE

III. German Versus American Films

Sample: 3,000 residents of the American Zone, over 500 West Berliners, and 300 people in Bremen.
Interviewing dates: November 1948. (7 pp.)

A larger percentage of people in AMZON, West Berlin, and Bremen had seen American films than had seen pictures made in either Great Britain, France, or Russia.

About half of the AMZON and Bremen moviegoers (45 per cent and 48 per cent, respectively) said that German films were better than foreign ones; in West Berlin only 30 per cent felt this way. Asked to compare the quality of the best American films with the best German films, most people (66 per cent in AMZON; 79 per cent in Bremen; 73 per cent in West Berlin) felt that they were of about the same caliber. Those who felt that German films were better said that they thought the contents more worthwhile. Those who rated American films more highly cited their technical superiority. Less than one-quarter (21%) of the AMZON moviegoers, however, thought that the best American pictures were being shown in Germany.

Although the majority of German moviegoers preferred to see German films, a sizable minority (37 per cent in AMZON) said that their evaluation depended on the nature of the film rather than its country of origin. Those preferring German films stressed the subject matter; they found German movies easier to understand, both from a cultural and a language point of view.

Report No. 174 (27 May 1949)

HESSIANS CONSIDER THE EFFECT OF LIFTING THE BLOCKADE

Sample: a representative sample of 475 people in Frankfurt, Giessen, and Kassel.
Interviewing dates: second week of April 1949. (9 pp.)

A large majority of Frankfurt (70%), Giessen (54%), and Kassel (70%) residents were aware of the fact that a parliamentary assembly had been meeting to draw up a constitution for the West German government. About three-fourths of these favored setting up such a government in the near future. Majorities in each of the three cities felt that plans for a West German government should not be given up if the Berlin blockade were lifted, primarily because this would not change the East-West conflict. Opinion divided quite evenly on whether or not lifting the blockade and dropping plans for a West German government would improve chances for uniting Germany.

A large majority of Frankfurt (67%) and Giessen (68%) residents and a plurality in Kassel (40%) felt that Frankfurt ought to be made the capital city. Almost no support existed in this survey for independent governments in the individual *Laender* as opposed to a centralized government.

Few people in the three cities thought that the Western Powers initiated the new West German government primarily as a bulwark against communism; the largest proportion of those with ideas on the subject thought it was designed for better administration and the return of order and normal conditions.

Report No. 175 (June 1949)

TRENDS IN GERMAN PUBLIC OPINION

Sample: an unspecified number of persons in the American Zone, West Berlin, and Bremen.

Interviewing dates: from October 1945 to February 1949 during which time sixty-seven full-scale surveys were conducted. (71 pp.)

This report summarizes in graphic form major trends of German opinion in the American occupied areas, covering ten major issues: cares and worries, reorientation, politics, economic affairs, food, international relations, Berlin, the occupation, media, and expellees.

Cares and Worries. Up to June 1948, the outstanding trend was the rise in anxiety over food. By April 1948, 54 per cent of the AMZON public mentioned this as the greatest worry. The next in importance was adequate clothing and shoes, which had risen to four in ten by 1948. Anxiety about prisoners of war and missing persons leveled off at about ten per cent in 1947. The category "unemployment and no means of support" dropped in 1947 to about 12 per cent.

The currency reform produced a remarkable shift. From the April 1948 high of 54 per cent, concern about food dropped to 19 per cent by July 1948, and by 1949 it was as low as ten per cent. Concern about clothing and shoes also sharply declined from 40 per cent in April 1948 to one per cent in February 1949. From July 1948, money trouble took over as the all-pervading claimed worry. Indeed, well over 60 per cent mentioned financial problems, far exceeding the peak figure of 54 per cent that had mentioned food as a major concern.

Reorientation. A plurality of Germans appeared doubtful of their ability to carry on democratic self-government. If forced to make a choice between a government offering economic security and one guaranteeing civil liberties, six in ten Germans said they would pick the former. The same number, however, said they would not give up the two civil rights of the franchise and freedom of the press; four in ten would do so.

In 1946 the average figure for the number of persons who felt that National Socialism was a good idea badly carried out was 40 per cent. In 1947 it had risen to 52 per cent and by 1948 it was 55.5 per cent. Given the choice between a communist and National Socialist government, the trend was from neither to National Socialism: In November 1946, 17 per cent selected National Socialism; in February 1949, 43 per cent preferred it, as against two per cent for communism. During this period the "neither" vote dropped from 66 per cent to 52 per cent.

From November 1946 until January 1948 majorities held that Communists had a right to radio time. From then on the trend changed and by February 1949 about six in ten opposed giving Communists a chance to air their views.

On the question of war responsibility, more Germans in January 1949 than in November 1947 blamed Germany for the outbreak of World War II.

Politics. The number of Germans who claimed to be informed about politics dropped from 1945 to 1947 and interest in politics remained consistently low at about four in ten. Disinterest did not, however, imply lack of opinion. Approval of the idea of a West German government was consistently high and most people felt that its establishment would not prove a permanent bar to unification. Although confidence in local government officials was not very high, there was a definite upward trend.

Concerning political parties, in AMZON the SPD continued to gain in preference over the CDU/CSU, although the gain was only marginal. In West Berlin the SPD got much higher preference than in AMZON. Since 1945 both parties lost favor among the population.

Economic Affairs. Popular opinion on economic matters mirrored the German economic recovery. The trend in confidence in the D-Mark was upward, gaining twenty points from

July 1948 to February 1949. Approval of currency reform measures remained at a very high level, averaging about nine out of ten. Although money and high prices in general were great cause for concern, after June 1948 majorities felt that prices would go down. In January 1949, 52 per cent of the AMZON Germans claimed to be better off than they had been a year earlier, at which time 57 per cent had said they were worse off than a year prior to that time. Nonetheless, in February 1949, 57 per cent claimed that they could not make ends meet on their income.

In January 1948, more people thought that conditions would get worse than thought they would get better, but immediately after the currency reform almost three-fourths expected an improvement in the near future. By January 1949, however, it had again fallen, but only to approximately the two-thirds level.

Well over half the respondents continued to feel that a local black market existed to a serious degree and majorities thought that local officials ought to increase their efforts to do something about it.

Food. In the spring of 1946 six in ten AMZON Germans claimed that they did not get enough food to do their work well. By January 1949 the situation had been reversed and only four in ten made this claim. Confidence in the fairness of the food-rationing system also appeared to be enjoying an upturn following a decline from the very high point registered in the fall of 1945 and spring of 1946.

International Relations. Since February 1948 majorities of varying sizes favored a Western European Union. The consistently large proportion of respondents with no opinion indicated concern over WEU's effect on future war or peace; within a period of eight months the majority tendency was that it would lessen the chances for war but, at the same time, the fraction seeing war as a possible result grew. During 1948 there was a steady upward trend in awareness of the Marshall Plan; by December the figure had risen to 83 per cent in AMZON. A majority consistently thought that the prime motive for

American aid to Europe was to prevent the spread of communism, although during 1948 belief in an altruistic motive rose nine points. Half the population feared that the United States would not adequately meet Europe's future needs; very few (about four per cent), however, ever stated that the United States would stop all assistance. Nearly seven in ten felt that the United States would have the most influence on world affairs during the next ten years. From August 1948 to February 1949, the proportion thinking that the Soviet Union would be the dominant world power nonetheless rose from 11 to 16 per cent. During the previous year, about six in ten people felt that there would be another world war in the next 25 or 30 years, but an optimistic three in ten said there would be a good chance to avoid it.

Berlin. Whereas about seven in ten AMZON Germans expected that the Americans would stay in Berlin, as many as nine in ten West Berliners held this view. In contrast, more AMZON residents than West Berliners consistently felt that the Western Powers were doing all they could to relieve West Berlin's distress. Both AMZON and West Berlin residents gave outstanding support (over 90 per cent) to the correctness of Western policy regarding West Berlin.

Occupation. Up to January 1948, majority opinion was that the United States should hasten the reconstruction of Germany to prevent its becoming a prey to communism. By February 1949 the figure had dropped from 57 per cent to 49 per cent; at the same time the view that the Germans should reconstruct their country alone rose from 16 to 20 per cent.

Whereas in November 1947 only 39 per cent had felt that the United States had furthered the reconstruction of Germany, by August 1948, 63 per cent thought so. In 1946 seven in ten said that the Allies would cooperate to bring about a united Germany before withdrawing. In February 1949, eight in ten said they would not do so.

Media. In January 1947, three-quarters of the population felt the news to be more trustworthy then than it had been during the war; by January 1948 the figure had dropped to 47 per cent, with the less trustworthy column remaining constant at about five per cent but the no opinion column growing steadily. Throughout the postwar period, more than seven in ten AMZON residents consistently claimed to read newspapers regularly or occasionally. The radio audience scarcely varied during the previous eighteen months. And approximately a fourth of AMZON adults claimed to read magazines.

Expellees. Both natives and expellees were in constant and almost unanimous agreement that the expulsions had been unjust. During the previous year, native residents tended to become more positive in their views on the ability of the expellees to get along with local residents. A corresponding trend was apparent in the expellees' attitudes toward their reception in Germany. There was little change in native opinion concerning the expellees' wish to return to their homeland; about nine in ten were sure that the expellees wanted to go back. The expellees themselves also expressed a desire to return, although the negative opinion was consistently greater among them than among the native born.

Report No. 176 (27 May 1949)

GERMAN OPINIONS ON THE "VOICE OF AMERICA"

Sample: unspecified number in the American Zone, West Berlin, and Bremen.
Interviewing dates: last week of April and first two weeks of May 1949. (3 pp.)

The study showed that 41 per cent of the adult population in AMZON listened to the "Voice of America" regularly or occasionally. Among those who never tuned in, almost seven in ten (68%) knew of the program while three in ten had never heard of it.

More than half (56%) of the AMZON audience considered the program good. Very few (3%) thought it was poor. The two most frequently cited criticisms offered by those who found the program fair or poor were that it was propagandistic and that it was dull or uninteresting. Of those who liked the program, four out of ten stressed that it informed them about life in the U.S., and another three out of ten merely found VOA interesting.

Report No. 177 (15 June 1949)

READERSHIP OF "HEUTE"

Sample: a cross-section of adults in all cities of 100,000 or more in the American Zone, as well as West Berlin and Bremen.
Interviewing dates: May 1949. (13 pp.)

The study reports on general critical reaction of readers of *Heute*, a publication put out by the United States Military Government in Germany, as well as reaction by these readers and the general magazine reading public to a specific issue of *Heute*.

Of the total sample, 32 per cent reported reading *Heute* (the next most popular magazine was *Quick* with 29 per cent) and of magazine readers the *Heute* readership was 62 per cent (57 per cent for *Quick*). Of the *Heute* readers, 58 per cent said that they usually read the editorials. More women (55%) than men (39%) claimed to read the serialized stories. A large majority (85%) liked the covers on the magazine. A majority (63%) thought the cartoons on the back page were good.

Heute readers were also asked whether they thought that the magazine should carry more information about their own country, the United States, and other countries. The largest proportion thought that the publication was fine in this regard, although more people wanted an increase in information than wanted less. On the general question of whether *Heute* had improved over time, 42 per cent saw no change, 27 per cent thought it had improved, five per cent felt it had gotten worse, and a large fraction could not make up their minds. Those with a university education, from upper socioeconomic levels, and men were more inclined than their counterpart groups to notice an improvement in the magazine.

Few (11%) of the readers claimed to subscribe to *Heute;* most (45%) bought it at the newsstand, while 21 per cent got it from friends or relatives. Almost all *Heute* readers (89%) said that others also read the copy they read.

As is the case with magazine readers in general, *Heute* readers were better educated, of higher socioeconomic status, and wealthier than the population as a whole.

All respondents – those who read *Heute* as well as those who read no magazines whatever – were asked to leaf through the 13 April 1949 issue of *Heute* and to indicate their interest in specific items. The items which the largest majorities regarded as interesting were a two-page spread of miscellaneous pictures with detailed captions (82%), the cartoons (80%), an article on students from Marshall Plan countries in the United States (78%), "Letter from Vienna" (74%), "Old French Actors" (72%), "German Fisherman" (68%), and the fashion section (65%).

Report No. 178 (30 June 1949)

GERMANS VIEW THE RUHR STATUTE

Sample: a representative sample of about 1,500 persons in the American Zone, 250 in West Berlin, and 150 in Bremen.

Interviewing dates: February 1949. (6 pp.)

A month after the announcement of the Ruhr Statute – a plan for international administration and control of the Ruhr area, proposed by the United States, Great Britain, France, Belgium, the Netherlands, and Luxembourg – a majority (54%) of those interviewed admitted that they had never heard or read anything about it. Among those who professed awareness of the plan, only half (27 per cent of entire AMZON sample) knew that Russia had not participated in drawing up the Statute. This informed group consisted primarily of men, the better educated, and those with high socioeconomic status.

Among all respondents aware of the Ruhr Statute, a strong majority (68 per cent in AMZON) disapproved of it. A majority of informed respondents in AMZON (62%) and Bremen (53%) and almost a majority in West Berlin (48%) felt that the economic effect on West Germany would be bad or very bad. Most admitted, however, that it would be good for Western Europe.

A major objective of the Ruhr Statute was the reconstruction of Western Europe. Almost two-thirds (65%) of the AMZON Germans recognized that the Ruhr Statute would further this goal, but 57 per cent thought that the Ruhr district could be used better. Of this latter group, the largest proportion felt that complete German authority would be the most efficient way to utilize the Ruhr for this purpose.

Report No. 179 (1 July 1949)

GERMAN DESIRES AND EXPECTATIONS ON FUTURE OWNERSHIP OF THE RUHR FACTORIES

Sample: aproximately 1,500 residents of the American Zone, 250 West Berliners, and 150 people in Bremen. *Interviewing dates:* February 1949. (11 pp.)

The survey had a twofold aim: to establish what the respondents hoped for with regard to future ownership of the Ruhr factories as well as what they expected to be the actual settlement of the ownership question.

A majority of respondents in AMZON (51 per cent, as contrasted to 66 per cent in West Berlin and 63 per cent in Bremen) were in favor of social ownership of the Ruhr factories either by the German national or *Land* governments or by the workers and employees of the factory in question. Of those in favor of private ownership (31%), the vast majority favored returning the factories to their former owners rather than giving them to new private owners. Sex, education, and age comparisons in AMZON indicated substantial similarity of attitudes on the ownership question — but not socioeconomic status, as indicated by the fact that 52 per cent in the upper classes supported private ownership. Viewed according to occupations, the greatest support for social ownership existed among governmental officials (69%) and master craftsmen (67%); the greatest support for private ownership came from farmers (45%) and business and professional groups (40%).

A sharp contrast characterized what Germans hoped for and what they actually expected the outcome of the ownership question to be. There was widespread belief (42 per cent in AMZON, 59 per cent in West Berlin; and 48 per cent in Bremen) that the Ruhr factories would ultimately be foreign-owned. Most people holding this view anticipated possession by foreign governments rather than by private foreign interests. Just as in the case of ownership preferences, no sex differences were evident in ownership expectations. Age comparisons, however, revealed that younger respondents were more likely to expect foreign ownership than were their elders. Similarly, half of the lower-middle class, those with greater income, and those with nine or more years of education anticipated eventual foreign ownership, as did pluralities from all the major political parties.

Report No. 180 (1 July 1949)

BONN AND BERLIN, GERMAN CAPITALS

Sample: 500 residents of the American Zone, 100 from
Bremen, and 100 from West Berlin.
Interviewing dates: May 1949. (4 pp.)

A majority (46 per cent in AMZON, 60 per cent in West Berlin,
and 66 per cent in Bremen) of Germans agreed with the choice
of Bonn as the capital of West Germany. While a vast majority
gave no reason for their view on the choice of Bonn, most
people who did comment specifically referred to aspects of the
city itself (e.g., university town, cultural center) or its convenient location. Those who felt that Berlin ought to be the
capital again at some future date increased in number over 1947
when the question had last been asked. In AMZON, the
percentage of those wanting Berlin to be the capital in the
future rose from 58 per cent in 1947 to 77 per cent in 1949; in
Berlin it increased from 93 to 97 per cent; and 93 per cent of
Bremen respondents expressed this wish in 1949. Of the ten per
cent in 1949 who did not think Berlin should ever again be the
capital, half thought that the choice should be Frankfurt, and
two per cent mentioned Munich.

Report No. 181 (7 July 1949)

THE RIAS AUDIENCE IN WEST BERLIN

Sample: a representative cross-section of the West Berlin
population.
Interviewing dates: May 1949. (3 pp.)

Among West Berlin radio listeners, RIAS (Radio in the
American Sector) continued to be the favorite station, having
increased its popularity from about 80 per cent in August 1948
to 91 per cent of the radio audience and 65 per cent of the total

population in May 1949. A considerable fraction (36%) noted an improvement in programs during the previous year, while 50 per cent felt the programs had remained qualitatively the same.

RIAS listeners exhibited no marked group distinctions as compared to the general public except with regard to their political interests. A large majority (76%) thought there was great interest in politics in Germany, 68 per cent took a personal interest in politics, and 92 per cent could correctly identify the mayor of West Berlin; comparable figures for nonlisteners were 54 per cent, 29 per cent, and 75 per cent, respectively.

Report No. 182 (11 July 1949)

GERMAN VIEWS ON DENAZIFICATION

Sample: 1,900 residents of the American Zone, West Berlin, and Bremen.
Interviewing dates: January 1949. (7 pp.)

Adverse criticism of the methods of denazification reached a high point in early 1949, as the denazification hearings approached completion. The predominant opinion (65 per cent in AMZON) was that the program had been badly carried out. Although exact comparisons with previously expressed attitudes were not possible because the questions had been phrased differently, there was a strong indication that approval of the methods and procedures had declined over the years. In November 1945, 50 per cent expressed satisfaction with the program. In March 1946 it rose to 57 per cent. By December of that year it had dropped sharply to 34 per cent, to 32 per cent in September 1947, and further to 17 per cent in May 1949. This decline does not necessarily imply hostility to the idea of denazification; critics based their objections on its laxness, rather than its harshness or unfairness.

Those who disapproved of the denazification procedures were most likely to come from upper income groups (83%), to be better educated (85%), have a higher socioeconomic status (90%), and they were more likely to be native residents (69%) than expellees from elsewhere (47%), "liberal" conservatives (84%), men (71%), and of course, former NSDAP members (78%) and their relatives (79%). Critics of the program claimed that it had treated the less important former members of the NSDAP more harshly than major offenders. People who approved the conduct of the hearings tended to talk primarily in terms of the justice of punishing the guilty for past crimes and misdeeds.

Generally speaking, majorities in each American-occupied area voiced their approval of the *idea* of denazification: 66 per cent in AMZON, 68 per cent in West Berlin, and 64 per cent in Bremen. Very revealing, however, is the fact that the opinion-leading and most vocal groups — the university educated (49%) and the upper socioeconomic groups (55%) — were most likely to express their opposition to the principle of denazification. Arguments of those who disapproved even the idea of holding supporters of Nazism responsible for the regime were scattered. The argument most frequently mentioned was that these people had been idealists and were therefore not deserving of punishment.

Report No. 183 (21 July 1949)

PEOPLE IN THREE HESSIAN CITIES CONSIDER THEIR RECONSTRUCTION PROBLEMS

Sample: a representative sample of 475 residents of Frankfurt, Giessen, and Kassel.
Interviewing dates: mid-April 1949. (6 pp.)

Asked about the main problem of their city, the largest number of Frankfurt and Kassel residents (59 per cent and 49 per cent, respectively) answered "construction of homes" whereas most of the others answered in terms of general reconstruction or removal of ruins.

Two-thirds (68%) of those living in Kassel and half (54 per cent and 48 per cent, respectively) of those living in Frankfurt and Giessen expressed dissatisfaction with the rate of progress in the reconstruction of their cities. Lack of money and incompetent officials were considered the main reasons for the lack of progress. In Frankfurt 11 per cent held the Mayor responsible.

There was little consistency between the way people felt public funds ought to be spent and the way they thought such funds were in fact being spent. Almost everyone felt that housing should be given priority over all other types of construction but most thought that in actual practice anything but houses was being built.

Report No. 183-S (26 July 1949)

KNOWLEDGE OF THE BONN CONSTITUTION

Sample: representative sample of more than 1,400 people in the American Zone, West Berlin, and Bremen.
Interviewing dates: late June 1949. (2 pp.)

Large numbers of Germans were not aware that a Basic Law had been framed for a West German Federal Republic. In AMZON only 18 per cent of those who did know that it had been completed knew something about it. In western Germany majorities could not say whether they would ratify it if given a chance to do so; in West Berlin, however, 60 per cent would vote for it. Significantly, among those respondents who were informed on the subject of the constitution, 70 per cent said that they would ratify it.

Report No. 184 (26 July 1949)

THE "VOICE OF AMERICA" AUDIENCE

Sample: approximately 1,400 residents of American-occupied areas of Germany.
Interviewing dates: late July 1949. (5 pp.)

The findings in this report were based on people who claimed to be radio listeners, said that they usually tuned in their radios at 7 p.m., and also listened to the "Voice of America." An additional group comprised those respondents who, when queried to the point, claimed to listen to VOA sometimes and correctly stated that it was aired at 7 p.m.

On an average, four in ten residents in all American-occupied territories (38 per cent in AMZON and West Berlin, 45 per cent in Bremen) stated that they listened to the "Voice of America" more or less regularly. VOA had not only the most extensive audience of any of the overt American information programs, but reached proportionately more of all segments of the German society.

In AMZON 64 per cent of the respondents said that they considered the programs good. Negative opinions (27%) rested primarily on the view that the programs were uninteresting, did not appeal to the listeners' interests, were not objective or were biased.

Majorities (65 per cent in AMZON, 74 per cent in West Berlin, and 76 per cent in Bremen) of the audience claimed to like the theme music "Oh, Susanna" played at the start of every program, but fairly large proportions, especially in Bavaria (27%) and Wuerttemberg-Baden (32%) said that they disliked it.

Report No. 185 (29 July 1949)

GERMAN OPINIONS ON A PEACE TREATY BEFORE UNIFICATION

Sample: more than 1,400 in the American Zone, West Berlin, and Bremen. .
Interviewing dates: late June 1949. (3 pp.)

Majorities varying from 57 per cent in AMZON, to 59 per cent in Bremen, and to 84 per cent in West Berlin would have rejected the proposal made by the Soviet Union at the Paris Foreign Ministers' Conference to conclude a German peace treaty prior to the reestablishment of a united government. It is worth noting, however, that considerable fractions in all places except Berlin would either have accepted the proposal or withheld judgment. Although the idea of a peace settlement was attractive to a minority, very few people (2 per cent in AMZON) appeared to trust Soviet motives in making the proposal, and most (82 per cent in AMZON) suspected ulterior purposes.

Within all population groups, majorities disapproved of the Russian proposal for a peace treaty at that time, but those most likely to approve were SPD adherents (27 per cent as opposed to only 15 per cent for CDU/CSU adherents), the less educated (24%), and those of lower socioeconomic status (24%).

Report No. 186 (22 August 1949)

GERMAN OPINIONS ON AMERICAN AID

Sample: unspecified number comprising a representative sample of Germans in the American Zone, West Berlin, and Bremen.
Interviewing dates: January and April 1949. (8 pp.)

The majority (68%) of Germans thought that Germany could produce half or more of the food it needed. However, a majority (55 per cent in January, 61 per cent in April) also felt that America was at that time supplying half or more of all rationed food then being sold in West Germany. In response to a question about America's motives in giving this aid, respondents most frequently cited humanitarian reasons (37 per cent in January, 33 per cent in April). Reasons of self-interest (bulwark against communism, to improve business, etc.) also received frequent mention. In all instances, the figures for Berlin were higher. Confidence that American aid to Europe would prove adequate appeared to increase between January and April.

Urban dwellers were more inclined to blame the farmers, and farmers were more inclined to blame inefficient distribution for the difficulties in the food situation – but there was a growing tendency to feel that there were no food problems, only a shortage of money.

Those who understood the background of the offer made in the fall and winter of 1948 by several foreign countries to supply Germany with certain foods in exchange for machinery were more likely to approve the rejection of the offer than were those who did not understand what had been asked in exchange.

Report No. 187 (23 August 1949)

CURRENT VIEWS ON A SUGGESTED WITHDRAWAL OF THE OCCUPIERS

Sample: 1,000 respondents in the American Zone, 200 in Bremen, and 200 in West Berlin.
Interviewing dates: late June 1949. (5 pp.)

The number of AMZON residents who favored Soviet proposals for withdrawal by the occupying powers rose from 34 per cent in November 1948 to 43 per cent in June 1949. An even larger percentage (46%), however, was opposed. Asked whether they thought such a withdrawal would endanger German security, 57 per cent responded negatively and 21 per cent positively. Of those who felt that withdrawal would leave Germany politically insecure, the most frequently cited consequences were civil war, disunity, and political chaos. Soviet aggression and/or a communist coup also received frequent mention, although fewer respondents tended to list this point in June 1949 (16%) than in November 1948 (24%).

Suspicion concerning Russia's motives in proposing the withdrawal of the occupying powers was very great (55%). Only one per cent in AMZON and Bremen and four per cent in West Berlin gave Russia credit for having a good motive in proposing the withdrawal, namely, to make Germany free and independent.

Report No. 188 (1 September 1949)

CHARACTERISTICS AND ATTITUDES OF THE GERMAN MOVIE AUDIENCE

IV. Appraisal of Movie Influences

Sample: a representative sample of 3,000 American Zone residents, over 500 West Berliners, and 300 people from Bremen.
Interviewing dates: November 1948. (6 pp.)

Opinions divided on whether or not American movies gave a true impression of how the average American lives, with 44 per cent of the AMZON residents feeling that this was the case and 42 per cent disagreeing. The largest group of those who said that the movies do not represent American life (13%) said that in general movies portray a world of unreality. When asked what they thought to be the basis for selecting movies sent to Germany, 16 per cent of those asked in AMZON replied, "to familiarize Germans with the American way of life," ten per cent felt it was "for democratic indoctrination," and six per cent mentioned their "cultural value."

In AMZON a majority (59%) thought that movies could strongly influence people's opinions. Problematic and political films were considered most likely to affect people's point of view.

Of those interviewed in AMZON, 74 per cent thought that certain movies were undesirable for children. Movies which might affect children's political attitudes were not considered as dangerous as those which might affect their behavior. There was little agreement on who should determine which movies children ought to be allowed to see: In AMZON 44 per cent felt it should be up to the parents, 46 per cent thought the decision should be in the hands of the authorities.

Report No. 189 (21 September 1949)

THE PUBLIC COMPARES PRESENT AND PAST ECONOMIC CONDITIONS

Sample: 3,000 in the American Zone, 500 in West Berlin, and 250 in Bremen.
Interviewing dates: July 1949. (4 pp.)

Most people (48 per cent in AMZON, 57 per cent in West Berlin, and 61 per cent in Bremen) felt that their economic situation was better in July 1949 than it had been a year earlier. Those who felt they were worse off (17 per cent in AMZON and West Berlin, 14 per cent in Bremen) were not any particular, well-defined, cohesive group. To be sure, many more people in the lower income brackets than in the higher brackets said that they were not getting along as well as they had in the previous year. Also, people with grammar schooling only, or those in the lower socioeconomic levels were more likely than the better-educated or upper social groups to make this complaint. But the differences were not usually marked, and in no case did a single group reverse the general trend of attitudes.

People who felt that they were worse off in July 1949 tended to view other related economic issues somewhat more pessimistically than did those who said that they were better off than in the previous year, or than did the AMZON population as a whole. They were inclined to take a bleaker view of future prospects in the American Zone of Occupation, although the plurality view was that conditions would be better. They were also slightly more pessimistic about future prices and the value of the Mark. Their buying expectations were substantially less, and considerably fewer of them claimed that they had enough food to perform their jobs adequately. Finally, many more said that they could not make ends meet with their current incomes.

Report No. 190 (17 October 1949)

THE MARSHALL PLAN AND WESTERN GERMANY

Sample: an unspecified number of respondents repre-
senting a cross-section of residents of the American Zone,
West Berlin, and Bremen.
Interviewing dates: last two weeks of August 1949. (8 pp.)

Large majorities (67 per cent in AMZON, 73 per cent in
West Berlin, and 76 per cent in Bremen) felt that economic
conditions in West Germany had improved during the previous
year. Foreign aid ranked second to currency reform as a
voluntarily stated reason for this improvement.

Seven in ten AMZON residents (69%) were aware of
American aid to Europe and majorities (53%) could identify
this aid program with the name Marshall Plan, ERP, or ECA.
Awareness that West Germany and West Berlin were receiving
Marshall Plan aid was very extensive (67 per cent of the total
population, 97 per cent of those who knew of an American aid
plan), particularly among men, the more highly educated, and
the upper socioeconomic groups. Along those aware of ERP, 71
per cent knew that the Soviet Union was not included and 62
per cent knew that the Soviets had not wished to participate.

Marshall Plan aid was generally (84 per cent in AMZON,
94 per cent in West Berlin, and 88 per cent in Bremen) regarded
as favorable to West Germany. A minority of AMZON Germans
(29%) felt that the United States would use the Marshall Plan to
influence political and commercial life in West Germany, and an
additional 45 per cent thought that the United States would
control the allocation of money and materials without any
interference in German affairs; only 17 per cent expected the
United States merely to provide the money and materials,
leaving their allocation up to the Germans. Few thought that
such aid was being given unconditionally. In AMZON 63 per
cent felt that the primary motive for giving assistance was
United States desire to curb the advance of communism.

Of those who knew about the aid plan and who also read newspapers regularly or occasionally, 88 per cent claimed to have seen articles on the plan. Among radio listeners, 66 per cent recalled broadcasts dealing with it. Majorities (52%) believed that the military aid program would not affect the economic recovery program. Among those who did see a connection between the two programs, 14 per cent felt the arms aid would result in increased economic aid. A large majority (67%) held that the economic slump during the summer of 1949 in the United States was not a cause of Europe's economic difficulties.

Report No. 191 (9 December 1949)

THE STATE OF GERMAN POLITICAL INTEREST AT THE OUTSET OF THE WEST GERMAN REPUBLIC

Sample: 500 to 3,000 in the American Zone; 100 to 500 in West Berlin; and 100 to 300 in Bremen.
Interviewing dates: several surveys, from May 1949 to September 1949. (21 pp.)

Widespread passivity characterized the state of German political interest at the outset of the West German Republic. Only 36 per cent of AMZON Germans indicated in May 1949 an interest in politics, a figure that dropped to 33 per cent in August 1949. By way of contrast, 64 per cent in May and 67 per cent in August preferred to leave politics to others. Less than two in five (38%) reported great political interest in Germany, almost half (48%) thought that there was little interest, and the remainder (14%) had no opinion on the question. Those who perceived great interest thought that there either was enough (49%) or should be more (35%), whereas those who perceived little interest were more inclined to say that there should be more (49%) rather than that there already was enough (40%).

Three in ten saw as the chief obstacle to democratic self-govern-ment in Germany the fact that people were not sufficiently interested. And, asked whether the low degree of participation in governmental affairs stemmed from the lack of opportunity or the lack of interest, only 22 per cent pointed to the former whereas 67 per cent cited lack of interest.

Low levels of information about politics bolstered conclu-sions about its low salience. As few as 58 per cent of the AMZON residents knew that the name of their *Land*'s Minister-President, although, it must be added, 96 per cent of West Berliners and 98 per cent of Bremen residents knew the name of their mayor. Less than one in ten in AMZON knew that their *Land* constitutions contained provisions for an initiative or were correctly informed about provisions for a referendum. About four in ten (39%) were aware of the fact that the Parliamentary Council had drawn up a constitution for the Federal Republic, and less than half of these (17%) claimed any knowledge of its provisions. Although 96 per cent of the AMZON Germans knew about the pending election, fewer than half of these (47%) knew what the election was about.

Lack of confidence in political parties and leadership contributed to low interest in politics. Only 20 per cent of AMZON residents felt that, if called upon to decide, political parties would opt for the good of the country, as opposed to 62 per cent who thought that the parties would pursue their own interests. Somewhat over a third (38%) felt that people could influence the activities of political parties. The bulk of those who perceived little chance of influence (34%) argued that the parties would do as they pleased without regard for the wishes of the people. Two-thirds of those who thought that the people could exert influence thought that this would be desirable, as did three-quarters of the more pessimistic. Regarding the *Land* parliaments, about four in ten (41%) thought their members to be in touch with public opinion, 30 per cent felt that their members welcomed expressions of opinion from the public, and 29 per cent felt their own interests as citizens sufficiently represented in these parliaments.

Nor were the prospects for political participation any greater. To be sure, three-quarters (76%) of the AMZON Germans indicated their willingness to work an hour daily without pay for the economic reconstruction of Germany. But an almost equally large percentage (71%) voiced their unwillingness to take a responsible position in the political life of their community if they were requested to. Only 40 per cent were aware of "citizens' meetings" in their communities; as few as 13 per cent claimed to have attended such a forum. Indeed, less than one in five (19%) had attended any political meeting since the end of the war. Roughly half this number (11%) had attended an election meeting during the campaign going on at the time of the survey.

In this election campaign, which culminated on 14 August 1949, 80 per cent of AMZON Germans indicated their intention to vote and, in fact, 78 per cent of those eligible did vote. Two weeks before this vote, 69 per cent had not decided for whom they would vote. Almost three-quarters (73%) of those who knew of the election had not seen the list of candidates for their voting district, and an equal percentage responded negatively or with no opinion to queries designed to find out if they were familiar with the electoral law. Over half (56%) of the AMZON residents could subsequently recall who won the election on the national level, 51 per cent were in general satisfied with these results, and 19 per cent were dissatisfied. The dissatisfied respondents were not only more knowledgeable about the electoral outcomes – which party and which candidate for chancellor had emerged on top – but they were also more informed about the aims of the individual parties. Asked why they voted, the largest number (27%) responded that it was their duty, 18 per cent hoped to defeat communism, an equally large percentage expressed partisan reasons (voting for or against a particular party), and 14 per cent hoped to achieve better conditions.

Despite their low level of political interest and participation, AMZON Germans gave expression to a norm of participation: Almost three in four (73%) thought it a good idea that people were able directly to make a proposal for a law; 65 per cent thought it "a good idea for the people directly to be able to vote on the acceptance of a law, instead of its going through the *Land* parliament"; 60 per cent considered political meetings desirable and 67 per cent even considered such forums to be worthwhile. As opposed to 23 per cent who favored a government by experts, fully two-thirds (68%) of the AMZON respondents thought it best that all the people determine the political direction that the government should follow.

INDEX

A NOTE ON THE AUTHORS

Anna J. Merritt, a freelance writer and translator, received her B.A. from Smith College. While studying on a Fulbright Fellowship she met her husband Richard at the Free University of Berlin where they were both exchange students. They have a common interest in the German people, and spend nearly every third year in Berlin.

Richard L. Merritt is professor of political science and research professor of communications at the University of Illinois. He received his B.A. from the University of Southern California and his Ph.D from Yale University. Honors he has received include a Woodrow Wilson National Fellowship, a German Government grant for graduate study, a Social Science Research Council predoctoral fellowship, and a Fulbright Research Professorship at the Free University of Berlin. A member of the American Political Science Association, Mr. Merritt served as editorial associate of *The American Political Science Review* from 1963 to 1967, and is program chairman for the association's 1970 annual meeting. He is also author of *Symbols of American Community, 1735-1775, Systematic Approaches to Comparative Politics,* and has co-authored several books including *Comparing Nations,* and *Western European Perspectives on International Affairs.*

UNIVERSITY OF ILLINOIS PRESS